THE AMIABLE MRS

The amiable
Mrs Peach

Celia Miller

with illustrations by Jean M. Smith

*Lasse
Press*

First published 2016
by the Lasse Press
2 St Giles Terrace, Norwich NR2 1NS, UK
www.lassepress.com
lassepress@gmail.com

ISBN-13: 978-0-9933069-0-7

Typeset in Garamond by
Curran Publishing Services Ltd, Norwich, UK

Printed in the UK by Imprint Digital, Exeter.

Contents

Illustrations

Foreword

Television has popularized some remarkable programmes about life in the 18th and 19th centuries. The novels of Jane Austen and others have attracted and engaged the masses, and have now been joined by the *Downton Abbey* saga. Celia Miller's account of the life of Betsy Peach is the result of much hard work and research into letters either written by Betsy or received from her numerous correspondents; her characters are not perhaps quite so distinguished or 'top drawer' as some of the better known fictional characters of the time, but they have the advantage of complete authenticity. Betsy is near to upper middle class, desperate to keep her position in society, constantly worried about money and the profligacy of her husbands and children.

The book traces the history of the Leathes family through the turbulent years of the last quarter of the 18th century up to the Battle of Waterloo in 1815, and is a very good read. It brings into sharp focus the economic travails of the age, emphasizes the dependency of middle-class society on agriculture and the extent to which Church livings were largely supported by the tithes extracted from the farming community. If the eldest son inherited the land and lived on the rents paid by tenants, the second son usually chose a career in the army or navy, leaving the third son to enter the Church – not so much as a spiritual vocation, but more as a means of obtaining an income commensurate with his status in society. The rural poor were kept poor by the avarice of the Church and it was not until much later, after mass agitation and the articulate courage of a Suffolk farmer, that the legislation of 1936 was passed. Tithes were finally abolished in 1977, when other arrangements were made to recompense the Church. It is extraordinary that even today there are many people who think that the Church of England is sitting on a pot of gold and requires little support from parishioners.

As a direct descendant of the Leathes family into which Betsy married I obviously found the book of great interest, although I have no wish to depend on the reputation of my ancestors. However, the book portrays so well the prejudices of society between town and country which continued to exist in milder form for another century or more. Tracing the origins and lives of ancestors has become a popular pastime and has historical importance, and Betsy Peach and her family were typical of their age. Celia Miller gives her an honoured place in a society which was beginning to make Britain the world's leading nation for the next hundred or more years.

Jim Prior
Baron Prior of Brampton

Preface

The Norfolk Record Office looks after many documents, all of which are part of the complex story of our collective past. This book tells the story of one woman and her family, reconstructed from one of the minor collections of correspondence and miscellaneous papers housed there, dating from the years between 1748 and 1815 and attributed to Elizabeth Leathes (née Reading), who married Edward Peach after the death of her first husband. Many of the letters in this collection were written to Elizabeth during her lifetime by members of her family and by her numerous friends; some were written by her and returned to her after the death of the recipient; others were copies of letters she had written, made by her before or after they had been sent. Such is the nature of the correspondence that her personality leaps from their pages, enabling the reader to enjoy the company of the intelligent, accomplished, pragmatic, determined and fun-loving woman who wrote them. Her correspondents are similarly brought to life, and it is a joy to piece together the interplay of their personalities in the context of a society that flourished more than two centuries ago.

Sadly, there is no other physical evidence of Mrs Peach's existence. The only known portrait of her, a miniature painted for her first husband, was given to her second husband and subsequently vanished, possibly sold or pawned before his death. She was buried in the Leathes/Reading family vault under the chancel of the handsome church at Reedham in Norfolk, and that too was lost during the fire that ravaged the church in 1981.

Elizabeth, or Betsy as she was known to her two husbands, was a prolific letter writer for most of her adult life, as were most middle and upper-class people in an era when letters were the only means of communication between friends and relatives who were separated by circumstances and geography. Because her correspondence was so voluminous, Betsy was forced to destroy some of it periodically to make it easier to store. After her death it was culled still further when three of her four children removed their own letters to her, plus other letters that referred to events they found distasteful or embarrassing. The surviving correspondence eventually found its way into the hands of Leonard Bolingbroke (1859–1927), lawyer, Norwich Diocesan registrar, antiquarian and local historian, whose collection was presented in 1959 to Norwich Central Library by his family. The deposit was transferred to the Norfolk Record Office in 1963, where it was augmented in 1974 by additional material deposited by Mr. B. O. L. Prior.

Like many other ladies of her class, Betsy also kept a small pocket diary for each year, in which she made brief notes of her daily activities and the many social events that she attended. Her diaries and correspondence became separated at some time after her death, and the diaries were packed in a sea chest which eventually found its way to an attic at Hargham Hall in Norfolk, the ancestral home of

Sir Thomas Beevor and his family. They were discovered in 1988, much damaged by insect activity and by water from the leaking roof, by Mrs Anne Carter, who was sorting and recording the Hargham archive. The 20 surviving diaries were in poor condition, but were salvaged by skilful conservation work at the Norfolk Record Office and are legible with the aid of a magnifying glass. They were eventually returned to Hargham Hall, where they were deciphered and transcribed by Mrs Carter. Sir Thomas Beevor kindly agreed to let me have access to the diary transcripts, and Mrs Carter gave generously of her time in taking me through them.

On their own, the diary entries are interesting, but one-dimensional; used together with the surviving correspondence they recreate the story of a relatively ordinary yet remarkable woman, her frequently troublesome family and the provincial society in which they lived. Betsy's legacy is proof that history is not written solely by the great and good, it is written by all of those people who have put pen to paper – providing, of course, that the paper has survived the ravages of time!

Acknowledgements

I am grateful for the support and help of many people during the years spent researching and writing this book, but most especially to the following individuals and organizations.

The former County Archivist, Dr John Alban; Frank Meeres and the staff of the search room at Norfolk Record Office.

Sir Thomas Beevor for allowing me to use the transcripts of Elizabeth Peach's surviving diaries and to Hugh Beevor for his cooperation.

Mrs Anne Carter for allowing me to use her transcripts of the diaries and for her help and guidance.

Baron Prior of Brampton (Jim Prior) for embracing the project, reading the manuscript and writing the foreword.

Jean Smith for her excellent drawings and for her support.

Clare Everitt, Picture Norfolk Administrator at Norfolk and Norwich Millennium Library, for her help and advice. Enjoy thousands of images of Norfolk's unique history at www.picture.norfolk.gov.uk

The staff of the search rooms at Bury St. Edmunds and Maidstone Record Offices for their help.

Jean Smith, Helen Hoyte, the Reverend William Hill and Hilary Hammond for reading the manuscript, detecting errors and offering helpful suggestions.

Susan Curran for seeing potential in this book and for her help and support.

Susan Yaxley, who also saw the book's potential but was prevented by illness from taking the project further.

Most important of all, my husband, Colin Miller, for his invaluable help as research assistant, critic, reader, photographer, chauffeur and supplier of unflagging support.

Illustration credits

Front cover illustration: portrait of an unknown lady, Kingston Lacy; reproduced courtesy of the National Trust.

Norfolk Record Office: pp. xvi, 177

Norfolk County Library and Information Services (Picture Norfolk): pp. 5, 17, 29, 94, 96, 110, 123, 124, 164, 168, 179

Reedham and District Local History and Archaeology Group, pp. 45, 65

Suffolk Record Office and Mrs Helen Sandon: pp. 51, 144

Jean Smith: back cover and spine, title page, pp. 2, 14, 42, 44, 50, 51, 53, 89, 98, 133, 151, 183

Colin Miller: pp. 20, 77

Author's own collection: pp. 130, 131.

If I have failed to obtain any necessary permission or omitted any person or organization from this list, I apologize and suggest that they contact me.

Editorial notes

The correspondence

The extant correspondence of Elizabeth Leathes (later Peach) is held at Norfolk Record Office in Norwich, reference MC 33314, BOL 2.

The diaries

The surviving diaries of Elizabeth Leathes (later Peach) are kept in the Beevor family archives at Hargham Hall, Norfolk, in boxes 31 and 32. They cover the following years: 1774, 1787, 1791–92, 1794–1802, 1804–1809, 1811 and 1815. The diary for 1812 was available in 1993, but has since disappeared, probably misplaced.

Editorial conventions

The following conventions have been used when dealing with excisions, parentheses and brackets in quotations from the correspondence and diaries.

* Quotations from the correspondence are identified by the use of indents and spaces above and below for the longer extracts, and quotation marks for the shorter extracts
* The author's excisions from the writer's text are identified by …
* The author's explanations for corrections to writer's text are identified by [ ]
* The writer's own parentheses are identified by ( ).

The original spelling and punctuation have been preserved in all quotations from the original documents.

Currency

Conversion to decimal currency

At the time of conversion to decimal currency in 1971, £. s. d became £. p, thus £1 (20s or 240d) became £1 (100p).
10s.became 50p.
2s.6d (half a crown) became 12½p.
1s (12d) became 5p.
1 guinea (£1.1s.) became £1.5p.

Historical currency conversion

This is a difficult and controversial area that is usually avoided by historians. It is, however, possible to get a general idea of relative values from the historical currency converter to be found at the National Archives website www.nationalarchives.gov.uk The converter was no longer being maintained at the time of writing, so the most recent values relate only to 2005. Where amounts of money have been converted to decimal equivalents in the text of this book, the calculations were made using this converter.

Abbreviations

The following abbreviations are used in the references and elsewhere in this book.

Diary The diaries of Elizabeth Leathes/Peach
HC   Norfolk and Norwich Heritage Centre
NRO   Norfolk Record Office
NC   *Norfolk Chronicle*
NM   *Norwich Mercury*

The Reading family

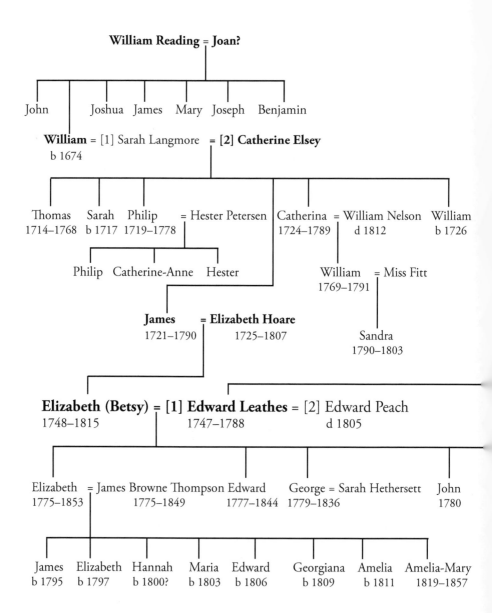

The Mussenden/Leathes family

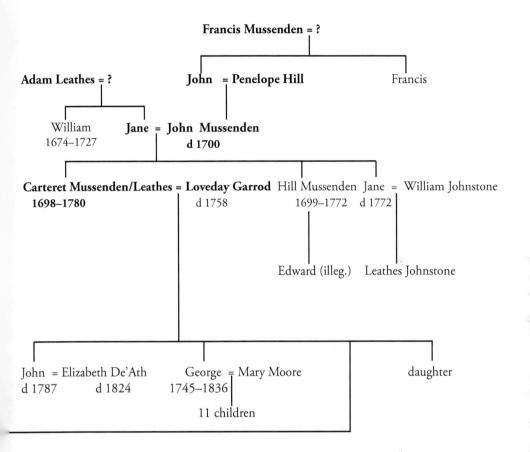

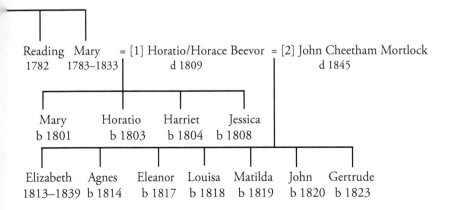

Jarnden. Saturday July 24. 1773 —

Notwithstanding what I said in my last, I think
I know too well my Edward's turn of mind to imagine a State of
suspence will be agreeable to him; 'tis therefore with pleasure I take
up my Pen to assure him of my forgiveness of his last offence —
A generous acknowledgement of a fault never fails to gain my
pardon & I hope you will find thro' life that I shall ever act
with that nobleness & goodness of heart which I could wish to be
the Characteristick of the Woman of your Choice —

I think my Edward I ever have avoided (& hope
I always shall) the being Captious & taking offence at trifles which
are not meant as such, but you must allow I had reason to
be out of humour, when after a silence of eight weeks, the only
excuse was my Aunts illness — I own I wrote my last in the height
of Passion & might perhaps make use of some expressions rather
too severe — however I shall say no more about it, as I am con-
vinc'd you will never be guilty of the like again —

I am in great concern about Mrs Nelson, pray
let me know how she does by the return of the Post —

I shall refer you to my last letter to my
Aunt for an account of the Oxford Encaenia, for I have
so much other News to send you that I have not time for
a repetition of that.

Mr Joveden was married to Miss Bryse last
Thursday senight at Pershore in Worcestershire where She has
been visiting for a month — I have seen them since, they both
enquir'd after you & desir'd their Comps: I shall pay them a
visit at Burscot soon, He has bought a very neat Chaise
which they appear'd in at Burford Races this Week —

Another piece of news is that Mr White
paid Miss Baynton a visit at Woodstock last week, the
consequence of which was that She set out for Town
last week monday — I imagine the match will either be
concluded immediately, or a time not very distant fix
on for it. We were all greatly surpris'd to see him, as

Letter from Elizabeth Reading to Edward Leathes, 24 July 1773.
(NRO, BOL2/5/21, 739x6)

*For Colin, to whom I owe more than I can say,
and for my mother, Edna Bushell,
who did not live long enough to see this book published.*

1   Love and marriage

Without thinking either of men or of matrimony, marriage had always been her object; it was the only honourable provision for a well-educated young woman, and however uncertain of giving happiness, must be the pleasantest preservative from want.

Jane Austen, *Pride and Prejudice*

Rejection in any form is hard to bear, but for a young woman who had been given good reason to expect an offer of marriage from a well-connected and personable young man with whom she and her family were well acquainted, it was an emotional and social disaster. After due consideration, the young man's parents rejected her as a suitable wife for their son because her father, a respectable if somewhat impecunious clergyman, had little to offer in the way of a dowry. Like many other ambitious middle-class parents, they thought their eldest son merited a wife who would bring to their family a reasonable amount of money. It was a painful and demoralizing lesson for a gently reared young lady, but it was certainly a fact of life in the 18th century.

This young lady was Elizabeth Reading, known to her family and close friends as Betsy, the daughter of James and Elizabeth Reading of Woodstock in Oxfordshire. Born on 10 May 1748, she had been brought up as a spoiled only child. From his combined employment as the master of Woodstock Grammar School, tutor to the children of the duke of Marlborough and rector of the nearby parish of Stonesfield, James Reading earned less than £200 a year in 1771, enough for a family of three to live on modestly but respectably. Clerical incomes differed greatly in the late 18th century, depending upon whether an individual church benefice, or living, was small and poor or large and rich. Some clergymen were pluralists, holding several good livings at the same time, whereas others counted themselves fortunate to hold one. Stonesfield was the only living in the duke of Marlborough's gift to which James had been appointed, but he lived in hope that the duke would one day recommend him for a wealthier one.

Betsy had been well educated. She was first taught at home by her schoolmaster father, after which she was sent to Mrs Wheatley's boarding school for young ladies in Oxford, where she learned deportment, needlework, English grammar, handwriting, mathematics, history, geography, music, dancing and French. She left boarding school at around 16 years of age, and as finishing school was beyond the purchasing power of her father's income, she was gradually launched into public social life. By the time she reached her 20th birthday she had acquired all the social skills needed to function effectively in polite society, and knew how to present herself to the best advantage. Her cultural accomplishments were typical of a young lady of her class: she played the harpsichord, read suitably improving

The Ancient House, Woodstock, as Betsy might have known it

literature, wrote letters that were both observant and witty, and was able to converse knowledgeably on a range of subjects. She had a large circle of female friends and acquaintances, and both she and her parents were on visiting terms with most of the genteel families in Woodstock and district.

Her father had three siblings, two older brothers and a younger sister. His eldest brother Thomas was assistant registrar at Sion College, London, where he lived in college accommodation; next in line came Philip, who had taken holy orders and then travelled to America to be a missionary; his youngest sibling and the only girl was Catherine, who had married another clergyman, William Nelson. When James visited Thomas at Sion College he occasionally took Betsy with him. Not surprisingly she looked forward to staying with her uncle because she was able to take advantage of the many opportunities that the capital city had to offer. It was during one such visit in September 1768 that Thomas Reading died unexpectedly and James Reading was forced to change his plans to return home because he was named as one of the three executors of his brother's rather complex will. The other named executors were his brother-in-law, William Nelson, and their good friend William Pocock, a leather seller with East India Company interests who lived and worked in Newgate Street, London.[1]

Thomas Reading was buried with due ceremony at Mortlake on 19 September 1768, and Betsy stayed on at Sion College with her father until mid-November to pack up the books and household effects that had been left to James in Thomas's will. During their stay in London James Reading made the acquaintance of a friend of William Nelson, Edward Peach, the absentee rector of Titsey in Surrey, who had a house on Cheapside. Mr Peach had two sons, Edward and Henry, and the families seem quickly to have become friendly during September and October, improving Betsy's social life quite considerably. After her father's departure to Woodstock in early October Betsy stayed on at Sion College under the watchful eyes of her aunt and uncle Nelson.

When he eventually returned to London, James Reading quickly realized that his daughter and Edward Peach junior were on the verge of becoming romantically involved, and the two fathers began to consider whether the match was a suitable one. The negotiations were lengthy, and Betsy returned to Woodstock while they were incomplete, to dream about her would-be suitor and gossip about him with her friends. But by spring 1769 it had become clear that the marriage negotiations were at an end. Edward Peach senior might have assumed that James Reading would benefit substantially from his late brother's will and that Betsy, as his sole heir, would inherit the money. Unfortunately Thomas Reading's estate was less valuable than anticipated. Catherine Nelson was the major beneficiary, and after debts, expenses, specific bequests and annuities had been paid, there was very little left for the two surviving Reading brothers. Money was clearly Mr Peach senior's main criterion of wifely suitability, and Betsy's prospects did not measure up to his requirements. Edward Peach disappeared from her life, and there is no further reference to him in her correspondence until many years later.

At the age of 21 Betsy was probably beginning to think that her prospects of marriage were receding into the distance. Women of her time were conditioned to believe from an early age that their main purpose in life was marriage, children and household management, and they were educated with that end in view. Spinsterhood was a relatively unattractive prospect, unless the woman concerned had a decent income in her own right. Betsy's father had a modest income, a house and a little money invested in government funds, but his income from both church and school would die with him. In the event of his death Betsy and her mother would inherit the small investment income and they would be able to sell the house and invest the proceeds, but this would yield only a slender income which was unlikely to support them adequately. About a quarter of well brought-up young ladies from gentry and middle-class families were spinsters, and those with little or no income had no alternative but to get jobs as governesses, companions and housekeepers, or to attach themselves in some capacity to the families of their more fortunate married siblings or relatives. This seemed to Betsy an undesirable fate, and it was one she was anxious to avoid.

James Reading visited London in late February 1771, but on this occasion he stayed at Nando's Coffee House near Temple Bar, and not at Mr Peach's house on Cheapside as he had previously. This is a good indicator of the rift between the two families following the collapse of marriage settlement negotiations. During his stay in London, James heard from friends that his brother-in-law, William Nelson, had been presented to a new church living worth £350 a year at Strumpshaw in Norfolk. Betsy was surprised to hear this, and became quite intrigued by the improvement in her uncle's fortunes. She therefore suggested to her father that it might be a good idea for her to pay a long-overdue visit to the Nelsons.

Fortunately for Betsy, her curiosity was soon satisfied. William and Catherine Nelson lost no time in removing to their newly acquired rectory at Strumpshaw, and in May 1771 they invited the Reading family to visit them. Mr. and Mrs Reading declined the invitation but Betsy, who was only too happy to leave Woodstock for the summer, accepted with alacrity. She left home in the middle of June and travelled to London, where she stopped off to visit her friend Mary Pocock and her parents at their town house. After an enjoyable two-week stay she left the delights of London and boarded a coach for Bury St Edmunds, where she had been invited to stay with Mr and Mrs Nelson at the grand house of his patron, Carteret Leathes. Betsy revelled in the fact that she was met by a coach at the stagecoach terminus in Bury St Edmunds and carried in style to the Leathes residence for a rendezvous with her aunt and uncle and the assembled Leathes family.

Carteret Leathes was a rich man. Born Carteret Mussenden in 1698, he had assumed the surname and arms of Leathes when he inherited the estate of his maternal uncle, William Leathes, who had prospered under the patronage of the first duke of Marlborough. His uncle's death transformed Carteret into a wealthy landowner with estates in Norfolk, Suffolk and Essex. As befitted his new status he then entered political life, and represented Harwich and Sudbury in several parliaments. In 1758 his wife Loveday died, leaving him with one daughter and three sons. By the time Betsy met him in July 1771 he was 73 years old, but still fit and active.

Betsy was introduced to two of the three sons of the house, both of whom made an impression on her, but for different reasons. She knew her parents would wish to know all the details of the places she had visited and people she had met, so she painted a pen picture of the Leathes brothers and of their father's Bury St Edmunds mansion in her next letter:

> The eldest [John] remembers to have seen you, my dear Papa, at Woodstock last Summer, just before Burford Races. He bears a most extraordinary good Character & his goodness of heart is very conspicuous in his Countenance. The second son, Mr. George, is an Officer in the army & is now with his regiment at Worcester. The Third Son, Mr. Edward, is very musical so I hope to improve myself in Singing as he returns to Strumpshaw with us tomorrow to stay the Summer .... Mr. L's house is an old Front, But a very good old House, one Room in particular is extremely elegant & furnished with a great many very valuable Paintings. The Garden is very pretty & remarkable for a fine Hot house, Green House & Pinery, of the goodness of which we have daily proofs.[2]

Strumpshaw Rectory, late 19th century

The week at Bury St Edmunds passed all too quickly, and by 10 August Betsy had arrived at Uncle Nelson's parsonage at Strumpshaw, near Norwich. She reported her observations on the house and its surroundings to her parents as soon as time permitted:

> My Uncle's House is very pleasantly situated, in a fine Country, very fertile & remarkable for producing good Wheat & Barley, & also fine Mutton. The Roads here are very good & the prospects very delightful, from a little eminence about two hundred yards from my Uncle's House there is a fine view of Norwich, & Yarmouth, & a most extensive prospect of the Country for many miles around. As my Uncle keeps a Post Chaise and a single Horse Chaise we ride or walk every day, visit a good deal, & spend our time very agreeably.[3]

Carteret Leathes' youngest son Edward had travelled with them to Strumpshaw, where he resumed his studies for ordination as a priest under William Nelson's tuition. The eldest son, John Leathes, was destined to inherit the family estate, and the second son George was a career soldier. As the third son Edward had no expectations of inheritance, unless of course his two elder brothers were to die before him, leaving no children. Having tried the navy for a short time and found it wanting, he had opted for another well-trodden career path for the third sons of the gentry and minor aristocracy, the church. Typically, the question of vocation appears not to have been involved in his decision to change careers, although he was averagely devout.

Studying was not high on Edward's agenda during the summer of 1771. A shared love of music ensured that he and Betsy found little trouble in passing the time together at Strumpshaw. Edward played the pianoforte, Betsy played the harpsichord and both of them enjoyed singing. No doubt the summer days flew by, filled with music and punctuated by visits to places of local interest and longer trips to Great Yarmouth and Norwich.

After staying for a week or so in Strumpshaw, the Nelsons, Betsy and Edward Leathes crossed the Norfolk border into Suffolk, and in late July they travelled to Herringfleet Hall to visit Edward's uncle, Hill Mussenden, and his illegitimate son Edward. Edward's illegitimacy was deemed a bar to his succeeding his natural father, so the Herringfleet estate, worth £1,800 a year, would pass to Carteret Leathes when his brother died.[4] Betsy enjoyed her stay at Herringfleet and the visits made by the party to Great Yarmouth, a seaport of some importance in the late 18th century. The town was also rapidly developing as a tourist attraction, thanks to its bracing sea air and facilities for sea bathing, a prescription highly recommended by doctors at that time.

Two weeks after their return from Herringfleet the Strumpshaw party travelled to Norwich, where they stayed for a week. The city was no longer as powerful and important as it had been in the past, but it was still wealthy and thriving. Betsy had stopped there briefly on her way to Bury St Edmunds at the beginning of July, and had been impressed by much of what she saw. She revisited the city in August for Assize Week, one of the most important weeks in the Norfolk social calendar, when the great and good of the county descended on Norwich to see and be seen at the theatre, the assembly house, and the pleasure gardens of the city. Betsy was a keen participant in the entertainments on offer, and enumerated the highlights of the week to her parents:

> The Town was very full of Company, which made it very Cheerful. We were at two Plays, one Assembly, a Concert, & the Publick Gardens. The Play House is exactly Drury Lane in miniature, the Assembly Rooms are very good neat Rooms & the Gardens are a good deal like Vauxhall. Our party from Strumpshaw consisted of my Uncle & Aunt, Mr. Leathes, Mr. Mussenden, Mr. Burney & myself; & we met several of our acquaintance at Norwich who join'd us occasionally.[5]

She ended her letter with a hint that her parents might not have to support her for too much longer. Having dropped this hint, she was still unsure how to tell her parents what had happened. Instead she persuaded William Nelson to explain to her father that she had received a proposal of marriage from an unnamed suitor, and that the match was a suitable one. Betsy restricted herself to assuring her mother she would never have encouraged a suitor of whom her parents would not have approved, and promised she would not marry without their approval. To do so, she said, would not only be ungrateful, it would also be a poor return for the love and kindness they had always shown her. Despite the suitability of the match, Betsy swore her parents to secrecy until the time was right, and asked to be allowed to stay at Strumpshaw until early November. The extra two months would be sufficient, she thought, to resolve any potential problems.

Mrs Reading quickly guessed that Betsy's mystery suitor was Edward Leathes, but her parents agreed to keep news of the engagement secret for the time being, and were happy for her to stay on at Strumpshaw. Edward was more fortunate than most men studying for ordination, she told them, because he would not have to wait for a suitable living when he was ordained. His father had reserved two church livings for him: the rectory of Reedham and the vicarage of Freethorpe, which were held temporarily on his behalf by William Nelson in anticipation of his eventual ordination. However, as is the way with mothers, Mrs Reading had spotted a significant omission in her daughter's letter. She asked Betsy whether the gentleman's family members were aware of the arrangements, and whether they approved of the match.

Betsy was aware that Carteret Leathes had already told Edward on several previous occasions that he was not free to choose a wife until he could support her, which effectively meant when he had been presented to the church livings that were being held in reserve for him. Until then, Carteret would not countenance any commitment Edward might be tempted to make. Their engagement therefore had to remain secret until the time was right to break the news to him, and marriage was out of the question. Edward would first have to be ordained deacon and then priest by the bishop before he could draw income from his church livings, a process that was likely to take at least one year, possibly two. So the lovers had a potentially long and frustrating wait ahead of them, much of which they were destined to spend apart, without the mutual affection and support that proximity could bring.

Betsy left Strumpshaw on 11 November and returned to her parents in Woodstock. She was desperate to receive Edward's precious letters, which all began with 'My Dearest Betsy', 'My Love' or 'My Dearest Girl'. Although his letters tended to be brief and were frequently short on punctuation, they were full of genuine emotion, affectionate philosophizing and banter. He also tried to prepare Betsy for the trials and tribulations that the future was likely to hold for them.

Edward had already encountered one reverse of fortune at Strumpshaw in the shape of Mrs Nelson, who for reasons best known to herself was going out of her way to be unpleasant to him. Betsy also had problems, because her parents were becoming increasingly unhappy that Carteret Leathes had not been made aware of the engagement. They feared he might attach some blame to them when he eventually found out. She was also worried about Edward's slow progress towards ordination, that crucial passport to married bliss.

Although Betsy and Edward were both over 21 and therefore legally able to marry without parental consent, it was usual in their era for people to wait for their parents' or guardians' consent before marrying. Respectability more or less demanded filial devotion, loyalty and respect for parental opinion in all things, including marriage. To conduct a clandestine engagement, or even worse to make a clandestine marriage, was not considered respectable. In addition Edward was entirely dependent on his father for an income until he was fully ordained, and his father could discontinue that income if he considered his son had married unwisely. In these circumstances it was a risky strategy for Edward and Betsy to enter into an engagement without the knowledge or consent of Carteret Leathes, and they would court financial disaster were they to follow it through.

If parents and other key relatives repeatedly opposed a marriage, the only recourse for the couple concerned was to ignore convention and marry clandestinely. Couples like Betsy and Edward, who were over the legal age of consent, could obtain a special licence which permitted them to marry in any church or chapel in a parish where one of them had been resident for a minimum of four weeks prior to its granting. Whatever the circumstances, this was not a course of action to be undertaken lightly.

Their relationship came under increasing fire from all sides, and the situation was not improved by Edward's confession of some of his past misdeeds. There can be no doubt that his behaviour before and after he met Betsy had been more than a little wayward. He was no stranger to the pleasures of the flesh, the bottle and the gaming table, behaviour that was not uncommon among men of his age and class. Polite society frequently turned a blind eye on youthful folly, although there was a fine line between testing and learning the boundaries of acceptable behaviour, and overstepping them. John Leathes had been concerned about his youngest brother's behaviour for some time, and had reprimanded him on at least one occasion. But when he received news of Edward's most recent exploits in Norwich early in 1771 he was forced to write to him once more, counselling him not to repeat his past mistakes. If he revisited his old haunts in Norwich it would only involve him once more in debts, debauchery and dissipation, a situation that would certainly lead to distress for all those involved.

Corroborating evidence of Edward's behaviour in Norwich during 1771 did not emerge until many years later, when an old letter shed a bright light on his escapades in Norwich during his years at Strumpshaw. In January 1779 his brother George wrote to Edward from his army camp at Guildford with news of an old acquaintance.

A few days since I went to dine at Godalming where two of our Officers are at present quarter'd, it seems by way of a Christmas Frolic they had each got a fine Lady down from London who din'd with us of course, during our Dinner time, I ask'd one of them to Drink a Glass of wine which she agreed to, & by way of Hob Nob she to my great surprise says, here's [to] all our friends in Norfolk. I star'd & cried Ma'am, I say Sir quoth She, here's Health & Long Life to your

<u>Brother the Clergyman</u>. I thank'd her very kindly but said no more till Dinner was over, I then sat next her and by a little conversation soon found she came from Norwich or it's Neighbourhood and that she was well acquainted with Mr. Edward Leathes during his Excursions from Mr. Nelson's to Norwich some time prior to his marriage, since when she seems to have lived with a Gentleman of the Law belonging to the Temple, by whose name she has sometime went. What was her Name when at Norwich she wou'd on no account inform me, her Christian name is Elizabeth, she is tall, well made, rather inclin'd to be lusty, dark Hair, & Eyebrows, which are large & thick, brown complexion, and fine dark brown Eyes, is about twenty two or three Years of Age or thereabout and all together a very fine Woman, she seem'd to know most of the Inhabitants of Norwich & its Environs. If you recollect her let me know who she was and the name she went by at Norwich, I fancy she was far above the common run that frequent Mother Jay's or the Duke's Head as she disclaim'd all knowledge of those Houses.[6]

In Edward's defence, the liaison referred to here could have predated his engagement to Betsy in 1771. So it is just possible, if not entirely likely, that he can be acquitted of infidelity to her. Betsy's reasons for keeping the letter instead of destroying it can only be guessed at.

The autumn of 1772 saw the next available ordination date come and go. Edward fell ill and remained in London with no word of explanation. However he had recovered sufficiently by 20 September to visit Woodstock, where he hoped to win over Mr and Mrs Reading. Unfortunately circumstances conspired to turn the visit into an unmitigated disaster. Edward seems to have made a largely unfavourable impression on Betsy's parents and some of their friends, the weather was awful, and the Reading household was suffering from a servant shortage. Within two days of Edward's arrival James Reading wrote to Carteret Leathes, thanking him for the kindness shown to Betsy when she visited Bury St Edmunds in 1771. James explained that although he wished to extend the same kindness and courtesy to Edward, he was unable to give his consent to Edward's request to marry Betsy without his father's knowledge and approval.

There can be little doubt that this was the first Carteret Leathes had heard of the engagement. His reply was brutally frank:

Your Daughter's genteel deportment during the short time she favoured me with her company here, merited more than the little civilities it was in my power to show her. I am obliged to you for the information you gave me of my Son's Views in his Visit to you, but I am sorry to acquaint you that I think him very undeserving of such fortune as to marry your Daughter. Not to enlarge upon the matter, I advise you to tender your own and your Daughter's future happiness to decline all closer connections with my Son. Believe me S^r, no dislikes to You, your Daughter, or Family, are the motives of the above advice, they flow from principles of Justice, to You and Her. With these, I beg leave to remain, with great obligations to you and y^r generous Cando[u]r, and with my best wishes for the young Lady's happiness.[7]

Some of their relatives and friends were also experiencing the tribulations of love, courtship and eventual marriage. Edward's cousin Edward Mussenden had married a Miss Adkin of Great Yarmouth during 1772. Unfortunately for him it quickly emerged that he had previously contracted himself to another young lady, who promptly sued him for breach of promise. This was a serious matter, and young Mr Mussenden had little alternative but to settle out of court to avoid the scandal of a court case, a course of action which cost him an annuity of £60 a year. Betsy's friend Margaret Pryse of Woodstock and her beau, Edward Loveden, were also experiencing problems with the attitudes of their relations. Loveden had declared he would marry Miss Pryse even if he had to abduct her to do so. Mr Pryse was clearly not happy with Edward Loveden as a prospective son-in-law, which is interesting because it is unlikely to have been for financial or cultural reasons. Loveden was the owner of a substantial estate at Buscot Park, near Faringdon in Berkshire, an accomplished scholar and a fellow of both the Royal Society and the Society of Antiquaries. No doubt Mr Pryse was doing his best to protect his daughter and her property, which was worth in excess of £1,000 a year.[8] Loveden prevailed in the end, and he and Margaret married in July 1773, perhaps clandestinely, when Margaret was on a visit to Pershore.

The path of true love continued to be a bumpy one for Betsy and Edward through much of 1773, governed as it was by the inflexible stance of both their fathers. The situation must have had painful echoes for Betsy of how her hopes of marriage to Edward Peach had been dashed in 1769. It is not hard to understand why these continued setbacks only served to make her more determined that history was not going to repeat itself. She was by now 25 and Edward 26, so it would be perfectly legal for them to marry without parental consent; the only negative consequence would be financial.

Betsy must also have realized that if she lost Edward now, her chances of making another 'suitable' match would be very few, a factor that almost certainly influenced her decision making. She told him that if they decided to elope, some positive action would be required of him. He would have to either obtain a special licence or take up temporary residence in Holborn, following which he could get the banns called there.

Edward was finally ordained deacon in London on 19 December, so 1773 ended on an optimistic note. If everything went according to plan he could now expect to be ordained priest within 12 months, meeting his father's main precondition for marriage and removing James Reading's objections.

Ordination apart, Betsy was unable to understand why Carteret Leathes was so implacably opposed to their marriage. Although she may have had some misgivings about Edward's spendthrift habits, she was blissfully ignorant of the scale of his debts and the extent of his previous extravagant behaviour. In February 1771 John Leathes had paid off about £200 of Edward's accumulated debts from Cambridge and Bury St Edmunds. John had subsequently written to Edward, warning him that he had been lucky to avoid debtor's prison and that his family would not come to his rescue a second time. He also reproached Edward for the unjust accusations he had made against their father during his Christmas visit to Bury St Edmunds, especially after his father had promised he would be presented to the livings of Reedham and Freethorpe as soon as he had been ordained. But references to Edward's penchant for gambling indicate that he had not managed to shake off all his bad habits. On 1 June 1772 he borrowed £700 from Henry Negus of Norwich, which reinforces that impression.[9] Had Betsy been aware of these financial problems, she might have understood why his father was so reluctant to let them marry until Edward had the means to support a wife and family.

August came and went with no mention of ordination, but the lovers were convinced that it would happen within the next few months. Perhaps this is what motivated them to abandon caution and plan an elopement. Betsy told Edward they would have a good opportunity in early September when she visited her father's friends, Mr and Mrs Holloway. The Holloways were planning a trip to stay with a Mr Middleton at Warborough for the duration of Abingdon Races on 13, 14 and 15 September, and planned to take Betsy with them. Warborough was a mere 40 miles from London, and the house in which she would be staying lay conveniently close to the coach road. Her old friend Ann Goldwyer told Betsy that her husband had offered to conduct the marriage service and that another friend had offered to give Betsy away. Mrs Goldwyer herself offered to 'throw the stocking'.[10]

On 14 September 1774 Benjamin Holloway sent a panic-stricken letter to James Reading:

> I take the earliest opportunity of informing you of what has much surprised me as well as given me great Concern. Mr. Lees [Leathes] has been to Warboro' & fetch'd away your Daughter in order to marry Her. I hope you will do me the justice to believe neither I nor my Wife were privy to this scheme. I remonstrated with Her on taking such a Step against your knowledge – she said after it was over it would all be well. He has a Licence in his pocket & they are gone to night to Miss Bayntun's at Highgate [&] propose being married & then going to Mr. Nelsons.[11]

Betsy's diary entry for Thursday 15 September reads: 'This morning went to London & was married to Mr. Leathes at St Andrews Holborn by Mr. Goldwyer. Mr. Bristow gave me away & Miss Baynton Bridesmaid. Mr^s G spent the day with us at the Queen's Head, Holborn.'[12] Her surviving correspondence includes a programme card for Abingdon Races that September. On the back of the card Edward Leathes wrote, 'Immediately upon her return from the Races, Miss Reading went to London and was married to the Rev[d.] Edward Leathes.'[13]

After three years of engagement and much tribulation, Edward and Betsy were man and wife at last.

2   The rector's wife

Betsy and Edward spent their wedding night at the Queens Head in Holborn, then boarded a coach bound for Norfolk the following afternoon. The Nelsons and several of their friends met them in Norwich, and they took tea there before travelling on to Strumpshaw rectory, the home of Betsy's aunt and uncle, William and Catherine Nelson. Arrangements had been made for them to stay there on a bed and board basis until Edward was fully ordained and could take possession of his livings.

Betsy lost no time in writing to her parents, telling them that her uncle approved of their marriage and that her husband was in the process of writing to his father with the news in the hope that he too would give them his blessing. Edward also wrote a short note to his mother-in-law, assuring her that her daughter's happiness would be his life's work, and that he and Betsy hoped to see them in Norfolk during the summer of 1775. Mrs Reading's reply left them in no doubt that she and her husband thought they should have waited until Edward had been fully ordained, although this did not prevent her from wishing them many years of happiness.

Carteret Leathes gave a cautious approval to the marriage. He took a dim view of Betsy's lack of dowry, but was prepared to be reconciled with the couple once Edward had been ordained priest. Edward's brothers, on the other hand, reacted very positively; they congratulated the couple and expressed the hope that ordination and complete reconciliation with their father would follow swiftly. But Betsy's parents were determined to have the last word, and James Reading's parting shot (in a letter undoubtedly dictated by him but written by Mrs Reading) left Edward in no doubt that in his opinion Betsy and Edward should have waited until they were in a position to marry with parental approval and with due ceremony. It was clear that both fathers had no intention of communicating or meeting with them until Edward was ordained priest, so all future communication would have to be through third parties: Betsy's mother and Edward's brothers. The newly-weds, however, were unrepentant. They were convinced they had taken the right step and confident that all their problems would be soon resolved.

While Edward studied for his ordination examinations and performed curacy duties at Reedham and elsewhere, Betsy spent her time writing letters to all her friends and relatives, informing them of her marriage and sending pieces of the wedding cake she had ordered at a cost of £1.2s.6d.[1] Etiquette demanded that a new bride should receive and return formal visits from her local acquaintances and friends to confirm her new social status. It was customary for the bride to make her return visits in new finery, so Mr and Mrs Reading offered to buy Betsy a new dress. She promptly ordered 22 yards of blue satin at 8s.6d a yard (less 5 per cent discount for cash) from the warehouse of Mr Vansommer in London, which was

Fashionable dress at the time of Edward and Betsy's wedding

made up in negligée style by a local dressmaker. The finished garment was greatly admired locally.[2]

Protocol decreed that Betsy fulfil these social demands, but it was equally important to put together the furniture, linen, tableware and kitchen equipment that would be needed for Reedham parsonage when Edward finally took posses-sion of the living. Ready money was lacking, so she asked her mother to send to Strumpshaw all the clothes, personal belongings and bedroom furniture she had left behind at Woodstock, and scrounged as many other essentials as she could from her parents. Mrs Reading had anticipated her daughter's dilemma, and promised to send much of her own surplus household linen to Norfolk. Betsy was very grateful, but continued to beg for anything more they could spare, especially beds and bedding for their servants. She was planning to engage a local farmer's daughter with some experience in service as a maidservant for £5 a year, which she claimed was the going rate in the area. Early in November the newly-weds spent a week playing house at Reedham, an experience they seem to have enjoyed. Betsy liked the parsonage, although she was not convinced it would prove suitable for them in the long term.

Edward's ordination was scheduled for December 1774, and during November he managed to obtain the four signatories necessary for his testimonium: John Arnam, rector of Postwick; James Carlos, rector of Blofield; Thomas Goddard, rector of Halvergate; and of course William Nelson, rector of Strumpshaw. It seemed everything was going according to plan, until on 23 November they received the news that the bishop had delayed the ordination on the grounds that he needed more time to think about Edward's suitability for the priesthood. This decision left Edward and Betsy in a very difficult position. Betsy had spent ten weeks at Strumpshaw in almost continuous motion, and the stress resulting from this and from the bishop's decision almost certainly contributed to her suffering a miscarriage at the end of November. Fortunately there were no long-term ill effects and she was back on her feet in a few days.

The financial implications of the bishop's decision were serious, because Edward would probably have to wait three to six months for another ordination opportunity. In the meantime they had no income other than the occasional cash handout from the Readings, who could afford very little, and John Leathes, who helped when he could. They were staying at Strumpshaw rectory on a bed and board basis, but fortunately William Nelson did not demand prompt payment and occasionally loaned Edward small amounts of money. However by December 1774 Edward owed £70 to William Nelson and had drawn heavily on the £700 loan he had negotiated with Henry Negus in 1772.[3] Every time the ordination goalposts were moved, Edward and Betsy sank deeper into a financial quagmire from which they would find it very difficult to extricate themselves. They had taken a substantial risk when they married in advance of Edward's ordination and without parental consent. Unfortunately for them the gamble had not paid off.

To make matters worse, the relationship between Betsy, Edward and Mrs Nelson deteriorated during their stay at Strumpshaw. In early December Betsy told her mother that her aunt had asked them to quit the rectory by Christmas. They were unable to rent a house for lack of money, so they intended to move to Reedham parsonage, where they could at least live rent-free. They had no money for more furniture and equipment, so Betsy asked her parents for two beds for their servants and £10 to buy some kitchen equipment, as both were urgently needed. She also asked them to dispatch the remainder of her bedroom furniture, the household linen promised by her mother and anything else that was surplus to requirements at Woodstock.

Betsy's parents were unimpressed by Catherine Nelson's ungenerous behaviour, not only because she was Betsy's aunt, but also because Edward's father was William Nelson's patron. Nevertheless Aunt Nelson must have enforced her decision, because the newly-weds moved to Reedham on Christmas Eve 1774. It may have been inconvenient, but perhaps the move was for the best because Betsy felt much more settled at Reedham, even though the house was sparsely furnished.

The village of Reedham lies on the northern bank of the River Yare between what was then the busy seaport of Great Yarmouth and the city of Norwich. Until the railway line was opened in 1844 the river was the main trading artery between the two places, and it was still well used even after the railway took some of freight that had previously been carried by boat. Wherries and keels (a type of river barge with a sail) were used to carry to Norwich goods transhipped from ocean-going vessels at Great Yarmouth. The return journey was loaded with goods destined for either onward transmission around the east coast or export abroad. The boats also called at the riverside villages of Thorpe St Andrew, Brundall, Cantley and Reedham to deliver and take on goods.

Reedham was a large parish, consisting of the village that clustered around the church and the riverside, as well as the hamlets of Witton Green, Reedham Ferry and Berney Arms, the latter some three miles downriver towards Yarmouth. Reedham Ferry lies about half a mile upriver from the village, and was then an important river crossing point, much more so than it is today. The landlord of the Ferry Inn owned and operated the chain ferry, which took carts, light coaches, horses, livestock and people across the river in both directions, significantly short-ening the journey to the Suffolk towns of Loddon, Beccles and Bungay.[4] Country roads were generally poor and sometimes impassable in bad weather, but it was fortunate for the newly-weds that the main Norwich to Yarmouth turnpike road, built in 1769, passed through Acle, some six miles from Reedham. Acle was also the nearest settlement for postal deliveries and collection.

The parsonage house or rectory at Reedham still stands next to the church and adjacent to the marshes that lead to the River Yare.[5] Betsy and Edward began to enjoy life there, free from Aunt Nelson's constant backbiting and troublemaking. Their farmer neighbours were obliging, pleasant and suitably deferential because they were nearly all tenants of Edward's father. They were also very generous, and gave the young couple butter, cream and turkeys, which went a little way towards easing the pressure on food bills at the rectory. Edward's financial situation was worsening. With no source of income, he had to buy clothes, food and other goods on credit, or more usually neglect to pay the bills. Debt was not Betsy's only worry in the first few months at Reedham; she may also have been a little lonely, because neither she nor Edward had yet had the time to build a network of friends and acquaintances in the area.

In February 1775 Betsy realized she was pregnant for the second time. This made Edward's need to access the income from his parishes even more pressing. His financial calculations were all predicated upon his ordination either at Lent or on Lady Day (25 March), but his plans were again thrown into confusion by the bishop's refusal to commit to a firm date. Carteret Leathes tried to argue Edward's case with the bishop, but without success. Edward and Betsy made an abortive trip to London to see him in early March 1775, and various family members,

Reedham Rectory, late 19th century

friends and even influential acquaintances lobbied him on Edward's behalf, but he continued to procrastinate. He also accused Edward of failing to take services in his churches on several occasions. One reason for the bishop's behaviour became clear when it was revealed that he and Carteret Leathes were involved in a lawsuit concerning a different matter.

Although the road to ordination was rocky, at least Betsy's pregnancy seemed to progress smoothly, and she began to make arrangements for her confinement and lying-in. Mr Leath, the surgeon-apothecary from Acle, who was highly regarded in the surrounding area, agreed to act as her man-midwife. Betsy also intended to book a nurse to look after her and the baby, because well-to-do woman were expected to 'lie in' for a month to recover from the rigours of childbirth before appearing in public.

Betsy was desperate to see both of her parents before she gave birth, and hoped that at the very least her father would allow her mother to stay at Reedham throughout her confinement and lying-in. But although Mrs Reading was permitted to make the long journey to Norfolk, James Reading stuck firmly to his decision to have no further contact with his daughter and son-in-law until Edward was ordained. He was clearly a man who put principles before sentiment, since he was well aware of the great risks involved in childbirth and knew he might never see his only daughter again.

On 29 May 1775 a deliriously happy Betsy gave her parents the good news that the bishop had at last accepted Edward's testimonium. His examination was scheduled for 8 June, and provided he was successful his ordination at Norwich Cathedral would soon follow. True to form, Edward complicated matters by breaking his collarbone on 7 June, but he attended the examination the next day, and passed it. William Nelson resigned his custodianship of the living of Reedham on 10 June, paving the way for Edward's presentation to the vacancy. With impeccable timing, Mrs Reading arrived in Norwich in time to see her son-in-law ordained priest at the cathedral on 11 June. She was pleased to see Betsy looking so well, and delighted with both the sights of Norwich and Edward's ordination.

Carteret Leathes was also extremely pleased to hear that Edward had been ordained at last, and in order to speed up the process of presentation to the two livings he sent £103 to help with Edward's examination and ordination expenses. Edward's ordination and the reconciliation with his father led at last to reconciliation between Betsy and her father, and on 20 June James Reading wrote to his daughter for the first time in ten months. Edward was presented to the living of Reedham on 20 June and formally inducted on 27 June. By 18 July he had also taken possession of the Freethorpe living, and could expect to receive his first income from tithes during the autumn.

The only person missing from the scene was the long-awaited baby. Childbirth in an age with improving, but still very basic obstetric knowledge, rudimentary antenatal and postnatal care, no antisepsis or anaesthetic and relatively few properly qualified and suitably experienced obstetricians, meant that women risked their lives with every pregnancy and delivery, and many of them died. In country areas childbirth was still treated as something of a female mystery, and many women invited female relatives and close friends who were themselves mothers to attend their labour, a gathering widely known as 'the groaning'. The collective knowledge and experience of those present presumably brought comfort and reassurance to the woman giving birth, and provided a degree of practical expertise.

James Reading sent a 'groaning cheese' and two bottles of Madeira to Betsy and Edward in anticipation of the birth, as he did on subsequent occasions. By the beginning of August it was clear that Betsy and the doctor had seriously miscalculated her due date. Betsy had grown to a huge size and was extremely uncomfortable. Her friend Margaret Loveden gave birth to a daughter on 15 August, and James Reading took this as an omen that Betsy would soon do likewise. At last on 27 August her labour began. Mr Leath left her in labour for 24 hours before correctly identifying that the baby was in breech position, a complication that could, and frequently did, end in the death of both mother and child. Fortunately for all those concerned his second attempt to turn the baby was successful, and after this long, painful and exhausting experience, in the early hours of Monday 28 August 1775 Betsy gave birth to a daughter, whom they also called Elizabeth.

Betsy made a good recovery, although she found breastfeeding very tiring. Edward was a proud and attentive father, pleased that both his wife and daughter had survived such a hazardous labour and birth.[6] Carteret Leathes was delighted to have a first grandchild and insisted on acting as her godfather. Although Elizabeth (or Bessy, as she soon became known) was a large and healthy baby, she was baptised soon after birth, common practice at a time when infant mortality was so high. This was done on 4 October during James Reading's first short visit to Reedham, and Mrs Reading, satisfied that her daughter's recovery was complete, returned to Woodstock with her husband a week later.

Little Bessy continued to thrive, and like most babies she exerted a powerful influence over her besotted parents, whose letters to her equally besotted maternal grandparents illustrate the growing involvement of well-to-do parents in the direct day-to-day care of their children in the second half of the 18th century. Bessy was weaned after about 11 weeks, allegedly because she would no longer feed from the breast, so Betsy had little alternative but to hope she would continue to thrive on a diet of bread and milk. Carteret Leathes was relieved to hear the news because it meant Edward and Betsy were free to visit him without her. Mrs Reading, on the other hand, was very concerned that the baby had been weaned so soon, although she appreciated the need for the parents to visit Edward's father at the earliest opportunity.

Betsy and Edward arrived at Bury St Edmunds on 4 December, leaving little Bessy at Reedham with her nurse. They were welcomed at the Northgate Street house by the assembled Leathes family. George Leathes had even travelled from London in order to meet them. Betsy enjoyed herself immensely. Because it was her first stay there as a bride, she was visited with due ceremony by all Carteret Leathes' friends and acquaintances, and etiquette dictated that she return all such visits in similar style. Betsy flourished in polite society; she loved the social life of the town and admitted to her parents that she would like to live there because it was agreeably genteel and the affluent atmosphere suited her. Edward and Betsy missed their little daughter very badly, but both of them felt that social obligations had to be fully honoured before they could return home, so they celebrated both Christmas and the New Year with Edward's family. The practice of exchanging Christmas gifts had not yet arrived in England, but those who could afford it often sent food at Christmas and New Year. Edward sent a turkey to his parents-in-law via the Birmingham coach, and told them it would keep for at least ten days after despatch. It was received safe and sound at Woodstock, the first of many such annual gifts.

The hectic round of visits, balls, card parties and other entertainments did not finish until mid-January, and even then Carteret Leathes was reluctant to let Edward and Betsy go. He did not agree to their departure until he became worried that Edward's continued absence from his clerical duties at Reedham might be construed as neglect by the bishop, even though temporary curacy cover had been

Carteret Leathes' house on Northgate Street, Bury St Edmunds

arranged before they left. They arrived back at Reedham rectory on 20 January 1776 to find that Bessy had outgrown all her baby clothes and had begun teething.

Nearly a month went by before Betsy confessed to her parents that she had suffered another miscarriage during their stay with Carteret Leathes. She attributed this to too much walking and dismissed it, but her mother worried that miscarriages could become a regular feature of her pregnancies.

Betsy and Edward's journey from Bury St Edmunds to Reedham coincided with a long spell of extreme winter weather. It rendered the roads almost impassable, and they were forced to use four horses to pull the carriage for most of the journey. It was lucky they travelled home when they did, because Reedham ferry closed on the following day. Conditions were worse at Reedham than they had been at Bury St Edmunds, and Betsy told her parents they could keep nothing from freezing inside their house. The weather was just as bad in Oxfordshire, where James Reading was unable to travel from Woodstock to nearby Stonesfield church to take services on three successive Sundays because the roads were blocked by deep snow. The Readings had also suffered from freezing conditions inside and outside their house, but all Mrs Reading worried about was Betsy's ability to keep herself and her child warm. The big freeze ended early in February 1776, when Betsy reflected that it had been the worst winter she had experienced during her lifetime.[7]

As soon as the cold spell had ended, Betsy began to plan their long-awaited visit to Woodstock to see her parents and the friends she had left behind when she eloped with Edward 18 months previously. After morning service on Sunday 5 May 1776, Betsy, Edward, little Bessy, her nurse and two manservants set off from Reedham. In 1775 Edward had acquired a coach from Messrs Gilbord, a firm of Norwich coach makers, although it was not paid for in full until 1777.[8] It was drawn by their own horses, with the family sitting inside and their manservants outside. Betsy's maid Betty travelled separately on the outside of the stagecoach from Norwich to London, and London to Oxford, and then by Bellenger's waggon from Oxford to Woodstock.

The Leathes family coach arrived at Woodstock without mishap on 11 May, no doubt making the desired impression on any Woodstock residents who saw it draw up outside the Readings' house on the High Street. The visit lasted until 20 August, and Betsy must have enjoyed herself hugely, making and receiving visits, showing off her husband and child to her Woodstock friends and acquaintances, and meeting up with old friends, particularly Margaret Loveden, who was awaiting the imminent birth of her third child.

Just before they left Woodstock Betsy found that she too was pregnant, and she spent much of the tedious journey home plagued by morning sickness. They broke their journey at Bury St Edmunds, where little Bessy celebrated her first birthday on 28 August, and arrived back at Reedham parsonage on Sunday 1 September:

> We found our Garden transform'd into a Wilderness & c^d scarcely get out the back Door for Weeds – the inside of the House made a different appearance & was perfectly clean & neat & has been preserv'd from the Damp &c better than we c^d have expected. We have a prodigious fine crop of Carrots, Parsnips, Onions, Potatoes, & Cabbage & our Artichokes tho' only planted last Spring bear finely & will afford us some nice Suppers. Our Turkey has produced seven & we have a fine brood of Chickens fit to kill which will suit Madam Bessy very well …. Our Parishioners express great Joy at our return & ran out their Doors to welcome us as we pass'd by their Houses & said they were sorely glad to see us. It was no small pleasure to us to view our Premises – there is a secret satisfaction in seeing one's own Property and I really believe I c^d. never prevail upon myself to quit Redeham unless it was for a Superior situation that was absolutely our own.[9]

Their stay at Woodstock had lasted more than three months and had cost £39.7s.6d, including £18.7s.6d for covering church services at Reedham and Freethorpe during Edward's absence.[10] This was a sum Edward could not afford. His already substantial debts had grown by some £400 in 1776, and topped £1,500 in 1777. His income from the Reedham and Freethorpe livings (including profits from the glebe land (whether rented out or farmed directly), tithes, fees and offerings) was probably between £350 and £500 a year. The income from both glebe land and tithes varied with prevailing agricultural conditions and prices, although by the late 1770s farm profits and clerical incomes were generally rising. An income of £350 should have been sufficient for a young couple with a growing family to live in a modest degree of style. But Edward and Betsy had begun their married lives in debt, thanks to Edward's extravagant bachelor lifestyle, and had accrued more debt over the subsequent year. Even if Edward took in £500 a year, it would take him many years to repay the debts after meeting overheads, taxes and the family's living expenses.

At first Betsy had done her best to equip Reedham parsonage economically, but this prudent approach did not last long. Edward evidently thought it necessary for them to have furniture, soft furnishings, silver, china, plate and kitchen equipment of a standard befitting the gentry. In many cases they delayed payment for the goods they acquired. Edward seemed equally unable to live without all the trappings of a gentleman: a coach and horses for travelling, riding horses and dogs for hunting and coursing, fishing rods, nets and a boat, and expensive guns for shooting game birds. Not surprisingly he experienced another financial crisis in March 1776. This time Carteret Leathes refused to bail him out, saying it was James Reading's turn to provide financial help. Edward and Betsy knew only too well that her father could not afford this, so Edward took out another loan to pay off a number of creditors who were making threatening noises.

James Reading hinted to Edward that it was beyond his means to keep a carriage and horses to draw it, and that perhaps retrenchment might be the answer. But Edward ignored his father-in-law's advice. When the first loan failed to solve the problem he put his name to two bonds, totalling £400, at 4 per cent annual interest.[11]

Edward's idea of a long-term solution to what he perceived as the shortfall in his income was to cease renting out his Reedham glebe land of around 80 acres and to farm it himself. Betsy's parents were dubious about the wisdom of this enterprise, which would require considerable expenditure on livestock, draught horses, equipment, fencing, drainage, seed and labour before any profit could be expected. It was a risky project for a man with Edward's financial track record and lack of farming experience. Mr and Mrs Reading were justifiably afraid that it would prove too much for both Edward and Betsy.

Financial windfalls were then, as now, always a welcome addition to any income. Like a great many of their contemporaries, Parson Woodforde included, the whole Leathes family had frequent flutters on the state lottery, and were always hopeful of winning the first prize. In December 1776 Carteret Leathes purchased five lottery tickets and gave his sons a one-fifth share in each of them, an act which prompted Betsy's mother to send her best wishes for a successful outcome. State lottery tickets cost £10 each and were frequently sold in small shares, bringing them within reach of a large number of people. Prizes were paid in cash in the 1770s, and the first prize was fixed at £20,000 (the equivalent of about £2.5 million today). The lottery was drawn in several rounds over 42 days, so the value of the tickets that survived successive rounds increased incrementally. Unfortunately Lady Luck did not smile upon the Leathes tickets: three of the five were blanks and the other two yielded a mere £20 each in prize money.[12] Carteret gave Betsy and her husband £10 of this. Betsy continued to buy lottery tickets throughout her life, always hoping to win that elusive first prize.

Betsy and Edward spent January 1777 at Bury St Edmunds, once again leaving Bessy at Reedham with her nurse. Edward fell ill with a bad cold almost as soon as they arrived, and this developed into a chest infection that continued to bother him for several weeks. Betsy enjoyed their stay at the Northgate Street mansion, and Carteret Leathes, who had developed a great fondness for his daughter-in-law, took care to ensure she had every comfort. During this uncharacteristically quiet visit Betsy encountered a new fashion in parlour games, known as charades, which livened up quiet Sunday evenings when card games were not allowed. She was very taken with the new entertainment, which seems to have been a precursor of modern charades, in which one guest set a verse riddle and the rest of the assembled company had to work out the answer. Betsy sent two examples of charades to her parents for them to solve, but either they were not cut out for the game or her explanation was unclear, because she eventually gave them the answers. Her second attempt at explanation was more successful. She sent several further examples to Woodstock and her parents wrote back with the correct solutions.

Betsy was due to give birth again in March 1777, but true to form the baby kept them waiting for a good deal longer. Mrs Reading arrived at Reedham early in March, but the month came and went without so much as a twinge, although there was little time for boredom because Bessy kept them all busy. She was clearly an active and demanding child, and it was agreed it would be best for her to accompany her grandparents back to Woodstock, leaving her parents free to concentrate on the new arrival. On 10 April Edward added a hasty postscript to his mother-in-law's letter to her husband, that Betsy had at last been delivered of a son and heir, whom they called Edward.

This was a very significant event for the Leathes family, mainly because the little boy was the first male of his generation, which put him in line to inherit the Leathes estates. Girls were seen as less important than boys in most families, so James Reading was only stating a self-evident, if somewhat cruel, contemporary truth when he congratulated his daughter on giving birth to a son:

I am very happy in the Opportunity of wishing You Joy of your Delivery, wch I hope has been auspicious & safe, and of the Birth of your little Son; and that You have been a better Woman than your Mother, who would never favour me, as You have your Husband, with a Son & Heir, but left these Conjugal Compliments to be paid, it seems, in the next Generation .... Your Daughter is a very fine little Girl, but I suppose She will no longer maintain the Preference in your Affections, (tho' she will lose nothing in your Estimation) because all Mothers are partial to a Boy. The Girls then of Course fall to the Grandmother's Care, till they get too cunning for them; and consequently Miss Bessy will be consigned to us, till she is big enough to chide her Brother for being naughty.[13]

Betsy was unwell for a short time after the baby's birth, and although she tried hard to breastfeed him she abandoned her efforts after about ten days. Fortunately young Edward was a strong and healthy baby who tolerated the change to a diet of bread and water. She then recovered quickly, but was unable to resume her social life until she had been churched on Sunday 11 May. The churching of women was a traditional celebration of thanksgiving for their safe return to church after the hazards of childbirth and lying-in. It had ancient and obscure origins, and survived in some places until as late as the 1950s. Whatever she may have felt about the social restrictions imposed by the custom, Betsy was certainly glad to regain her freedom and to enjoy the fresh air once more.

Betsy's relatively swift recovery was fortunate for James Reading, who was not managing very well on his own at Woodstock. Quite apart from missing his wife, he confessed to her that he had had servant trouble during her absence and was not sure he could cope for much longer:

I am sorry to acquaint You that my Domestic Affairs are greatly embarrassed by the bad Behaviour of your Servants. I made a Discovery a few Days ago, that there are two keys to the inner Cellar, & that it is in a great Measure stripped of its Contents, I mean Candles, Liquors & Cheese. I suspected the Candles walked off by the Dozen a little before this, and accordingly kept an exact Account, and was too soon satisfied that my Suspicions were well grounded. I wish You would send me Word what Ale you left me in Barrel. Your Maid has been seen to go loaded to a neighbouring House, and more than that at an unseasonable time of Night; for she watches me go to bed, steals down, takes the keys of the Gates & spends her Night abroad. One, was the Night before our last Fair. Upon this I secured those Keys, & the Consequence was, she introduced her Gallant at Midnight at the Hall Windows. Now, if they spent their Night in our Kitchen, I can partly account for the Consumption of Ale, Candles & Fire. In short, since this discovery, I am afraid to go to Sleep, and therefore You must not wonder if You find her discharged, for I do not think myself safe.[14]

The offending servant was dismissed, and by the time Mrs. Reading returned home she had been replaced by a maid who came with a recommendation from previous employers of known respectability.

Household management was generally seen as the function of married women throughout society; only the very wealthy and the aristocracy employed house-keepers. A married woman's duties included the hire, management and firing of servants, as well as their instruction and supervision in all aspects of work in and connected with the household: cleaning the house, buying food and drink, and managing the kitchen, the bake house, the brew house, the dairy (if there was one), the nursery and the sewing room. Housework gradually became more demanding as items of furniture, new soft furnishings and decorative materials were introduced during the 18th century, adding even more work to the house-maid's traditional repertoire. Not surprisingly the demand for servants increased as a result, while the supply began to dwindle because it was becoming easier to find alternative employment. Servants also tended to be more mobile, and rarely stayed more than one or two years in the same household during the second half of the 18th century. Maintaining a constant supply of good servants became every wife's nightmare, and most wives experienced the all-too familiar problems of absenteeism, theft, drunkenness, impertinence ('sauciness') and in the case of female servants, unplanned pregnancy. Servants and the problems asso-ciated with their employment were the common currency of conversation and correspondence between married women.

Mrs Reading finally returned to Woodstock on 5 June, accompanied by 22-month-old Bessy. Once she had been installed at her grandparents' house the little girl became the centre of attention for several local ladies. She received presents from her admirers: a one shilling share in a lottery ticket from Mrs Hindes of Hampton Gay, where she went to stay with her grandmother, plus a watch from Lady Anne Spencer and a doll's house from Lady Charlotte Spencer, the daughters of the duke of Marlborough. She was sadly missed by her Leathes uncles, and her Uncle George wrote to Betsy demanding her return:

> I shall insist upon Mr. & Mr⁺ Reading returning little Betsy by the month of November, or I make no promise of spending any time at Redeham next Winter. I doubt not but my Nephew grows a very fine little Fellow, but yet the young Lady has taken such a strong hold on my Heart that I shall not know what to do without her.[15]

Baby Edward took up much of Betsy's time, but this did not prevent her from worrying about her daughter, far away in Woodstock. Her doting grandparents described her progress in all their letters to Reedham. Their greatest concern was grandma's failure to persuade Bessy to put aside her 'baubaw' or 'mock breast'. In return, Betsy wrote of Edward junior's progress in great detail. According to her he was a good baby who rarely cried, and although he was very active he gave her very little trouble. She often mentioned details of his diet. He liked pheasant with bread sauce, rabbit, mutton, dumplings, potatoes and buttered muffins –

precocious tastes for a child of seven and a half months. Betsy was lucky to have two such fit and healthy children. Her friend Margaret Loveden was much less fortunate, for her ten-day-old baby boy and her youngest daughter died within a few days of each other in November 1777.

3 For richer, for poorer

Lack of ready cash was a permanent problem for Edward and Betsy. Edward's solution was to ignore the problem, pay off a few of his more pressing creditors and then borrow even more money. As the youngest son of a well-to-do gentry family, he evidently felt he had to maintain their social position. Although the two church livings his father had given him were together worth between £350 and £500 a year, that was an insufficient income to support his lifestyle and pay off his debts. Life would have been easier, of course, if he had followed his father's wishes and waited until he was ordained priest before marrying Betsy.

He reached a crisis early in 1777. Richard Bacon, a man from whom Edward had previously bought goods and borrowed money, was declared bankrupt.[1] His creditors took formal action against Edward and two of Bacon's other debtors in the Court of Common Pleas, which meant that Edward had to settle the debt (of £124) or suffer considerable social embarrassment and possible imprisonment.[2] John Leathes intervened at this point. He and Edward jointly took out a loan from Roger Kerrison, the Norwich banker, and the loan from Bacon was repaid.

Later that year, John realized that drastic action had to be taken if the family were to avoid similar situations in the future. So he loaned Edward £503.10s via a formal bond, a sum which met the most urgent of Edward and Betsy's outstanding debts and bills up until July 1777 and paid off the remaining bills himself. In effect John was writing off the money, since it was unlikely Edward would ever repay it. In fact this covered only part of the total debt. When Betsy drew up an account of the couple's unpaid bills on 25 August 1777 (not including the £503.10s paid by John in June), they amounted to approximately £1,700, excluding a further £100 or so of bills not yet presented.[3]

In this situation they absolutely had to make domestic economies, but Betsy's attempts at retrenchment in her household expenditure were few and lacked enthusiasm, despite her protestations to the contrary in her letters to Woodstock. At Michaelmas they replaced Edward junior's nanny with a strong maid of all work who could turn her hand to farm work if necessary. They reduced their grocery and alcohol bills by the dubious expedient of buying highly taxed luxury goods from smugglers. The secluded creeks of the Norfolk coastline and the rivers and marshes of the Broadland area were ideal for smugglers, who specialized in goods that attracted high levels of import duty, such as gin, brandy, tea and coffee. Wherrymen were often involved in carrying smuggled goods, and as Reedham lay on the important river route from Yarmouth to Norwich, the village was probably kept well supplied.

Edward's initial contribution to the retrenchment was to restrict his wine consumption. He also made a resolution not to visit the public house. His only serious plan to boost his income involved increasing the number of cows on his glebe land, but this necessitated further expenditure on stock and farm workers. It also involved hard work, late nights and equally early mornings, features of farming life which were distinctly unpopular in the Leathes household.

By early November 1777 Betsy and Edward's enthusiasm for both retrenchment and farming had waned. Their former life of ease beckoned, and Betsy soon wrote to her mother to say that they intended to revert to a lifestyle more befitting their status. Edward let out most of his glebe land once more and sold off some of his livestock. He continued to farm on a much reduced scale, paying others to do the work.[4] Any pretence of economy was soon abandoned, and Betsy and Edward resumed their lives where they had left off only a few months before.

The difficulties associated with road travel and Reedham's distance from Norwich and Yarmouth meant that much of the young couple's socializing was limited to nearby villages. They visited and were visited by neighbouring clerical families on a regular basis to dine, take tea, stay for a short period, or a combination of these. William and Catherine Nelson, Betsy's uncle and aunt, were part of this circle, as were John Arnam (rector of Postwick), Charles Gogill (rector of Brundall), James Carlos (rector of Blofield) and Samuel Browne (rector of Acle), their wives and children. The families met on a regular basis, taking it in turns to host dinners. Sometimes more elaborate parties, known as routs, were held. Betsy attended two 'grand routs' in March 1778, one at Mr Arnam's house and one at Mr Carlos's house. The second grand rout seems to have been an ostentatious affair to which many local families had been invited, and the supper included some expensive and out-of-season food such as pigeons and asparagus.

Reverend and Mrs Leathes were well integrated into the social life of the area around Acle and Brundall by 1778. Local social functions and trips to the Leathes mansions at Bury St Edmunds and Herringfleet were punctuated by occasional trips to Yarmouth and Norwich, sometimes to visit friends, but more often to attend the parties, assemblies and events that were the highlights of the county's social calendar. One such treat was a trip to Yarmouth to attend an assembly held in Yarmouth to mark the King's birthday. Edward gave his parents-in-law an amusing, if somewhat idiosyncratic, account of the occasion:

> We were soon immers'd in a crowd of Beaus Nasty, Fops Foolish, Young Flirts Poor & Proud, some newly married Dames, few Matrons, Stinking Tarrs, & the Cambridgeshire Dirty Militia, the Rest of the Group consisted of Yarmouth Whiting, Red Herrings & Cod's Heads & Shoulders with a rare Band of Unharmonious Cat-Gut Scrapers. Sick of our Amusement after a Game at Whist we retir'd to Mr. Warmington's to supper & soon after to rest; the next day we din'd at Acle with Mr. Browne & in the evening return'd to Reedham.[5]

Betsy thought the assembly had been most agreeable, and told her mother that Edward's jaundiced account was his idea of humour.

St Andrew's Hall, Norwich; drawing by James Sillett, 1828

For Betsy, the high point of their social life in 1778 was the mayor-making ceremony held in Norwich on 16 June. The mayor-elect was Mr (later Sir) Roger Kerrison, the banker, and the occasion seems to have been not only very elegant but also a very conspicuous display of wealth:

We ... were sumptuously entertain'd with every rarity that could be procur'd, a delightful Band of Musick playing the whole time which render'd it extremely cheerful. The Hall [St. Andrews Hall] is a noble Room which held the Company (tho' very large) very commodiously. The Crowd of Coaches was so great that our carriages tho' order'd at Six could not get to the Door till nine.... The Ladies were all elegantly dress'd especially Mrs Mayoress who had a very pretty Brocaded Lutestring Suit of Cloaths with a very large Hood, richly ornamented with silver Fringe & Beads & Gauze strip'd with Lylack – a beautiful pair of Point Lappets very long – Ruffles & Tippet the same, with handsome Diamonds & Pearls in her Hair & Ears – The Mayor was in a Lylack Silk Suit of Cloathes gently trimm'd with Silver – They have two Daughters & a Son, the eldest not more than eight – the little Boy had on a blue silk spotted Suit of Cloaths, the little Girls had fine silk work'd Muslin Frocks trimm'd & border'd with Silver over a pale pink Lutestring with fine Mecklin Lace – I was extremely pleas'd with my Days entertainment, it was quite a new thing to me

& different from any thing I ever saw. Everything was conducted with great order & decorum & the Mayor & Mayoress behav'd with great politeness to all the Company.[6]

Even Betsy's children were occasionally subjected to the rigours of fashion. A child's cap made of black silk was sent to Woodstock for little Bessy to wear. She did not like it, but such caps were fashionable in Norwich, and as Betsy pointed out to her mother, it would not show the dirt! She also made her own clothes and her children's clothes, doubtless with considerable help from her maids, who were expected to help with sewing tasks. She made herself an expensive black silk cloak lined with white, but was annoyed to see an advertisement for satin inter-lined cloaks in all colours on sale at £1.16s each – a great deal cheaper than it was possible for her to make them. She therefore offered to give the cloak that she had made to her mother, in return for the most genteel of the advertised cloaks.[7]

Bessy thrived at Woodstock, and at 4 years old was a sturdy, healthy, active little girl with an exceptional understanding of language and a correspondingly preco-cious vocabulary, according to her grandparents. James and Elizabeth Reading were grateful for the distractions provided by their beloved granddaughter at a difficult time in their lives. James's tenure as master of Woodstock Grammar School (1743–89) was punctuated by periods of difficulty with his employers, Woodstock Corporation. He was charged with neglect of his duties on at least one occasion, and was actually dismissed on another occasion following allega-tions of 'lewd acts' with his female pupils, although he was later reinstated.[8] These difficulties did not help his chances of improving his income when the living of Woodstock and Bladon fell vacant early in 1778. Although James acted as tutor to the duke of Marlborough's children, the duke did not consider him for either the living or the curacy, and he was left with only the occasional curacy that he had held under the previous incumbent. His social standing declined as a result of these cumulative difficulties, and James found himself publicly slighted by some of his erstwhile friends and acquaintances.

Events in the world beyond Reedham and Woodstock emerge intermittently from the letters received by Betsy and her father. News of the death in America of his brother Philip reached James Reading at the end of April 1779.[9] Philip Reading had travelled to America in 1746 as a missionary for the Society of the Propagation of the Gospel in Foreign Parts (SPG) at a salary of £60 a year. He had died a bitter and disappointed man in 1778 after more than 30 years of faithful ministry in Appoquiniminck (later Middletown), Delaware. Towards the end of his ministry he was mistrusted and finally rejected by his parishioners because he had remained loyal to his ordination oath during the turbulent months preceding the American Declaration of Independence on 4 July 1776. Philip's decision to continue to pray for the king and the royal family during church services, as required by his oath of ordination, was seen by the majority of his parishioners as a refusal to espouse the cause of independence. It led directly to the closure of his church and indirectly to his death in October 1778.[10]

His son, Philip Reading junior, had been born in Delaware and seems not to have shared his father's principles; he stayed on in Middletown, married and set up a tannery.[11] The SPG, on whose behalf Philip had laboured so long in America, was as ungrateful as his parishioners. Far from rewarding his loyalty to them and to the British Crown, they failed even to pay the pension due to his widow after his death. As late as 1789 Philip Reading junior was still seeking help to secure the money due to his mother from the SPG, and it is doubtful whether he ever succeeded.[12] When they received news of the death of Philip Reading senior his remaining siblings mourned for him, but their grief was effectively diminished by the length of their separation and by the vast distances involved, which had in reality estranged them many years before.

Closer to home, the health of some family members, friends and family servants gave Betsy cause for concern. People at all levels of society were at the mercy, to a greater or lesser degree, of the limited and sometimes downright fraudulent medical and pharmaceutical treatments available in the late 18th century, and the ability to pay for the best possible treatment was no guarantee of a cure. In 1778 Edward Leathes was troubled for the first time by gout in his toes. Gout was a disease of affluence for which medicine then had no cure. Its occurrence was known to be associated with protein-rich diets and high alcohol consumption, especially wine and fortified wine, but abstention was not a popular remedy. The number of those who suffered from gout reached epidemic proportions by the 1780s, mainly among males in the upper echelons of society. It was believed that gout could travel around the body, in which case it was known as 'flying gout'. Gout in the vital organs was considered to be the most serious kind, but 'dropping gout', or gout that had settled in the extremities, was thought to be a means of evacuating gout from the body and therefore beneficial, if somewhat painful.

Pregnancy and childbirth were continual topics of conversation among women of childbearing age and their friends and families. Betsy's friend Margaret Loveden was seriously weak following the traumatic premature delivery of her second son in 1777, which had been swiftly followed by deaths of both the baby and her youngest daughter. Her letters to Betsy indicated that she was exhausted as a result of continual pregnancies, and she expressed the wish that Betsy try to make sure she did not suffer the same fate.[13]

In April 1778 Betsy told her parents she did not intend to have any more children, but in July she wrote to tell them they could expect another grandchild in February 1779. Edward was delighted that he was to be a father for the third time, but Betsy was more concerned about where the baby was going to sleep. They were beginning to run out of room at the parsonage, and she joked that Edward might have to turn the barn into a nursery. The pregnancy seems to have been trouble-free until September, when she suffered several falls, sustaining an injured back on one occasion and a sprained ankle on another. Fortunately she recovered from her injuries quite quickly and without any lasting adverse effects. James Reading again permitted his wife to stay with Betsy for her confinement and lying-in month, but on this occasion he decided to accompany her to Reedham, together with little Bessy.

The Readings' travel arrangements were the subject of great debate, for Betsy regarded herself as something of an expert in this field and could not resist giving her parents the benefit of her opinion regarding the best route:

> I think Cambridge the most inconvenient Stage you can take from London, as you must hire a Chaise to carry you from thence to Newmarket, a dreary Road of 16 Miles. I should think the best Scheme would be to take either the Norwich two Day Coach by Colchester or Bury which would set you down by Harleston where our Chaise might meet you & bring you to our House by daylight – but there is another one which I think still better than that, which is the Yarmouth, it reaches Bury (from London) the first day where it stays all night & next morning at seven proceeds on its Journey & reaches Bungay by twelve o Clock where our Chaise [will] meet you & bring you to Redeham to Dinner .... this Coach leaves London Mondays Wednesdays & Fridays, this would also be the least expence as the Fare from Bury to Bungay is only eight Shillings – I don't know exactly what it is from London to Bury .... The Norwich Coach thro' New Market is the most inconvenient, because it w^d be too late for you to reach Redeham that night.[14]

Betsy was anxious for her parents to arrive in Reedham by the beginning of February at the latest, but her father was adamant that they could not travel to Norfolk until 11 February at the earliest. They dithered so much that they almost left it too late, and eventually arrived at Reedham only hours before Betsy gave birth to a second son, George Reading Leathes, on 19 February 1779.

Betsy made a reasonably good recovery from the relatively easy birth. Her parents stayed at Reedham for the bare four weeks of her lying-in period, and returned to Woodstock with Elizabeth junior towards the end of March, despite their daughter's pleas for them to stay longer. All was well for the first few months, then disaster struck the parsonage in late June, when both Betsy and baby George succumbed to the strain of smallpox that was ravaging the surrounding villages. Betsy's nephew Billy Nelson, who had contracted the disease at Norwich earlier in June, was making a good recovery by early July. Betsy and George seem to have recovered equally quickly, although Betsy told her mother that her face had been left permanently scarred. Edward junior, who was cutting some teeth at the time the smallpox struck and had not quite got rid of the whooping cough he had caught earlier in June, was packed off to board with a smallpox-free family nearby until Reedham was free of the disease. Betsy believed in the value of inoculation against smallpox, and thought the disease was best treated by isolating those who were infected and limiting them to a strict physical regime and a Spartan diet. Her father held diametrically opposed views, and thought Betsy reckless in her attitude.

Smallpox was not the only illness to befall the family at the parsonage, and Mr Leath, the Acle surgeon apothecary, became a frequent visitor during 1779. In May Edward Leathes fell ill with a fever, attributed by Mr Leath to the frequent colds he had suffered during the preceding months. Edward failed to respond to Mr Leath's treatment and his father became very concerned about his condition. So he set about finding an additional church living for Edward, one that would provide a parsonage in a more salubrious location than low-lying, marshy Reedham, which he considered an unhealthy place to live. He also recommended that Edward seek a second opinion from the best physician in Norwich. Betsy was also extremely worried about her husband's illness, and told her parents it was the only cloud on her otherwise perfect horizon:

> I believe that I have one of the best Men in the World for the Partner of my Life, his Intelligence & kindness to me in every respect, claim my sincerest gratitude & I hope I shall always make it my Study to make his Life happy & comfortable. A Better Heart never fill'd a human Breast, his Acquaintance all esteem him, his Parishioners & servants adore him – may the Almighty spare his Life many, many Years to be a blessing to us all.[15]

No sooner had Edward recovered from his debilitating fever than gout struck him down again, this time in both feet. Carteret Leathes, whose own health was steadily failing, was true to his word, and although he failed to secure the living of Caister by Yarmouth for Edward, he did manage to buy the living of Limpenhoe with Southwood, worth an additional £140 a year.[16] The small village of Limpenhoe and the hamlet of Southwood lay close to Reedham and Freethorpe, so Edward's three livings were conveniently grouped together. Unfortunately the new living, to which Edward was formally presented in September 1779, did not include a parsonage, so the family would have to continue living at Reedham for the time being. However Carteret Leathes still had plans to find a better house for them somewhere nearby. By late September Edward was again very ill, and Betsy and Edward travelled to Norwich soon afterwards to consult Dr Manning, although he must have made a swift recovery because he went on a shooting expedition three days later.

Carteret Leathes was by now 80 years of age, a very old man in 18th-century terms, and his health had deteriorated noticeably during 1779. At the beginning of October he became so severely ill that he was not expected to live, and was effectively confined to his house at Bury St Edmunds. By mid-November he was still in considerable pain and was so weak that he could not walk more than ten yards unaided and had to be lifted into his carriage. Even though he was unable to write, he was desperately eager to see his son and daughter-in-law at Bury St Edmunds for the post-Christmas and New Year festivities. His sons felt the best option was to visit him as usual, even though he would be unable to play any part himself. On their arrival at the Northgate Street house, Edward and Betsy found that the once lively old man had become very weak and forgetful, but despite his serious condition he remained a gregarious and generous host.

Their host's illness did not deter Betsy and Edward from enjoying themselves at Bury St Edmunds, and Betsy made good use of the room he had provided for her to entertain tea visitors and organize small card parties. They attended routs, balls, the theatre, several dinner parties, and Edward accompanied his brothers on organized shooting expeditions. Fashion was one of Betsy's keen interests, and she lost no time in assessing both the quality and contemporary style of the great and good of the locality. Although she enjoyed the social life she did not neglect to attend regular church services, even if she was unable to resist commenting on preaching style after witnessing a performance that she considered overly theatrical:

> The Sermon was wrote in the most pathetic Style you can imagine – quite Poetical, the manner & action of the Preacher entirely Theatrical, & I c^d. not help wishing that Mr. Dupré would exert his powers on the Stage especially as there seems to be at this present time a great want of Capital Performances. This Gent. is of Oxford & I think of Merton Coll. quite young & only a Visitor in this Place. In short the Theatrical mode of Preaching is so much in vogue amongst our modern Clergy that in great Towns it is become a common practice & I think now & then it is pleasing enough when the Action is proper & not over done, it is apt to keep up the attention & make a greater impression on the mind of the Hearer.[17]

Towards the end of March 1780 Carteret Leathes' condition deteriorated so much that he was not expected to live more than a few days, and Edward was summoned to his father's bedside. Carteret passed away in the early hours of 28 March. Edward told Betsy his father had been in great pain for most of the day until he lost consciousness for about four hours, after which he slipped away peacefully. Edward was very fond of his father, but neither he nor his brothers attended the funeral because locally accepted custom dictated that close relatives did not accompany the body to the graveyard. So having done as much as he could, Edward left Bury St Edmunds on 29 March and hurried back to Betsy, who was pregnant with their fourth child.

The provisions of Carteret Leathes' will were predictable. The bulk of the estate was left to his eldest son John, after payment of debts, funeral expenses, annuities and legacies. His second son George (who had risen to the rank of major in the

Light Dragoons) received a legacy of £10,000, and Edward received £4,000. Betsy's uncle, William Nelson, must have been held in high esteem by his patron, for he was left £1,000.[18] Payment of the legacies was not immediate but had to be made within three years of the date of his death, although the will provided for the payment of interest at 5 per cent on the capital sums, at half yearly intervals during the interim. Some of the surviving letters indicate that the payment of interest continued until 1791, when the legacies were finally paid in full, clearly indicating that the execution of the will had been far from straightforward. The interest payments were a welcome and much-needed addition to Edward's income, as his expenditure still had a pronounced tendency to exceed his income.

Betsy had arranged for her parents to visit her in May, when the marshes were green again and the countryside around Reedham came into its own. Although she did not expect to be confined until August, she was conscious that her mother's previous visits had been spent running the household, and she had had little or no time to enjoy herself. A May visit meant that Betsy could get out and about with her parents before her pregnancy was too far advanced. She would be able to introduce them to her friends so they could enjoy social engagements together. The visit was eventually brought forward to early April because James Reading wished to assist Edward with his church duties during the period following Carteret Leathes' death. Elizabeth junior travelled to Reedham with her grandparents, and the Leathes children were reunited for a month or so.

The visit seems to have passed uneventfully and all too swiftly for Betsy, who was faced with the prospect of waving farewell to her son and daughter, who were due to travel back to Woodstock with their grandparents. Mr and Mrs Reading left Reedham for Woodstock on 7 May 1780, accompanied by Elizabeth junior, aged 5 and Edward junior, aged 3. They broke their journey in London, where James Reading was amazed at the confidence with which his young grandson greeted the bustling city:

> Edward was embarked in a new World, and followed the pure Dictates of Nature; he seized the Oranges that were exposed to Sale in the Street, with one hand, and the Nuts with the other, without troubling himself about the Price. We went into a Pastry-Cook's to buy Biscuit for our Journey, and he began to serve himself with everything within his Reach. I never saw a young man of three years old introduce himself into the World with so little Ceremony.[19]

Unfortunately Edward junior fell ill shortly after his arrival at Woodstock. His grandparents thought at first that he must have contracted smallpox, but it soon became apparent that both children had tapeworms, a not uncommon complaint before the second half of the 20th century. Little Elizabeth did not seem to be very badly affected by them, but Edward passed three tapeworms of considerable length in two weeks before his condition began to improve. As usual, Betsy and her father disagreed about the most effective treatment for tapeworms. Betsy recommended the recipe given to her by 'an eminent Surgeon':

> For a Child of 3 y$^{rs.}$ old mix 10 or 12 Grains of Aloes with a Quarter of a Pint of Milk & give it as an Injection in the morning early, repeating the same Quantity six successive mornings & afterwards purge him with 6 Grains of Julap & 12 Grains of coarse Sugar, repeated 3 times.[20]

Predictably James Reading ignored this advice and dosed the children with a medicine containing 'the bark' (quinine), usually used to treat fevers but regarded as something of a cure-all. Because Edward recovered after he had passed the tapeworms, James Reading felt his treatment was vindicated and told Betsy there was no need to use her remedy, although he did promise to try it if the children developed tapeworms again.

News of Margaret Loveden's miscarriage saddened Betsy when it reached her early in May 1780, for her friend had already lost her father, brother and her three youngest children during the previous two years. It may also have worried her because she expected her own confinement in August. Betsy scaled down her social commitments after her return from a visit to Bury St Edmunds in June and rested at home, waiting for her confinement. On 6 August 1780 she gave birth to a baby boy, John, who lived for only 40 minutes. Having given birth to three children who had survived the perils of infancy, Betsy was devastated by this death. She seemed at first to accept what she saw as God's will and to recover well from the birth, but a few days later Edward wrote to James Reading with the news that she had caught a cold, following which she had lost the use of one leg and then lapsed into a fever, bouts of sweating and a violent headache. Her condition worried Edward so much that he called in Dr Manning from Norwich, who thought Betsy would eventually regain the use of her leg, although the illness was likely to leave her very weak for some time to come. It is possible she was suffering from white leg, sometimes known as milk leg, a type of deep vein thrombosis that occurs in pregnant women in their third trimester or just after giving birth. The condition is potentially very serious and can be fatal.

Betsy's parents were very worried about her, and although she had told them there was no need to travel to Norfolk, Mrs Reading insisted on doing so. It was the first time she had failed to attend her daughter's confinement, and the first time anything had gone wrong, so she was very uneasy about the situation. Poor James Reading was left in charge of his two oldest grandchildren, with the help of only one servant.

Betsy's recovery was slow. Six weeks after the birth her leg was still swollen and painful, and in mid-September she and her mother moved to Herringfleet Hall at John Leathes' invitation so that she could convalesce. However, Betsy's illness did not prevent the two women from taking little outings during their stay at

Herringfleet. One such outing took them to Lowestoft, where Mrs Reading was greatly impressed by the quality and cheapness of the porcelain manufactured there. Lowestoft soft-paste porcelain-ware may well have been comparatively inexpensive in 1780, but a number of factors, including the short life of the factory, the low survival rate of its product and the passage of time, have done much to increase its value since. Despite the short course of mercury treatment administered by Mr Leath of Acle when she returned home to Reedham after her mother's departure in September, Betsy made a good recovery in a surprisingly short space of time.

1780 had not been a good year for the young Leathes family. Death and illness had been all too prominent, and they must all have hoped that better times lay ahead.

4   For better, for worse

Betsy had recovered sufficiently from her illness by late December 1780 to travel to Bury St Edmunds, where the whole Leathes family had congregated at the Northgate Street house to celebrate New Year. George Leathes had married Mary Moore of Worcestershire in 1779, and his wife and baby son also joined in the family festivities. This was probably the first time Betsy had come into contact with her new sister-in-law, and she told her parents her first impressions were not favourable:

> The Want of Education in a certain Lady not an hundred miles from us, where Mind seems to be entirely devoted to Dress, Visiting & Cards without one rational Thought – I fear there is but little Prospect of Amendment as She seems to look upon herself [as] too clever to follow the Example of others .... You will suppose from what I have said ... that the acquisition of a new Relation does not afford me so much pleasure as I expected.[1]

Edward Leathes was equally unimpressed according to Betsy, and thankful that his own wife gave him no cause for embarrassment.

Although the New Year period was usually spent with the Leathes family at Bury St Edmunds, this did not mean that Betsy forgot her parents and her children at Woodstock. They usually exchanged gifts of food, and sometimes small individual presents such as ribbons and handkerchiefs, between Christmas and the New Year. The gifts were packed into hampers and sent by stagecoach; they usually reached their destinations on time and in good condition, but occasional accidents and delays caused problems. The Christmas turkey dispatched from Norwich on 20 December 1779 did not reach Woodstock until New Year's Day 1780, by which time it was not fit for consumption. The art of buck passing by carriers was clearly well developed in the late 18th century, because when James Reading enquired at Oxford about the reason for the late delivery he found that each carrier in the sequence passed the blame down the line.

Just before Christmas 1780, Edward and Betsy dispatched a large hamper to Woodstock containing a turkey, a large ham, eight bottles of rum, almonds and raisins, tea, coffee, and some small gifts for the children. This was followed by a New Year hamper sent by Edward from Bury St Edmunds containing another turkey, some sausages and mince pies. The first hamper was dispatched from Norwich on 21 December but met with a slight accident on the way to Woodstock, where the turkey was found to be well preserved, thanks to the contents of a broken bottle of rum. The second hamper seems to have arrived without mishap. Mr and Mrs Reading usually reciprocated by sending a hamper from Woodstock to Reedham or Bury St Edmunds. Given the state of 18th-century roads and the frequent overloading of stagecoaches, it is surprising that food hampers arrived unscathed and on time as frequently as they did.

Grandma and Grandpa Reading sent frequent bulletins to Betsy and Edward about the progress and development of Elizabeth junior (who turned 6 in August 1781) and Edward junior (who was 4 in April 1781). Both children were being taught by James Reading at home in Woodstock, and were making good progress in learning to read and write. Elizabeth, according to her grandfather, had become something of a tomboy, while Edward seemed to have embraced his feminine side with enthusiasm:

> He irons a Handkerchief, and almost the Sleeve of a Shirt; he sews a Doll's Cap, and, considering his Age, hems tolerably; he washes pretty well, but is apt to use too much Soap; he makes a very good Crust to a Mince-Pye; mixes Plumb-pudding, beats an Egg, and makes a Puff ... he wants nothing to compleat him, but to be introduced into the Dairy, to the Butter and Cheese.[2]

Young Edward had a good singing voice, and James Reading predicted that he would one day excel at the choral singing so typical of exclusively male social occasions. He had asked for a black doll to play with, and Betsy even went so far as to make one for him as a Christmas present. No doubt both parents and grandparents heaved a sigh of relief when his interests developed a more masculine bias after a year or so.

Betsy planned to visit her parents and the two children at Woodstock in April 1781. Unfortunately towards the end of March she took to her bed with a bout of 'the ague', a form of malaria. The disease, often known as the tertian ague, usually lasted for two months or so, and consisted of bouts of fever accompanied by vomiting and diarrhoea which lasted for between two and six hours each and returned on every third day. Patients with the ague usually became anaemic and jaundiced. It occurred frequently in parishes bordering the River Yare, where there was a good deal of the lush marsh grazing that provided an ideal breeding ground for mosquitoes. The marshes were drained in the late 18th and early 19th centuries, after which both the mosquito and the disease gradually disappeared. Edward Leathes drained the Reedham marshland owned by the Leathes family and the marshland pasture of his glebe between 1784 and 1787, too late to save Betsy from the attacks of the ague that had plagued her in the preceding years. The standard treatment for the ague in the 1780s was quinine (usually in the form of Peruvian bark) for the fever and laudanum for the other painful and unpleasant symptoms.[3]

Edward Leathes senior succumbed to another bout of unspecified illness at around the same time that Betsy had the ague, while little George had an eye infection. Ill though she was, Betsy medicated herself and the rest of the family. Many housewives were accustomed to treating minor or recurrent illnesses themselves, and had an impressive knowledge of the basic herbal pharmacopoeia. They frequently compiled their own collection of tried and trusted recipes for linctuses, poultices, ointments and cure-alls acquired from family and friends over the years. Betsy kept her own collection of recipes for conditions such as scurvy, gout in the stomach, 'eruptions', deafness, warts, constipation, rheumatism, worms, toothache, coughs and colds, chilblains and the ague.[4] To modern eyes the ingredients look a little strange to say the least, and some of the resulting concoctions might well have done more harm than good, but little else was available at the time, and faith in their curative properties might well have had a beneficial effect.

The visit to Woodstock had to be postponed until everyone was fit and well again. It was not until 30 April 1781 that Betsy, Edward senior, little George, their coachman-cum-manservant and Betsy's maid left Reedham, in their own coach drawn by their own horses. They reached the Leathes town house on Northgate Street, Bury St Edmunds that evening, and stayed there until 5 May, when they set out for London. They spent several days in the capital, where they attended to their financial affairs, picked up the interest due on their investments, made new investments, shopped for items that were difficult to obtain in the provinces and gave their horses a rest. The party finally arrived at Woodstock on or around 10 May. After a fond and welcome reunion with their two eldest children and her parents, Betsy and Edward began the usual round of making visits, receiving visitors, renewing friendships, contacting acquaintances and attending local events.

During their stay at Woodstock they visited their friends Mr and Mrs Loveden, and doubtless admired the extensive building work in progress at their home, Buscot Park near Faringdon.[5] Edward Loveden had employed the architect James Darley to design and supervise the enlargement of the old house at a cost of £20,000. He had also spent a good deal more money buying land to increase the size of his estate, saddling himself with a large debt despite his substantial income. Margaret Loveden was expecting yet another baby and had begun to suffer from severe headaches. During the summer Betsy found that she was pregnant for the fifth time, so the two friends had much to talk about.

After a most enjoyable summer Betsy and Edward finally set out for Reedham with Elizabeth junior and little George in late August. They travelled via Newport Pagnell, Cambridge and Newmarket, reaching Bury St Edmunds on 1 September. The family stayed for two weeks at the Leathes town house before making their way back to Reedham, where they arrived on 15 September. Not surprisingly Betsy declared she was thoroughly tired of travelling, and wished to enjoy home life for some time before taking to the road again.

Although she declined an invitation to stay at Bury St Edmunds in November 1781 because she felt too heavy and uncomfortable to travel, Betsy seems to have kept well throughout her fifth pregnancy. She was very worried about Margaret Loveden, whose pregnancy was beset with problems. Not only was her friend still suffering from continual headaches, there were also signs that her baby had died in the womb. Poor Margaret refused to acknowledge the obvious truth, and in October she told Betsy that she still believed herself to be seven months pregnant, no matter what other people thought. But by December she had suffered a miscarriage.

Betsy, on the other hand, was planning ahead, making sure that her mother would be on hand at Reedham for her own confinement. Travel arrangements were made and Mrs Reading duly arrived at the parsonage on 4 January 1782. Betsy was very grateful to her father for allowing her mother to visit because she had begun to feel unwell and uncomfortable, thanks to her large size. Her mother thought she might give birth to twins. Fortunately all went well and on 16 February 1782 Mrs Reading wrote to her husband to congratulate him on the birth of another grandson, privately baptised Reading in his honour.

Baby Reading was formally christened at Reedham Church on 28 April 1782, where the service was performed by his great-uncle, William Nelson. James Reading, Mrs Pryse of Woodstock (Margaret Loveden's mother), and William Nelson stood as godparents, although neither James Reading nor Mrs Pryse was able to travel to Reedham for the occasion and both nominated substitutes to attend the service. Mrs Reading returned to her long-suffering husband at the beginning of May. She was much missed by the family at Reedham, especially Betsy, who sincerely thanked her mother for the kindness and care she had received from her:

> We all lament your loss very much & never a day passes but we are wishing for Grandmama – This being washing week, I am head Nurse, therefore only take up my pen for a few minutes while my little Boy sleeps, he is now in the Cradle by me, perfectly happy as health & innocence can make him, Elizabeth is setting a few more stitches in Dolls bed-gown & George rolling upon the Carpet …. he often burst out in a fit of crying & exclaim'd, I'm sorry poor Grandma is gone, His Sister endeavour'd to conceal her grief & to soothe him & took upon herself the Woman very much.[6]

Grandmama was clearly a born organizer, for she soon restored order to the Woodstock household after her return, sorting out her household, her husband and her oldest grandson. It was customary for male children to wear dresses until they were about 4 or 5 years old, after which skirts were abandoned for breeches. Edward's parents and grandparents agreed that it was time for him to undergo this rite of passage, so the 5-year-old was duly measured for a suit and formally breeched on 23 May 1782. The little boy enjoyed this change in his status and the resulting admiration of the ladies so much that he became particularly fond of dressing and undressing and wanted to go to bed during the day so he had an excuse to do so. Edward's progress was not confined to the physical; his grandfather also observed a significant improvement in his capacity for learning in general

A gentleman's day dress of the 1780s and the less fashionable dress of a clergyman

and his enjoyment of reading in particular, but regretted his tendency towards sulkiness.

George Leathes, Betsy's brother-in-law, sold his commission as major in the Light Dragoons for 5,000 guineas and left the army early in 1782, intent on living the life of a gentleman of leisure. John Leathes, the eldest brother, ran the family estates through a land agent and bailiffs, but as the youngest brother, Edward Leathes had to work for a living. Services at Freethorpe and Reedham churches were held every Sunday, while there were services at Limpenhoe and Southwood churches on alternate Sundays, therefore on any one Sunday Edward had to conduct services in three churches. As there were also services on the numerous feast days and saints' days in the church calendar, the job was not exactly a sinecure. Many sermons were needed for these services, but the task was rendered less onerous by the relatively common practice of borrowing sermons from other clergymen. Edward borrowed James Reading's sermons at regular intervals, and occasionally James borrowed some of Edward's. James's father William Reading had published three volumes of sermons during his lifetime, and James made Edward a present of these in 1782.[7] Edward also worked his way through William Reading's manuscript sermons, which had been loaned to him by James, and had them bound before returning them.

Edward Leathes was a reasonably conscientious clergyman, and he was conscious of his duty to the poor of his parishes, particularly in Reedham, as befitted the brother of the squire. He organized subscriptions of money to support the poor of the parish in long periods of bad weather and chronic unemployment, and he frequently donated food to the poor when times were hard. When he travelled to Bury St Edmunds in March 1782 Edward left Betsy to supervise the distribution of half a bullock between 36 poor families in the parish. She described to Edward the joy involved in this episode of charitable giving, as well as some of the more practical problems involved in the distribution:

> You lost a great pleasure by not being at home to see them flock from your house with cheerful Countenances & grateful Hearts, there is certainly a heartfelt satisfaction in doing a charitable Action superior to every other pleasure. I only wish it was in our power to experience it oftener. I endeavour'd to have your orders executed as nearly as possible in the division of it & hope you will be pleas'd with my management. It afforded a very handsome Lot for every one according to the size of their Families & they were all well satisfied – except Mrs. Jane Capps, whom upon several accounts I did not consider as an Object of Charity, therefore had not enter'd her on the List, but She attended my Levee this morning without invitation & I believe I should have order'd her a piece but She was very saucy – however tho' I am out of her favour I fancy you are not, for She said She was sure if the Parson had been at home he wd. have given her some.[8]

As head of the Leathes family John Leathes had a duty to marry and produce an heir. He had been engaged since 1780 to Elizabeth De'Ath, thought to have been the daughter of a Herringfleet farmer, and the couple finally married at the beginning of May 1782. Edward, Betsy and Elizabeth junior were invited to stay at Bury St Edmunds, where members of the Leathes family were to congregate in order to celebrate the return of the newly-weds from London in June. News of the squire's wedding was received in time-honoured fashion at Reedham. 'Half the Parish have been ringing to Day for the Squires Wedding & Mr. Leathes has treated them very plenteously with strong Beer – Some of them are so very Tipsey that they are forc'd to be lock'd in the Barn all night – & the rest are oblig'd to lead each other home.'[9] Edward was dependent on his eldest brother for any further increase in his income, in the shape of loans or the gift of more livings.

Fashionable lady's dress, 1780s

Betsy was therefore assiduous in her cultivation of John Leathes and his wife, not only on her husband's behalf but also on her father's behalf – the gift of a modest living to her father would have been very convenient after he fell out of favour with the Marlboroughs. She also lost no time in urging her father to write to John and congratulate him.

John Leathes sent Betsy 28 and a half yards of silk, to be made up into a gown suitable for accompanying the new Mrs Leathes when she returned her bride visits at Bury St Edmunds. Edward also made his wife a present of some silk for another dress to wear on formal occasions. Betsy sent her mother a sample of the fabric provided by her brother-in-law, but asked her not to show it to anyone at Woodstock because she wanted people to think it was a new dress when she next visited her home town. She was much more impressed with her new sister-in-law than she had been with George Leathes' wife, writing that 'I have the pleasure to find my new Sister a very agreeable Sensible Woman & one of the most elegant Figures I ever saw – as she has a remarkable good Taste in Dress, her Cloathes are very handsome & well chosen, very proper for her Situation in Life.'[10] Because his new wife had fashionably delicate health, John Leathes decided to visit Tunbridge Wells so she could take the waters.

Baby Reading and young George were left at Reedham in the care of a nursemaid while Edward and Betsy were staying at Bury St Edmunds, and at first all seemed to be well. But on 26 June 1782 Edward, who had been to Herringfleet Hall with his brother for a short visit, wrote to Betsy with some terrible news:

My Dearest Life
The bad news I have to inform You of will I am afraid affect You beyond measure I therefore pray You to summons to your assistance & aid all your Courage fortitude and reason, for I know not how to soften or palliate that story which you must hear, and I must relate, but to relieve from all suspence know then that Charles arrived at Herringfleet this morning with the affecting & disagreeable account of my poor child Readings having been taken in the night or early this morning with a very bad stoppage under which the dear dear

Infant went off, for Godsake my Dear bear this unfortunate unexpected blow with Patience & Resignation to the Divine Will & Pleasure.[11]

Reading was buried at Reedham on 28 June by his father and his great uncle, William Nelson. Later letters indicate he had died after having a fit, so his young nursemaid was not in any way to blame. Betsy and Edward were devastated, having lost two babies in less than two years. To make matters worse Betsy succumbed to another bout of the ague and was unable to return to Reedham for another two and a half weeks. Her parents would have liked her to convalesce at Woodstock, but Betsy preferred to accept the invitation of her brother- and sister-in-law to accompany them to Tunbridge Wells, where she could recuperate and take the waters. Edward, whose own need for rest and care was probably equally pressing but whose pockets were insufficiently deep, had to stay at Reedham to carry out his ecclesiastical duties.

Arrangements were made for Elizabeth junior to attend a suitably genteel school in Bungay during Betsy's absence. She began to learn to dance during her stay there, and seems generally to have been very happy. George was moved around between his father at Reedham, John and Elizabeth Leathes at Herringfleet, and George and Mary Leathes at Bury St Edmunds. Betsy's departure for Tunbridge was delayed by a severe injury to Edward's leg, a deep gash which had laid bare both the tendon and the joint. He also suffered another attack of the gout, and he was still far from well when Betsy set out for Tunbridge on 22 August to join Mr and Mrs John Leathes. It did not take long for her to decide that all aspects of spa life were beneficial, and she described the place, the people, the social round and her convalescent routine to Edward in some detail:

I am very much pleas'd with the Place & the Country round which is romantick

*Exterior of
St John the Baptist Church,
Reedham, 20th century*

beyond description & as it abounds with Hills the prospects are delightful, the Air is particularly pure & salubrious. The Wells are at this time remarkably full of Company, & that of the genteelest sort, indeed none but People of Rank & Fortune ought to come hither, for the Expences of the Place are greatly beyond a moderate fortune – every thing is gay & chearful & you would not suppose any one resorted hither for the sake of health, Pleasure seems to be the chief Object, for the gratification of which there are a continual round of Amusements from the time we rise till the hour of returning to rest – Publick breakfasts, Publick Tea-Drinkings, Raffles innumerable, Balls twice a Week, Publick Card Tables every day & what I admire very much is a Publick Walk close to the Well (called the Pantiles) I suppose from its being pav'd, where a band of Musick plays at certain hours, on one side is a row of very entertaining Shops & on the other two or three fine rows of Trees, when it is lighted up of an Evening it puts me in mind of Vauxhall & what renders it very convenient for this Wet Season is that half of it is under a Covering which secures one from the frequent Showers & also from Catching Cold – The number of Subscriptions are a very chief part of the Expence & are things one cannot avoid without appearing particular. I subscrib'd to a Charity Sermon for repairing the Chapel on Sunday & on Monday to both the Rooms in consequence of which I had a visit the next morning from Mr. Tyson the Master of Ceremonies, which I find is customary & in return for his Politeness we are going this Evening to his Ball, which has the same regulation as at Bath, that begins at seven & ends at eleven an agreeable circumstance to us who are fond of regular hours. I assure you we are such sober folks that we declin'd an invitation to a private Ball on Monday merely on account of the late hours we must necessarily have kept, for as we are oblig'd to rise early it makes us little inclin'd for sitting up late – my Sister drove me out upon the Rocks yesterday morning as soon as we had drunk the Waters & the clear air of Mount Ephraim gave me a particular relish to my breakfast …. I forgot to tell you we have the same Master of the Ceremonies here as at Bath, & like Bath here are two Sets of Rooms which are continually open alternately for the reception of the Company.[12]

Despite her protestations that she was leading a quiet life, Betsy had to ask Edward to send her more money on two occasions to cover 'unforeseen' expenses and presents. Edward was distinctly unimpressed. Not only was Betsy enjoying all the comforts and diversions of Tunbridge, she had declared her intention of moving on to Woodstock when she left, and had asked him to send Elizabeth and George, plus servants, to London in their coach so that she could meet them there and proceed to Woodstock in the coach. Edward was unwilling to go along with this plan, and Betsy eventually travelled to Woodstock alone by stagecoach, arriving on 20 September 1782.

It is not surprising that Edward was unhappy about Betsy's costly travels. He had continued to suffer at home with an ulcerated leg throughout August and early September, enduring the attentions of Mr Leath, which included purging, constant doses of quinine for the fever that accompanied the ulcer, and a short course of mercury. Despite the fact that he was sick, worn out and depressed, he had managed to serve his churches throughout August and September. His perseverance was rewarded by a temporary lull in his afflictions at the end of September, and he left Reedham for Essex to join his brothers for a shooting trip, followed by an excursion to Newmarket races and from there to Bury St Edmunds in time for Bury Fair.

Towards the end of her stay at Tunbridge Wells Betsy realized she was pregnant yet again. Morning sickness began to plague her, spoiling her visits to Woodstock and Buscot Park. When Edward received news of the pregnancy in mid-September he offered to send some 'good Geneva' (gin) to Tunbridge or Woodstock, possibly as an abortifacient. It seems he too found it difficult to entertain the possibility of another dead baby. By mid-October both Edward and Betsy were feeling the need to be reunited as a family in their home at Reedham, and Edward planned to travel to Woodstock in their coach in order to collect her and bring her back. Unfortunately he fell ill again, the plan was abandoned, and Betsy finally travelled to Norwich by stagecoach, reaching Reedham on 16 November. She was delighted to be back at home with her husband and children, although poor health continued to trouble Edward throughout the winter months.

Back home at Reedham Betsy was glad to relax, sit back and indulge herself with a good book. She told her parents she had spent most of her time since she returned home reading Fanny Burney's runaway bestseller *Cecilia*, which she had enjoyed enormously. Christmas was a quiet affair spent at Reedham parsonage, although Betsy and Edward went to Bury St Edmunds for the New Year festivities. Betsy and Mrs George Leathes were both pregnant, and Mrs John Leathes was her usual delicate self, so all three women spent a very quiet time at the Northgate Street mansion during January 1783.

Her return to Reedham at the end of January saw Betsy in reasonably good health for this late stage of her pregnancy, and she began to prepare for her confinement, which was expected in April. Unfortunately Edward then fell violently ill, and it was three weeks before Betsy was able to tell her parents that he was on the road to recovery, causing Mr and Mrs Reading to speculate yet again about the cause of Edward's frequent illnesses.

Mrs Reading's visit to Reedham for her daughter's confinement was eagerly awaited by the Leathes family. Her journey was planned to coincide with the full moon between 18 and 23 March, a common practice amongst seasoned coach travellers, who knew that the light of the moon gave better visibility, making poor road surfaces and highwaymen much easier to see. She left Woodstock for Oxford on 19 March and travelled overnight to London, where she changed coaches and travelled on overnight to Norwich, arriving on 21 March without having had an overnight stop at all, quite a feat in those days. Betsy met her at Norwich and was surprised to find her hale and hearty, despite her lack of sleep.

After a false labour on 8 April, Betsy finally gave birth to a healthy baby girl on 12 April 1783. The baby was privately baptized Mary on the same day. This precaution was often taken by parents in case the baby died during the first few months of life, while the formal christening usually took place three to six months later. Betsy seems to have recovered very quickly, and was soon breastfeeding little Mary and complaining of sore nipples. Edward fell ill yet again shortly after Mary's birth. He seemed to have recovered by the end of April, but relapsed early in May. Betsy's month of lying-in after the birth passed without any further mishap, and she was churched on 11 May. After so much heartache in the previous two and a half years, Betsy and Edward were happy to watch Mary thrive, and to hope that this time they would be fortunate enough to see her grow up.

James Reading, who had been preoccupied with his problems at Woodstock, finally arrived in Reedham at the end of May, too late to officiate at his grand-daughter's christening. The doting grandparents enjoyed the summer months at Reedham, and returned to Woodstock with their two eldest grandchildren at the end of September. The Leathes children were growing fast, and the three eldest were developing as personalities. In the opinion of his Uncle John and Aunt Elizabeth Leathes, Edward had a 'sweet and generous' disposition. Elizabeth, they said, seemed to be the favourite of both Betsy and her father, while their grand-mother loved them all and had no clear favourite. 'Rebel George' was his Aunt Elizabeth's favourite and had the first claim on her affections.[13]

By the end of November 1783 baby Mary had cut two teeth and was making good progress. She was still being breast fed but had begun to take solid food in the form of 'pudding' and vegetables, bread and butter, toast and occasionally finely minced meat. She was fond of beer, which she had nearly every day, and her parents frequently gave her a little red wine. Not surprisingly she was strong and active, and had become so heavy that Betsy could scarcely carry her. Four live and healthy children from six full-term pregnancies was a good average for the late 18th century, and the Leathes family at Reedham parsonage could be considered blessed in that respect.

5   In sickness and in health

In January 1784 Betsy received news that Margaret Loveden, her childhood friend, was gravely ill. A physician had been summoned from London, but was able to do little for her, and she died at the end of the month, leaving a husband and three children. Her friend's death upset Betsy greatly, and she went into deep mourning, as she would have done for a close relative. In ten and a half years of marriage her friend had suffered two miscarriages and given birth to six live children, three of whom had died in infancy. There could be little doubt that the debilitation resulting from the combination of illness, frequent pregnancy and childbirth had contributed to her premature death. Betsy herself, now aged 36, was hoping that Mary would be her last child, having had eight pregnancies in nine and a half years. Edward Loveden was broken-hearted for a few months but by the end of the year he was already looking for a new wife, preferably an heiress who would be able to subsidize his building habit.

The winter of 1783/84 was notoriously cold and the usual New Year visit to Bury St Edmunds had to be cancelled. Betsy caught a bad cold, which she attributed to her attendance at a bankruptcy sale in Great Yarmouth, and this laid her low for most of January. At the same time Edward came down with gout, rheumatism and gravel, and he too was ill for much of January and February. The cold, snowy weather and icy conditions were an inconvenience to the better off, but to the poor who lived at subsistence level they were a disaster. Bad weather meant no work, no work meant no money, and no money meant little or no food, other than that provided by parish poor relief and private subscription.

At Reedham riverside some keels, or river barges, on their way from Norwich to Yarmouth became marooned when the River Yare froze over, and the keel men, who carried only food sufficient for their journey, began to feel the pangs of hunger when it ran out. They walked to the parsonage to beg for charity, and Edward responded by giving them some pork and peas which, together with other food they acquired by similar means, was just about enough to keep body and soul together. The poor of Reedham were also hungry and cold, so Edward raised a subscription for their relief; he put in two guineas himself and the wealthier farmers and other residents who could afford to do so followed suit. The money was used to buy food and fuel for the poorest families, which was augmented by doles of beef, bread and beer from Edward and a few other Reedham residents. Even at the end of March the weather was still cold and the snow lay in deep drifts over the whole district. To make matters worse, the spectre of smallpox began to stalk the villages around Acle, and Betsy began to fear that it would spread to Reedham.

The four Leathes children were growing up fast, and education began to play an important part in the lives of the two eldest, who were currently living with their grandparents at Woodstock and being tutored by James Reading. James held strong views about what was best for them in the long term, favouring a genteel boarding school for Elizabeth and a public school for Edward. He was unsure of their parents' views and felt that in Elizabeth's case, private dancing lessons with local masters and continued home tuition might well provide a temporary solution. James thought private tuition might also answer for Edward in the short term, but it was finally agreed that he should attend school at Woodstock and receive supplementary tuition from his grandfather. It was becoming obvious that while he was extremely intelligent and very able, Edward was headstrong, obstinate and difficult to control.

Betsy agreed that Elizabeth should continue to receive dancing tuition, and Edward too if he showed any inclination to do so. She wished the dancing master to concentrate on drilling Elizabeth in the arts of 'a graceful Carriage & an easy genteel entrance into a Room, I look upon these things to be of more Consequence than dancing, as they will be of advantage to her every hour, Dancing is a Thing which does not occur so often, not but that I wish her to excel in that too.'[1] Elizabeth's posture and figure became something of an issue following a derogatory remark made by one of the Woodstock ladies, and 'stiff stays'

were the recommended solution. Thankfully Betsy thought this too extreme a measure for a 9-year-old girl who already wore a junior version of adult stays. It was finally agreed that Mrs Reading should have a steel collar made for Elizabeth and ask the stay maker to add extra stiffening to her existing stays.

George Reading Leathes had begun to attend school at Reedham in mid-January 1784, just before his fifth birthday. His attendance must have been somewhat irregular as he spent a fair amount of his time with his uncle and aunt Leathes at Herringfleet, where he was pampered and made much of. They were very fond of him and seem to have assumed some parental responsibilities, especially where his education was concerned, for by late May 1784 he was attending school at Herringfleet. It was at Herringfleet that he came down with the 'Water-Pock' (chickenpox), and he had to return to Reedham to be nursed by his mother. After his recovery he stayed at home for much of the rest of the year. Betsy was conscious

Stays and chemise, 1770s–90s

Herringfleet Hall in the 1830s. The house inherited by Carteret Leathes in 1772 is the older block to the right of the picture; the square south range with the three-sided bay to the left of the picture was erected by John Leathes in the mid-1780s and the entrance elevation was added as part of the improvements made in the 1830s. The drawing is based on a photograph supplied by Suffolk Record Office (HG 402/3/83), courtesy of Mrs Helen Sandon

that George was in need of regular and consistent schooling because he was falling behind with his reading, and she did not have the time to help him.

Little Mary, the baby of the family, reached her first birthday on 12 April 1784 and began to walk unaided two weeks later. It was fortunate that she was healthy as well as good natured because her constitution was severely tested in the latter part of 1784 and early 1785. First her leg was burned at the beginning of June 1784 when a careless nursemaid let her play too close to the open fire, then two weeks later she came down with chickenpox, probably caught from her brother George. Worse was to come in December 1784 when she came into contact with a virulent strain of smallpox which had already killed a woman in Limpenhoe, a woman and child at Cantley and a woman at Acle. Betsy was very worried because Mary was teething at the time and was also suffering from a cold, so she decided to 'prepare' her for the onset of smallpox by putting her on a strict diet of potatoes, toast and water and isolating both the child and herself while she cared for her. The disease struck soon afterwards, but on 2 January 1785 Betsy was able to tell her parents that Mary was over the worst. The little girl made a complete recovery, much to the relief of the whole family.

As head of the Leathes family, John Leathes owned both the mansion house at Northgate Street, Bury St Edmunds and Herringfleet Hall. He used the former as his residence during the Bury social season and on those occasions when he was obliged to visit the town on official business in the locality, while the latter became his main residence. The two younger Leathes brothers had growing families, and both felt the need for larger, and in George's case more prestigious, accommodation. George and his family had moved into rented accommodation in Bury St

Edmunds after he left the army, but this became too small for his needs, so he and his family took up temporary residence at the Northgate Street house while he searched for a suitable gentleman's residence to rent. He eventually decided on Kirby Cane Hall, between Beccles and Bungay, and the family moved in during October 1784.

Edward and Betsy had the largest family but the smallest income, so the only viable solution for them was to extend the house in which they lived, an option that was finally forced on them when the smoking kitchen chimney had to be knocked down, exposing a severely damaged gable end wall. The whole wall had to be demolished, conveniently providing the opportunity to add an extension. Typically, Edward and Betsy did not confine themselves to a modest addition to their living accommodation but built on a grander scale, adding a new parlour, a study and bedroom for Edward, a larger kitchen, bigger and better outhouses, and a suite containing a parlour and bedroom for Mr and Mrs Reading – an incentive to either visit more frequently or take up permanent residence. It was anticipated that the building work would last at least a year, so Betsy and Edward were forced to cancel their planned visit to Woodstock during the summer. The final cost of the extension was more than Edward could comfortably afford, so it is likely that John Leathes footed at least some of the bill because the house was a Leathes family asset and not Edward's own property.

Spending money was something Edward was rather good at, even though he did not have an income commensurate with the scale of his spending. Edward and Betsy's social life was busy, consisting mainly of dinner and tea visits, card parties and card visits, parties and balls at neighbourhood level, plus visits to Herringfleet, Bury St Edmunds and Norwich, where rather grander company was involved. Fashionable clothes were a necessary part of their social life, and they were expensive. Betsy and her maids, together with Mrs Reading and her maid, sewed basic clothes for the children and for themselves, but 'best' clothes usually required the skills of a tailor or a dressmaker, often known as a mantua maker in the 18th century. The attentions of a hairdresser were needed for special occasions in order to create and maintain the tall hairstyles that were so fashionable for ladies during the 1770s and 1780s, when hair was arranged over a high frame or a pad of tow, often with the addition of false curls and ringlets, and the whole edifice was lavishly powdered.

Betsy described the preparations necessary before stepping out for public inspection during Bury St Edmunds Fair week in October 1784:

> The greatest part of the morning after our arrival was spent in adjusting our Dress & modernising ourselves that we might make our appearance at the Fair without the hazard of being pointed at for our awkwardness. The first & chief Personage employ'd in assisting in this important Article is the Hair Dresser who comes down from London on these occasions & is equal in extravagance

Left to right: a white cap under a straw hat, an elaborate hairstyle,
and the Gainsborough or Marlborough hat

to those in all publick Places & what with Powder Pomatum Pins Combs & Cushions I suppose his Bill will be as much as w^{d.} maintain my whole Family for a month.[2]

Fair week was an important regional social occasion. Betsy loved it – the promenading, the lectures, the plays, the dances, the parties, the balls and the church attendances – and described it to her mother in some detail:

After sauntering in the Square which is built for this purpose upon the Angel Hill with Shops round where You may purchase all kinds of Things & great temptation to Draw the Money out of your Pocket, the next amusement was an Exhibition of stain'd Glass which was really very curious & a new way of taking Likenesses, very well worth seeing. In the Evening we attended the Lecture upon Elocution & upon Hearts which I should have thought very clever had I never seen Alexander Stevens, but these kind of things always appear flat upon a second hearing – As this was ended by eight o'Clock we thought it too soon to return home therefore to keep up the true Spirit of the Beau Monde we drove to the Playhouse & were just in time for the Farce of 'Dead Alive' which is a very laughable thing – The next Morning (Wednesday) we went to a Concert for the Benefit of Leoni which did not answer my expectation as I have heard the same Musick perform'd in a much more capital Style – & Leoni's Voice is not near so good as when I heard him last, Master Hague the other Vocal Performer pleas'd me better his Voice is exactly like Spences who sung at the Musick Room at Oxford. The Amusement for the Evening of that Day was an Assembly & a very genteel one, & as none of our Party were Dancers, after the Minuets were over we retir'd to the Card Room & play'd a Rubber at Whist, the Party at the next Table to us were the Duke de la Cour Lady Hunt the Recorder of Bury & Miss Vanneck we left the Rooms about two – next Morning (Thursday) walk'd in the Fair receiv'd & paid morning Visits, in the Evening we went to see the Comedy of the Rivals with poor Vulcan – the Play was extremely well acted the Characters well supported the Story interesting & a great deal of true Comic humour runs thro' the Whole, I think it is wrote by Sheridan – Friday Morning was chiefly spent in preparing for the Ball in the Evening.[3]

The ball held at the Assembly Rooms was the highlight of the week:

The Room was exceedingly crowded being near five hundred People & not one Tradesman or Tradesmans Daughter, the Ball was open'd by Lady Mary Cornwallis who (according to the fashionable Phrase) comes out this Fair, & S[r.] John Rous, & the Hon[ble.] M[rs.] Sandford & S[r.] Gerrard Vanneck – Minuets being always danc'd at both ends of the Room. The dresses were extremely elegant, Diamonds & Pearls in great Profusion, a number of fancy dresses by which the Ladies shew'd their Taste for they were most of them well chosen & display'd their Charms to a great advantage, one Lady who was extremely ornamented with Diamonds & Pearls Flowers Feathers gold fringe &c was in our Party & Bride to Counsellor Mingee [Mingay] of Thetford, her Name was Corall a Kentish Lady of large Fortune so the family of the Mingees seem to be in a flourishing State. Yesterday Morning we pass'd in paying & receiving Visits sauntering into the Square Shopping & putting into Raffles. In the Evening we were willing to give ourselves a little Rest & sat quietly at home to recruit our Spirits. This morning we have been to hear a Sermon by a famous Preacher Dr. Harrison, The Sermon was a good one but his manner & action was so very Theatrical that I could not help fancying myself in a Playhouse instead of a Place of Worship. There was a Collection for the Charity Children & I dare say a very good one for there was a very genteel Congregation.[4]

Even in the provinces, social life at this level could only have been expensive.

Fashion had come to mean much more than clothes and hairstyles by the second half of the 18th century, when buildings, furnishings, interior and exterior decoration, food and household goods of all kinds were all subject to the demands of progress and style. Retail outlets were needed to supply both the home-produced and the imported goods needed to meet the growing requirements of fashion and good taste amongst the rich and the middle classes. Shops and warehouses were opened in increasing numbers by enterprising tradespeople, craftspeople and entrepreneurs during the late 17th and 18th centuries in order to meet the demand. The practice of shopping for non-essential but fashionably modern goods had arrived, and a consumer society had come into being. Betsy and Edward embraced both fashion and consumption with enthusiasm, although their tastes invariably exceeded their income.

According to Betsy's accounts, between 1774 and 1787 she and Edward spent a total of £919.13s.7d on furniture, carpets, china, glass, musical instruments, iron-mongery, brassware, silverware, linen and other fabrics, books, coaches, saddlery, fishing nets, boats and guns.[5] The list is not comprehensive and Betsy's accounting and addition were somewhat hit and miss, but it does give some idea of the scale of their spending, especially when the equally lavish sums spent on food, alcohol, clothes, schooling, entertaining, horses, dogs and so on are taken into account. The imperatives of class, gentility and fashion were such that Edward and Betsy felt they had little alternative but to live on the credit extended to them by traders and retailers and then to borrow from money lenders to pay those bills that could not be met from their income.

Money and possessions were precious to Edward and Betsy, and like many other people with taxable assets, they resented the direct and indirect taxes levied by the government on their property, lifestyle and purchases. But Britain's wars were expensive, and the government's need to raise as much revenue as possible to meet the expenses of war and to service the national debt had increased as the wars proliferated. The first budget of William Pitt the Younger in June 1784 not only increased existing direct and indirect taxes on goods and services, it also introduced new taxes. As a result it became more expensive to employ servants, use horses and coaches, have windows in houses, go shooting, buy gentlemen's hats, ribbons, silk gloves, fabrics, newspapers, writing paper, and post letters.

Before the advent of railways and the introduction of the penny post in 1840, the British postal system was slow and expensive. Postal charges depended on the distance travelled by each letter and the number of sheets of paper it contained; the charge was paid by the recipient, who had to collect the mail from the nearest post office. Betsy recorded the cost of every letter she received that was subject to postal charges. Both she and her correspondents complained loudly every time costs rose, and made frequent attempts to reduce the number of sheets of paper they used in their letters by confining themselves to one sheet and writing both across and down it in small script, a practice known as crossing. The middle and upper classes attempted to reduce their postage costs by making use of the system of 'franks' whenever they could. (MPs and peers of the realm were able to use their parliamentary privilege of franking letter covers for friends and political contacts; letters covered in this way travelled free of charge.) Betsy, her family and her friends were often successful in their efforts to acquire franks, sometimes in quite large numbers. Any threat to restrict the use of franks met with fierce resistance from all those involved.

Needless to say, the Leathes and Reading families were typical of their class in their vociferous disapproval of any attempt to increase taxation. In practical terms, the 19 windows in Reedham parsonage cost Edward Leathes senior £2.10s.0d a year in tax after 1784, as opposed to £1.11.6d in 1784. Their servants cost them £4 a year in tax after 1784, their four-wheeled carriage £6.17s.2d, their three horses £1, and Edward's shooting licence £2.10s. Their average yearly tax bill prior to 1784 was around £30 but after 1784 it rose to around £40. Their total tax bill for 1786 was £41.10s.8½d, including new and increased government taxes, land tax, ecclesiastical taxes and parish poor rate.[6] Such was the determination of James Reading and Edward Leathes to reduce the amount of tax they had to pay that James blocked up five of his windows and Edward took the springs off his whisky, a type of two-wheeled carriage drawn by two horses, transforming it into a vehicle that did not incur carriage tax.

The same whisky was involved in a road accident in May 1784, when Edward was badly injured. He suffered considerably afterwards with a broken clavicle, and it was several weeks before Betsy was able to tell her parents that he was on the road to recovery. Edward's health, which had already taken a battering from gravel, rheumatism and gout earlier in the year, remained poor after the carriage accident. He came down with a bad cold, followed by yet another attack of gout in September, and then by an unidentified but worrying illness in October, when Betsy said that he was suffering from bouts of acute breathlessness. James Reading made reference in his letters to Edward's frequent chest and breathing problems, plus several other recurrent complaints – too many for comfort for a man still three years short of his fortieth birthday.

Much of Betsy's correspondence with her parents between 1780 and 1784 concerned the ups and downs of the relationship between her father and the duke of Marlborough. James Reading had tutored the children of the duke and duchess on a regular basis since 1771, when the duke's agent had first asked him to visit Blenheim Palace in that capacity. Although he carried out his tutorial duties conscientiously and well, payment for his services was at best infrequent and at worst non-existent. He made no reference in his surviving correspondence with Betsy and Edward to a fee having been agreed in the first place, or of ever having received any payment, and he had certainly received nothing since 1780. He received frequent invitations to dine at Blenheim Palace with the Marlboroughs and regular presents of venison from the park. He was treated as an intellectual equal by the duke, a keen amateur astronomer, who had relied heavily on James's help in setting up and running the observatory in Blenheim Park. The duke was clearly happy to deal with James as a gentleman, but discussion of payment for his services did not fit comfortably with the niceties of rank or gentility.

James had already been passed over as a candidate for several of the wealthier church livings in the duke's gift when the living of North Leigh fell vacant in 1783. Unfortunately for him, he was passed over yet again. By this time his income from other sources had also shrunk, reducing his total income by about £50 a year and leading to a degree of financial embarrassment. So in 1784 James was left with little alternative but to try to collect some of the money he considered to be owing to him and to put his tutoring work at Blenheim Palace on a salaried footing. He therefore approached the duke's agent with this request and an invoice for his services over the previous four years and two months. This greatly displeased the duke, who made it clear that if James put a price on his services then he would dispense with them. James paraphrased the formal response that he received from Blenheim Palace in a letter to Betsy. It was brutal in its frankness and left him in no doubt about their graces' attitude to paid employees, as opposed to gentlemen who performed a service:

> Their Gˢ. had turned the Matter in their Minds, and resolved not to proceed upon an annual Stipend, but to keep to the Track of single or double Lessons, and to pay accordingly; that their Gˢ. Employed Dancing Masters, Musick Masters, Drawing Masters, and Mr. Bailley a Geography Master in Town, and paid them for occasional Attendance …. This explains the Light in which they have all along viewed, or wished to view me; and tho' I was aware of this, and did all in my Power to obviate the Unimportance of my Services, by striking into the most liberal Communication of useful Knowledge, yet they have tacitly enjoyed these Advantages, and industriously excluded me from turning them to my own [advantage]. In short, I see that no Endeavour of mine however exerted, have infused into them one generous or kind Thought towards me; and that their Denial of every little Favour asked either by me or my Friends, has arisen from secret Contempt, and Abhorrence of apparent Obligation.[7]

James's invoice was soon paid, with an added bonus of 40 guineas, and there his relationship with the Marlboroughs ended. He felt totally humiliated and was haunted by the malicious gossip that was circulating in the town, so he began once more to think of turning his back on Woodstock and moving to Norfolk. Edward and Betsy continued to encourage her parents to move, but it was not easy to find a Norfolk income for her father and a suitable house to go with it. James was willing to talk about moving, but reluctant to do anything positive, although he complained incessantly about the treatment he continued to receive at Woodstock. Betsy and Edward had found suitable Norfolk houses for him in the past, plus potential livings and curacies, only to find they did not meet with his approval.

Edward thought his search was over when the living of Wickhampton, next door to Reedham, fell vacant in March 1785. The living was in the gift of John Leathes, who was aware of the situation, so Edward had good reason to hope it would be offered to James Reading. But it seems that John had already promised the living to his friend, Charles le Grice of Bury St Edmunds, and to make matters worse, George Leathes voiced the opinion that John had a right to bestow the living wherever he wished, regardless of family claims on it. Edward was furious, and a rift opened up between the brothers. William Nelson, Betsy's uncle, was also offended because he claimed the living had been promised to him in the past. Fortunately the disagreement between the Leathes brothers lasted for only six months or so, and normal brotherly relationships had been resumed by September.

Mr le Grice chose to be an absentee rector, so Edward tried once again to lure his father-in-law to Norfolk with the promise of the curacy of Wickhampton, plus the curacies of one of his own livings and of Cantley, which was shortly to become vacant. James himself attributed his unwillingness to commit himself to the move to his advancing years, which he said would make it so much more difficult to adjust to a radical change in circumstances. The Wickhampton curacy, worth £15 a year, was eventually given to William Nelson, with the proviso that he give it up to James Reading at a later date. Edward himself took the Cantley curacy on James Reading's behalf until such time as his parents-in-law eventually moved to Norfolk, adding to his own burden. Betsy spent a good deal of time looking for a house for her parents, but despite her best efforts her choices always failed to find favour in her father's eyes. The effort of house-hunting for her parents, preparing the newly renovated and extended parsonage house, together with her hectic social life, may well go some of the way towards explaining why Betsy suffered her third and last miscarriage in September 1785. She did not seem particularly unhappy about it, however, probably feeling that six live births, two infant deaths and three miscarriages in 11 years of marriage were quite enough for her.

6   Until death us do part

The extension to the parsonage house at Reedham was finally completed late in the summer of 1785 at a cost of £1,400, excluding interior decoration and furnishing. Edward and Betsy continued to lead a full and expensive social life, including another costly trip to Woodstock in their carriage in late May, returning in late August. Edward had again begun to accumulate substantial arrears in outstanding bills, and had taken out a number of loans on which he was paying annual interest. This was not a new state of affairs, as he had been dangerously close to financial disaster for three or four years.

In November 1783 an action for an undisclosed amount of debt had been brought against Edward in the Court of King's Bench by Henry Brittan Esquire. A warrant for his arrest was issued in May 1784 but this threat was averted when Jonathan Layton and Mr Tuthill, Reedham farmers of some substance, stood bail for him. The case was scheduled to come to trial in July 1785, but it seems to have been settled out of court. Edward agreed to pay damages to Brittan of £52.10s plus costs. The total cost of the case to Edward was over £300, after which he must have reflected that it would have been cheaper to pay the debt in the first place.[1]

The court case alerted John Leathes that his brother and sister-in-law were in a first-class financial muddle once more. At the beginning of April 1785 Edward had outstanding debts amounting to £1,621.10s, all in the form of notes of hand and loans, so John gave him £2,000 to pay off the loans and some of his outstanding bills, then deducted it from the as yet unpaid £4,000 legacy from his father. Edward had therefore halved his legacy in five years, and unless he curbed his financial behaviour in the future he could expect to have little or nothing left by 1790. Most of the accounting and other paperwork seems to have fallen to Betsy's lot; she kept all the household accounts and the tithe accounts, helped out with the parish registers and found other clergymen to deputize for Edward when the need arose. Whether or not she was fully aware of the full extent of Edward's debt is debatable, but she must have been aware that they were living well beyond their means.

Edward's financial affairs were complicated by the fact that he was a generous host. He and Betsy entertained frequently, not on a lavish scale, but certainly well and consistently. Much was expected of the squire's brother in Reedham village, and at Edward's annual tithe feasts, harvest frolics and on special occasions the scale of his hospitality did not disappoint. The parsonage accounts indicate the comfortable standard of living that was enjoyed there. Looking through the pages of Betsy's account book, it is not the purchases of clothes, household furniture or food that are particularly striking, but the amount of alcohol that was bought and consumed. The accounts show that in the two-year period 1786–87 Edward bought the following from three wine merchants, Isaac Barnes, A.C. Fayerman of Loddon and Pain of Acle:

34 gallons and 1 pint of cognac	£23. 2s. 4d
10 gallons of brandy	£ 4. 14s. 0d
6 gallons and 1 pint of Holland gin	£ 4. 1s. 9d
2 gallons of Maidstone gin	14s. 0d
2 gallons of rum	£ 1. 1s. 0d
6 dozen bottles of red port	£ 6. 12s. 0d
2 dozen bottles of Carcavalla Lisbon	£ 2. 8s. 0d
2 dozen bottles of Carcavalla	£ 2. 2s. 0d
Total cost	£43. 17s. 1d[2]

The varying prices probably indicate that cheaper wines and spirits were offered to visitors of a lower social class. The more expensive cognac, Dutch gin and Carcavalla Lisbon were kept for personal consumption, or offered to family members and socially demanding visitors; the Maidstone gin may have been purchased for the servants. Beer, in the form of strong ale and small beer, was still brewed at home in larger and more affluent households in rural areas at the end of the 18th century, and was consumed by the whole household. Brewing took place at regular intervals at Reedham parsonage.

Edward continued to stay afloat financially solely by delaying the payment of bills for as long as possible. The distress that this could cause to small tradespeople, craftspeople and artisans is illustrated in a letter written to him on 26 August 1786 by Daniel Coppin, or Copping, a Norwich housepainter, about work he and his men had done at Reedham parsonage in April 1785. Coppin sent his son to Reedham with the letter, asking Edward to pay either on the spot or without fail the next day:

[I] am at this Present Without any Cash ... and have Several Men to Pay which Want their Money and Dair not tell them that I have it not for then it Woud be Attended with a bad Consequence it Woud be all over the County by to Morrow Night that they Could not get their wages and made my Whole dependence on your Paying it this Week and as being within a few Miles have sent my Son for it as I cannot do without it at this time hope you will excuse my not Coming its attended with a Great Expence I came three times before it cost me 2 Guineas With loss of time which is more than the Profit of the Job and it was begun your Job April 1785 and our Merchants will Credit us only 4 Months Nesessity Oblidge me as woud not Trouble you or must be Oblidge to draw on you on Monday at the Bank if Honourd Sir you thought Proper to send me a Draft will send it by the Bearer to Norwich immediately if you have no Cash but it will Suit self and Family return you thanks and Madam we Little Tradesmen if our Credit is touch'd Either by Merchants or Men its never to be recover'd Again so beg you will not be Angry and Shall Always be happy to Serve you or Madam in a Days Notice from your Obedient and Humble

Servant to Command D Coppin Painter at the Rev^d Mr. Nichols Blundston Saturday Night 26th Aug^st 1786.[3]

Fortunately for all concerned, Edward paid the bill on 27 August.

It is difficult to judge whether it was more or less expensive to educate the children at Woodstock, where they had the benefit of their grandfather's extra tuition and their grandmother's care, or at boarding schools closer to home. Educationally Woodstock may well have been a wise choice, as the results indicate James Reading was an excellent teacher. Edward (aged 9 in April 1786) was proficient in both English and Latin grammar and had begun to learn Greek. Elizabeth, who reached 11 in August 1786, had been privately tutored in the feminine arts of dancing, music and needlework, and had also benefited from her grandfather's tuition in English and Latin, although probably not to the same level as Edward. George, who had not had regular schooling, had been sent to his grandfather for remedial education, a move which was bearing fruit as he finally learned to write before his seventh birthday in April 1786. Even so, he had some way to go before he could match either of his siblings at the same age.

Betsy was able to implement her plan to inoculate her two eldest children against smallpox when they travelled back to Reedham with one of her Woodstock friends, Miss Medcalfe, in 1786. By the time they arrived at Reedham in late April smallpox was rife in the locality, so she acted quickly. The inoculation usually consisted of taking matter from the pustules of a patient with a mild case of the disease and inserting it into shallow cuts or pricks in the skin of an otherwise healthy patient. Many patients survived the disease that resulted, although there were some fatalities. By 3 May the two children were unwell, had lost their appetites and smallpox pustules were beginning to make their appearance. Within two weeks they were over the worst, and Betsy allowed her parents to travel to Reedham with George.

The whole family and Miss Medcalfe were then able to enjoy the summer at Reedham, with added social opportunities and entertainment provided by the arrival of the East Norfolk Militia at their summer camp in Reedham in July. Betsy's parents finally left for Woodstock in early October, taking Edward and George with them. Miss Medcalfe stayed on until early November before she too reluctantly left the parsonage to travel back to Woodstock.

In late November 1786 John Leathes became seriously ill while he was staying at Great Yarmouth. He was expected to die, but rallied sufficiently to be able to return to Herringfleet Hall, although he relapsed swiftly after his arrival there. His treatment had involved drawing fluid from his body by making cuts in the skin on his feet, a painful process according to Betsy. By mid-December John was again dangerously ill and his scarified feet had turned black, possibly as a result of gangrene. He died at Herringfleet Hall on 6 January 1787, aged 48, and was buried with great ceremony in the family vault at Herringfleet church on

15 January. In the absence of information about his original illness it is difficult to say what killed him, but the treatment must have been a contributory factor.

The future financial health of Edward Leathes and his family was at least partly guaranteed by John Leathes' will.[4] The four children were each left £1,000, to be paid when they reached their majority at 21; until then they were to receive interest of 4 per cent a year on the capital, paid on a quarterly basis. The will also specified that the church livings held by Edward Leathes, plus the living of Wickhampton when it fell vacant, should be reserved for his two sons in the event of their father's death, guaranteeing each of them a modest income should they choose to become clergymen. Edward himself received a legacy of £1,500 to be paid three years after John's death; interest of 4½ per cent was to be paid quarterly until then. John left Herringfleet Hall and its estate, the property at Bury St Edmunds and his personal possessions to his wife for her lifetime, and also granted her £2,000 a year for life. All this would revert to George Leathes or his heirs after her death. George inherited what was left of the family estate, an asset which would be greatly reduced by the need to sell the Essex estate to pay outstanding debts and fund the substantial legacies.

Edward and Betsy were truly devastated by John Leathes' death and grieved sincerely for him. John had been the most generous of brothers. He had forgiven his youngest brother's irresponsible behaviour on several occasions, and had done his best to make adequate provision for Edward and his family in his will. Betsy however was more astute than her husband, and was only too well aware that John's early death had robbed them of continued financial protection, and their children of the means of professional advancement beyond the church livings specified. John had left to George a much smaller income than that he had enjoyed himself, so George was much less likely to be willing or able to protect Edward's family in the way that John had. Edward calculated that John's legacy would raise his annual income to approximately £1,000 a year, a somewhat hopeful estimate but more than enough for a family to live on in modest style with prudent financial management. But prudence was not Edward's strong suit, and Betsy was soon telling her mother about the splendid new chaise (a two-wheeled carriage) they had acquired. This did not augur well.

When stability eventually returned to family life at Reedham after John's death, Betsy again turned her attention to persuading her parents, particularly her father, that it would be their best interests to sell their house at Woodstock as soon as possible and move permanently to Norfolk. The Readings travelled to Reedham with young George on 12 April, and stayed there until 25 September 1787. This provided the ideal opportunity for Betsy to demonstrate all the familial, domestic and social advantages of a move to Norfolk. Visits, tea visits, dinners and card parties were exchanged with Sir William and Lady Gordon of Norwich and London, Sir Edmund and Lady Bacon of Raveningham Hall, Sir Thomas and Lady Beauchamp Proctor of Langley Park, Mrs John Leathes of Herringfleet,

Major George Leathes and his wife, together with some of their extensive gentry connections, and of course with the circle of local clerical families and the more prominent farming families of the district.

The West Norfolk Militia's annual camp at Reedham during June and July offered one of the best opportunities for rubbing shoulders with the well-to-do and well connected. Its commanding officer was George Walpole, third earl of Orford (grandson of Robert Walpole, Britain's first prime minister), who lived at Houghton Hall in Norfolk. He was very eccentric but nevertheless well regarded in the county. Relations between Lord Orford and his officers and the Leathes family were very cordial, and there was a good deal of social contact.

Betsy's efforts must have been successful because by the time the Readings returned to Woodstock on 25 September 1787 they had made a positive decision to leave Oxfordshire, subject to their finding a suitable house near Reedham. Young George returned to Woodstock with them so he could continue his education under the supervision of his grandfather. Edward Leathes junior had reached the age of 10, and was sent to board at Norwich Grammar School. He seemed to settle in quickly, and Betsy was soon able to report to her parents that the head-master, Dr Samuel Forster, thought highly of him. Preparations were being made for 12-year-old Elizabeth to travel to London, where she would attend Miss Olier's school for young ladies in Bloomsbury. Mary, the baby of the family, turned 4 in April 1787 and was sent to board at Miss Banyard's school in Yarmouth in July.

Edward senior's health continued to deteriorate in 1787. Between February and April he suffered from a painful episode of gout, followed by a fever. Mr Leath, the Acle surgeon apothecary, travelled frequently to Reedham to treat him, and Edward was bled, blistered, given emetics, purgatives, febrifuge powders (to reduce his fever), pain-relieving medicines, cordial stomach mixtures, sudorific mixtures (to make him sweat) and gargles. In mid-April 1787 he developed a severe and persistent sore throat, for which Mr Leath bled him under the tongue. Between bouts of fever, gout and 'weakness' Edward tried hard to lead a normal life, serving his churches, socializing, hare coursing and shooting, but these efforts caused frequent relapses, followed by periods of confinement to bed and more treatment by Mr Leath. Betsy called in Dr Manning of Norwich at the end of June, but it seems that he had little more to suggest, because Edward relapsed so severely at the beginning of October 1787 that he made his will. The pattern of rally and relapse continued into December, and Edward grew weaker by the month.

James Reading was more of a hindrance than a help to his daughter and son-in-law, since he began to drag his feet when Edward set about buying a house in Freethorpe on the Readings' behalf in early November 1787. Just when his help was most vital and Edward had agreed a price of £130, James first pleaded illness then dithered about the size of the house, which he might well have seen and approved before he left Norfolk. He continued to find excuses not to complete the move, even though Edward had offered the house to him rent-free. Betsy, who was already worried about her husband's health, lost patience with her father and told him they needed his help urgently.

The situation was exacerbated by the sudden disappearance of the curate who had been installed at Cantley to deputize for James Reading:

> It seems Mr. Jackson [the deputy curate] is so much in debt that he was oblig'd to leave Norwich very hastily – he call'd here last Sunday & told us a plausible Story of his having the Offer of a Curacy in Lewes in Sussex of 55$^£$ p^r Ann. & a House, but on Tuesday Mr. Papillon came over & acquainted us with the real cause of his decampment, & also demanded Surplice Fees which Mr. Jackson told him Mr. Leathes had promis'd to make him a Present of but Mr. Leathes declares he never made him any such promise.[5]

The curate had also absconded with £5 of recent advances from Edward.

By mid-December 1787 the house purchase was complete, leaving Edward so short of money that Elizabeth junior's fragmentary formal education had to be postponed, and she was sent to stay with her wealthy aunt at Herringfleet Hall. James Reading refused to take the house rent-free, so a rent of £6.10s a year was agreed, but Betsy had begun to doubt whether her father would ever leave Woodstock. Edward was by this time very sick, and it was becoming more and more difficult for him to even try to serve his churches. It was also difficult to find deputies for these. William Nelson was prepared to deputize for James Reading at Cantley, where services were held once every two weeks, but refused to help Edward with any of his livings. Betsy had run out of informal curacy options and was forced to keep begging favours from clerical friends and acquaintances as need dictated.

James Reading continued to prevaricate for the first three months of 1788. First he blamed the time it was taking for repairs to his Woodstock house prior to letting it, then he found difficulties with arrangements for the transport of his household goods to Norfolk, and finally he encountered problems with letting his tithes at Stonesfield. At Reedham, Edward was close to collapse in January 1788. Betsy's pleas for help met no response, and she began to realize her parents would only move to Freethorpe if she went to Woodstock to help them. She was making arrangements for her trip when Edward collapsed and took to his bed, exhausted and gravely ill. Betsy wrote to her father begging him to settle his affairs in Oxfordshire swiftly and travel to Reedham as soon as possible. Again James Reading ignored her pleas, and told her he was unable to move until matters were settled to his satisfaction. At last he agreed to leave Woodstock with his affairs unsettled, and he, Mrs Reading, their maid Patty and their boy Will arrived at Reedham in late April 1788.

Despite her husband's illness Betsy made great efforts to maintain a correspondence with her closest friends, finding that news from the outside world helped to distract her from more serious affairs at home. Interesting reports of the marital career of Edward Loveden, the widower of her great friend Margaret, came occasionally from her friends and family in Woodstock and Oxford. Following Margaret's death in January 1784 he was rumoured to have courted Lady Elizabeth Ashbrook (probably the widow of William Flower, second Viscount Ashbrook) and even to have married her, although that is highly unlikely. It is more certain that he married a Mrs Nash in 1785 and that she died in 1787 or early 1788, leaving him a widower for the second time. In June 1788 news reached Betsy that he was to be married yet again, to the daughter of Whitbread the brewer.[6]

Valiant attempts were made to maintain a semblance of normal social life at the parsonage. Lord Orford brought the West Norfolk Militia to Reedham once more for their annual summer camp. Betsy occasionally called at the camp to take tea with the officers, who reciprocated by visiting the parsonage on Edward's better days. But she found it virtually impossible to participate in the social round at Reedham Camp while trying to cope with her sick husband's growing demands. Sadly Edward's condition worsened throughout May and June, and he died at the parsonage on 13 July 1788, aged 41.

He was laid to rest in the newly built family vault under the chancel floor of Reedham parish church on 19 July. William Nelson conducted the burial service, which was attended by his grieving widow in a black mourning dress with apron, bonnet, gloves and even a handkerchief in unrelieved black. No doubt the children were also suitably dressed in mourning clothes. The vault was completed and sealed after the burial and the communion table was positioned on top of it.[7] After almost 14 years of marriage, Betsy was a widow with four young children to support.

Interior of St John the Baptist Church, Reedham, 20th century

7   A second chance

Under the terms of Edward's will, Betsy inherited his whole estate including money, household goods, carriages, horses and live and dead stock for life. After her death the estate was to be divided between their surviving children, with the exception of the house bought for James Reading in 1788, which was left to George Reading Leathes. Betsy was named as the legal guardian of the four children, who were each left £100 to be invested on their behalf until they came of age. Other bequests included 5 guineas each to buy gold mourning rings for Mrs John Leathes, George Leathes and his wife Mary, and James and Elizabeth Reading, as well as one guinea to buy a mourning ring for his old friend Jonathan Layton of Reedham Hall Farm. The giving of mourning jewellery (frequently rings) to commemorate the death of a family member or valued friend was a centuries-old tradition. Betsy was named as sole executrix of the will, which was proved at Norwich on 4 August 1788.[1]

Edward had also stipulated in his will that all outstanding bills and debts be paid by Betsy out of the estate within three years of his death. Not surprisingly, clearing up the financial mess he had left became Betsy's first priority, because she would have no idea how much was for her and the children until his debts were cleared, the bills paid and the money for the bequests set aside. She gathered together all the bills and notes of hand she could find, sorted them into bundles and paid them as money became available, a process that extended well into 1789. Some of the unpaid bills, for goods and services of all kinds, went back several years. Mr Leath's medical bills were paid relatively quickly in November 1788, as were several bills for church duty performed by neighbouring clergymen from December 1787 to August 1788. The rest were left until last.[2] All in all, the job of executrix was a formidable one for a woman simultaneously attempting to deal with her own grief and to look after her children and her elderly parents.

Until such time as Edward Leathes junior and George Reading Leathes were ordained, it made sense for James Reading to take over the livings of Reedham, Freethorpe and Limpenhoe with Southwood, even though he was 67 in July 1788 and in poor health. A proposal to consolidate the livings of Reedham and Freethorpe was approved by the bishop of Norwich in October 1788, and Reading was duly instituted in November. The bishop of Oxford had given permission for him to continue to hold the living of Stonesfield, Oxfordshire in conjunction with the Norfolk livings, making him a substantial pluralist for the first time in his life. He still held the curacy of Cantley, which was one church duty too many for him, so a young deacon, William Farley Wilkinson, was appointed as his deputy there. Wilkinson came from Harwich, where Carteret Leathes had once lived and for which he had served as member of Parliament. The young curate had a small independent income, so the low salary of £25 a year from the Cantley curacy was not a problem. James Reading quickly saw the advantages of a deputy, and Wilkinson was appointed curate of Limpenhoe with Southwood later in 1788, then in 1789 the curacy of Reedham with Freethorpe was added to the list.

Betsy's precarious position soon became apparent to her. Much of the income she had enjoyed during her married life had died with Edward, although it was fortunate that her father held the church livings on behalf of her children. She seems to have reached an agreement that he would allocate part of the income to the support and education of her four children. The exact amount was never stated, but it was probably in the order of £50 for each child. Betsy's remaining income consisted of the quarterly and half-yearly interest payments on investments and legacies, yielding approximately £350 a year. This meant the family had a total income of about £550 a year, around half as much as the £1,000 a year Edward had reckoned was available to him in 1788.

It was advisable for Betsy to be on good terms with the trustees of the trust protecting part of her income. Of the four trustees John Leathes had named for his legacies, the Reverend Francis Bowness of Lowestoft was Betsy's main point of contact. Their business acquaintance grew into a lasting friendship with considerable regard and some affection on both sides, although Mr Bowness occasionally became exasperated with the extravagance and lack of attention to mundane financial details that not only Betsy, but also her children as they grew up, tended to show. It became evident quite early on in her widowhood that Betsy would have great difficulty in tailoring her tastes, preferences and aspirations to her reduced income.

The education of her children was a key indicator of her financial difficulties. Edward, who had reached 11 in April 1788, continued as a boarder at Norwich Grammar School at an average yearly cost of around £35 between 1788 and 1790. This was well within the £90 a year that Betsy could make available to educate each of her children. In August 1788 Elizabeth, who had just passed her 13th birthday, finally took up a place at Miss Olier's school for young ladies in Bloomsbury, after this had been postponed at least twice while her father was alive. This proved expensive, perhaps because Elizabeth required additional private tuition to make up for the years of formal education she had missed. Miss Olier's bill for the six months from 13 August 1788 to 13 February 1789 was £53.6s.3d. It included £15.15s for basic board and instruction, £11.16s.3d for extra classes in 'writing', dancing, drawing, music and French, £6.1s.3d for extra board (furniture, a reserved pew at church, pocket money of 13s, washing, starching, tea and sugar), £4.11s for books and equipment, and £15.2s.9d for clothes, shoes and sundries. For the following half year the bill was £66.16s.7d, making a grand total of £120.2s.10d for 12 months. Elizabeth had also run up additional bills for clothes, hats, shoes and sundries, including one for 10 guineas from Mr E. Madden for 'dressing and cleaning' her teeth.[3]

At the end of January 1789 Betsy left Reedham for London to take Elizabeth back to school after the Christmas holidays. Mrs John Leathes accompanied them, and the two widows embarked on a concentrated programme of visiting and being visited by acquaintances and friends old and new, dining out, and attending the theatre, the opera and other entertainments. Betsy had been careworn, depressed and in poor health for long periods since Edward's death, and Francis Bowness hoped the restorative powers of London society would improve both her health and her disposition. For two weeks she stayed with her sister-in-law in lodgings at Islington Place, London, before moving to 20 Warwick Court in Holborn to stay with her old friend Ann Man (née Loggin), whose second baby was due within a few weeks.

During this four-week stay Betsy made contact with her old flame Edward Peach, whose business interests included management of the late Thomas Reading's estate in Cheam on behalf of James Reading and William Nelson, the trustees. The couple had not met since 1769, when his parents had decided that she was unsuitable to be his wife, but the old chemistry was still there, and the renewal of their friendship after 20 years soon developed into romance. On 10 March 1789 Betsy responded to a (presumably amorous) letter she had received from him:

> The receipt of your letter my dear Friend has thrown me into such an agitation that I scarcely have power to answer it, the candid & generous manner in which You have express'd yourself greatly adds to the esteem which I have ever entertain'd for You & as I have many things to say of a material conse-quence which I cannot communicate by letter, I beg you will let me see you immediately … your sincere & affectionate Friend Eliza Leathes.[4]

Their romantic idyll was rudely interrupted by news of the death of Betsy's paternal aunt, Catherine Nelson, at Strumpshaw on 13 March. His sister's death brought James Reading a financial windfall in the shape of the £1,500 invested in govern-ment stock that their late brother Thomas had left to her. James said he was unable to travel to London to deal with the transfer of the stock into his name, and asked Betsy to see whether Mr Man would undertake the task. Mr Man agreed, and Betsy turned her attention to getting her father to sort out the necessary docu-mentation. Although her aunt had severely tried Betsy's patience and loyalty on several occasions, Betsy was very upset by her death. She told Edward Peach her peace of mind had been blighted by the news, which had brought back all-too-recent memories of her own bereavement, so much so that she took to her bed for five days with violent headaches. But her grief soon faded; she arranged to meet him and their romance continued to blossom.

Betsy was acutely conscious that Peach planned to return to his home at Sundridge, Kent on 28 March. They met on 27 March, just before he left, and they spent a happy day together, so happy that he immediately wrote to express the depths of his feelings for her. Betsy was equally explicit in her next letter to him:

The Melancholy which hung over me at parting with You my dear Sir was soon dispell'd by the pleasing reflection on the friendly manner in which we parted and I look'd with a truly grateful Heart to that kind Providence who has safely conducted me thro' so many severe Trials & Afflictions & at last bro.̃ me to a State of Happiness – It gave me real satisfaction to hear You was pleas'd with your Walk on Friday, and I think You are sufficiently acquainted with my History & my Sentiments to believe me when I say that the last Week was the happiest I ever experienc'd.[5]

While Betsy was writing this letter, Mrs Man went into labour and eventually gave birth without mishap to a healthy daughter. Betsy attended the birth and immediately thanked God that she was past such things! With her work in London completed and without Edward Peach to persuade her to stay longer, she then said goodbye to Mr and Mrs Man and returned to Reedham. Speculation about her romance and impending marriage was rife among her London-based friends, and rumours were soon disseminated far and wide.

Betsy received an enthusiastic welcome from her three Norfolk-based children when she arrived back at Reedham parsonage on 9 April 1789, but her delight was marred by the sight of her father, who had been transformed by a combination of illness and the harsh Norfolk winter weather into a sick and broken old man. Fortunately the arrival of spring saw him rally a little, and he was able to travel to London in mid-May with William Nelson and Betsy to sort out the final formalities of the stock transfer.

Betsy met Edward Peach all too briefly during their stay in London, before travelling on with her father to Woodstock, where they were to make arrangements for letting the former family home. They took rooms at the Bear, a popular coaching inn, where they were impressed with the standard of comfort. They arranged for the clearance and cleaning of the handsome double-fronted stone house on the corner of High Street and Park Lane. It has survived to the present day as the Ancient House, and is still a prominent feature of Woodstock High Street. When the house was ready it was let to Charles Heynes, a Woodstock surgeon apothecary, for £15 a year, payable half-yearly. The tenant agreed to pay the parochial taxes and land tax, not to sublet the house and to give six months' notice to quit; in return the landlord agreed to keep the premises in good repair.[6]

Betsy had pinned her hopes on meeting Edward Peach in London on their way back to Norfolk, but he was busy with local affairs in Sundridge, where he was a justice of the peace, and unable to spare the time. But he wrote affectionately to Betsy and advised her to keep herself busy when she arrived back at Reedham instead of sitting at home moping.

By the early months of 1789 Betsy was finding it difficult to keep solvent. Her friend and trustee Francis Bowness advised her that the difficulties involved in settling Carteret Leathes' estate had finally been resolved, and the remaining

£2,000 of Edward Leathes' legacy from his father would be paid as soon as the necessary documents had been signed. Unfortunately his optimism was premature: various administrative bungles meant the bank draft was not deposited in Betsy's account at Kerrison's bank in Norwich until July. Betsy was then able to wind up Edward's estate by paying off his remaining debts. With Bowness's assistance she invested the residue of the legacy in government stock, known widely as 'the Funds', and looked forward to receiving the interest at half-yearly intervals.

Betsy was also keen to improve her access to the other components of her income, including the £500 'dowry' her maternal grandfather had left her before her marriage. The money had been invested for her by her father in his name, so she had to wait for him to pass on the half-yearly dividend. Unhappy with this inconvenient arrangement, she had twice tried to persuade him to arrange for her to receive the dividends herself, but both times James Reading had become very upset, feeling the request implied she did not trust him. Francis Bowness, however, thought it entirely reasonable for Betsy to seek a more convenient arrangement, and with his support she overcame her father's objections.

The four trusts created to safeguard the children's legacies would remain in place until each one reached their majority, and that could not readily be changed. Betsy then transferred her attention to obtaining payment of her husband's £1,500 legacy from his eldest brother. She believed it would soon happen because Carteret Leathes' estate had been settled, which meant the settlement of John Leathes' estate could not be far behind.

Her income might have stretched further if she had been more organized in managing her financial resources, her children had been less demanding and her concept of what was appropriate for them more modest. Her worst problems were associated with their education. In 1789 and 1790 Elizabeth junior's school bills rose again. It was claimed she needed extra lessons in French, history, music and painting. She also had larger bills for dressmaking, shoes and accessories, in line with her physical growth and the demands of fashion and etiquette. Betsy was acutely aware that a young lady of good family but slender means needed a thorough education in the social arts to appear to good advantage in polite society and secure a husband with good prospects, so she might have felt this justified the extra expenditure on Elizabeth. The school bills were reduced to around £50 a half year when Betsy moved to London with her son George in September 1789 and took lodgings in Red Lion Square, Holborn. Elizabeth could then attend Miss Olier's as a day pupil at rather than boarding.

But this small saving was a drop in the ocean, and Francis Bowness advised Betsy to be more cautious in her future approach, although he realized the problem was not easily solved, especially for the boys. Betsy's intention was to teach George herself until she could place him in a reputable London school. James Reading was none too sure her teaching abilities were equal to the task, and advised her to send George to 'a good Latin Grammar School' as soon as possible.[7] However

Betsy soon found that the affordable schools in London were socially undesirable, while socially acceptable ones were unaffordable. So she told her father she would carry on teaching George herself until they returned to Reedham for Christmas, then send him to join Edward at Norwich Grammar School. Elizabeth was to stay with Miss Olier for at least another half year, as she was making such good progress, but Mary was to leave Miss Banyard's school at Yarmouth and be taught by her grandfather at Reedham. As her children grew up, Betsy continued to find paying for their education an area fraught with problems, and one that made disproportionate demands on her income.

Following their fond parting in London on 27 March, Betsy was able to meet with Edward Peach only twice in May. Both meetings were brief and unsatisfactory. They wrote to each other regularly, although Betsy occasionally complained that his letters were insufficiently frequent, and found it difficult to cope with his apparent preoccupation with the pressures of business at Sundridge. When she moved to London with George in late September she felt certain Peach would rush to her side, and was sadly disappointed when he failed to do so.

Very few of their letters written between October and December 1789 have survived, so it is difficult to say exactly what passed between them then. Any problems cannot have been serious, because rumours of their impending marriage had reached Francis Bowness in Lowestoft by mid-November, causing him to comment on her slyness.

Betsy's health was as variable as her moods. Sometimes she was prostrate with headaches and general weakness, while at other times she seemed happy and reasonably healthy. These inconsistencies probably reflect the stressful nature of her situation: constant money worries, a new relationship, and towards the end of the year a very sick father.

James Reading had been in poor health for at least three years. The move to Norfolk and the resulting increase in workload had probably been too much for him. He struggled to cope with his parishes and relied more and more on his curate, Mr. Wilkinson, to help with church services and managing parish affairs. Even the day-to-day running of their home seemed to present a problem. Perhaps servants in Norfolk were more intractable than those in Oxfordshire, because Mrs Reading experienced great difficulty, and a procession of indifferent or downright poor servants passed through Reedham parsonage in the year from September 1788 to 1789. James's health continued to decline in January and February 1790. His previous medical problems returned to trouble him: gout, kidney stones, gravel and bleeding from the bladder. His condition was serious enough to prompt solicitous enquiries from family and friends, together with advice on the best way to manage his condition, most of it bad.

Ever the realist, Francis Bowness was fearful of the outcome, and began to make arrangements for a succession to the livings in the event of James's death. Betsy returned to London with Elizabeth in February 1790. She had no illusions about the seriousness of her father's illness and begged him to send for her if she was needed. Mrs Reading tried to tempt his capricious appetite with little delicacies, while Major Leathes offered to send anything that James desired from his kitchen or cellars. By 22 March Betsy was back at Reedham, and Francis Bowness warned her to be prepared for the inevitable outcome. James Reading died on 31 March 1790, and was buried on 7 April in the Leathes family vault in Reedham church.

Bowness had not yet managed to arrange a succession to the livings of Reedham with Freethorpe and Limpenhoe with Southwood, so the diocesan administration appointed sequestrators to ensure the revenue, including tithes, church rates and Easter offerings, was paid to the diocese during the vacancy. The trustees of Betsy's children's trust expressed a preference for Mr Wilkinson to be appointed, partly because he and his family were well known to the Leathes family, and partly because he already held the curacies and expected soon to be ordained priest. Arrangements for his presentation were kept on hold until he was privately ordained by the bishop of Norwich on 29 September 1790, after which he was formally instituted to the livings on 5 October.

Betsy's uncle William Nelson, rector of nearby Strumpshaw with Braydeston, bitterly resented this, not least because Betsy had given her consent. He had assumed he would be the automatic choice for at least one of the livings, and also felt he needed the extra income more than Wilkinson, as unlike the other man he had no private income. Having secured the rather mischievous support of Betsy's brother-in-law George Leathes, he wrote to Betsy in May 1790 asking her to request that the trustees pass one of the livings to him. Betsy refused because the trustees thought it in the best interests of the children for the livings to be kept together, and in any case the business was already settled. Nelson refused to acknowledge that Betsy's first duty was to her children, and bore a grudge for the rest of his life.

The trustees, and no doubt Betsy herself, were keen to secure some income from the livings for the children during their minorities, and Mr Wilkinson agreed to pay £50 per child a year (in half-yearly instalments of £100 to Betsy) until they each reached 21. This arrangement probably reflected the agreement Betsy had had with her father, and was the best deal that the trustees could secure. It is doubtful whether William Nelson would have parted with any of the income.

The sequestration of the livings at least gave Betsy and her mother sufficient breathing space to make new accommodation arrangements. They had to move out of the parsonage to make way for Mr Wilkinson, his wife and their young baby, but this was sure to worsen their financial position because taking lodgings would add rent to their outgoings. Mrs Reading's only income came from the quarterly dividend on the £1,500 invested in government stock she had inherited from her husband, the half-yearly rent on three small properties in Oxford, the annual rent on the Woodstock house, and any money her husband had put aside. This probably came to no more than £150 a year in all. Betsy's income remained steady at around £550 a year, thanks to Mr Wilkinson's contribution to the children's education, but it was becoming increasingly clear that her financial juggling act was being compromised by Major Leathes, who continually fell behind with the interest payments on John Leathes' £1,500 legacy.

Betsy believed her life would be easier if she could get her hands on this legacy, and the three years specified in the will had elapsed, so she asked George when the capital was likely to be paid over. She had not known that John Leathes' will was proving even more difficult to settle than his father's. The legacy and the interest payments were the least of Major Leathes' worries at that time, although he promised to pay up as soon as he was able.

By June 1790 he was a year in arrears with her interest payments, and Betsy was growing desperate. A sympathetic Francis Bowness loaned her some money on account, until the arrears were finally paid in November 1790. This enabled her to keep afloat financially at a time when her outgoings were increasing.

Towards the end of April 1790 Betsy and her mother travelled to London, partly to visit Elizabeth, who was boarding once more at Miss Olier's, and partly to provide the documentation needed to transfer Mrs Reading's stock (the legacy from her husband) to a trust. Mrs Reading returned to Reedham when her business was completed, but Betsy stayed on in London for a few more weeks. She met with Edward Peach at least once, and on 19 June he sent what was clearly a very affectionate letter to her, so affectionate that Betsy cut away all the text! It is possible he proposed to her, but if so she either refused him or found some sort of objection, because by the time she returned to Reedham at the end of June the relationship seems to have been at a standstill once more.

Betsy wrote to tell him she and her mother would be glad to see him visit Reedham, because she was in great need of his advice and assistance with her preparations for leaving the parsonage. Unfortunately he declined the invitation on the grounds that he was short-staffed and could not leave his house at Sundridge until he was able to hire more servants at Michaelmas, so Betsy had to cope alone with her removal plans and selling her surplus furniture. At the end of July she started making and receiving leave-taking visits in Reedham, the surrounding district and Bury St Edmunds, a process that distressed her greatly and emphasized the separation between her old life and the new life she must soon begin.

Happily, by 4 August 1790 Betsy was once more discussing the pros and cons of marriage with Edward Peach. The discussion came to a premature end when she misinterpreted the contents of one of his letters, and she had to be prompted by him before she finally replied in somewhat cool tones on 31 August. Edward then became confused, and they continued at cross-purposes for the next two weeks or so, during which time Betsy and her mother moved into lodgings with Mrs Dordoy at Tombland in Norwich.

Betsy's unwanted furniture and effects were auctioned at Reedham on 20 September. Unhappily the auction failed to realize the amount she had hoped for. Although she was physically and mentally exhausted by this time, at least she had been able to rectify her misunderstandings with Edward Peach, who was delighted that she seemed to trust him at last:

> I can most truly assure you that <u>You</u> are the only Woman upon Earth with whom I can be happy; and I do flatter myself our attachments are in every respect reciprocal towards each other, and that much time will not elapse before we meet together to adjust matters to the satisfaction of each of us.[8]

So she could now look forward to marriage to Edward, but she told him their intentions should remain secret until Mr Wilkinson was in possession of the livings and all the necessary financial arrangements were in place. But by the time Mr Wilkinson was ordained at the end of September Betsy had once more succumbed to a combination of violent headaches, hot and cold sweats and fainting fits, and this prevented her from moving far. She was treated by Dr McQueen of Norwich, who attributed her illness to fatigue and anxiety, and recommended rest and liberal doses of quinine.

Betsy's illness did not, however, prevent the lovers from exchanging declarations of devotion. On 5 October 1790 Edward described to her his hopes for the future. 'I do look forward to many years of happiness with you my dearest Betsy and I do trust in the Divine Providence we shall be so in sincerity of heart & affection toward each other,' he wrote.[9] Betsy's response echoed his sentiments. 'I hope with You that we may look forward to many happy Years, I do not doubt but the desire of rend'ring each others Life comfortable is <u>reciprocal</u> & will be <u>lasting</u>, & is the surest foundation for happiness.'[10]

After a few weeks spent languishing in her Norwich lodgings, Betsy felt fit enough to travel to London, where she took up residence in a lodging house off Red Lion Square in Holborn and began to lay plans for her wedding to Peach. First a marriage settlement had to be drawn up and a trust formed to protect Betsy's income, in the same way that the legacies left to Betsy and her children by John Leathes and their father were protected. Arrangements for the formation of the trust were well advanced by mid-November, when Francis Bowness and another man, John Love, agreed to be co-trustees. The negotiations were complicated by Betsy's position as a widow with four children, but any doubts about their future security were eventually assuaged by Edward Peach's declaration that he would be 'liberal' towards them. Because the Kentish custom was for widows to inherit half of their husband's estate in the event of his death, Francis Bowness advised Betsy that it would be advantageous for her to accept that as part of the marriage settlement, rather than a fixed annual pension.[11]

The approaching nuptials were no longer a secret in Norfolk, Kent, Oxfordshire or London, and premature letters of congratulation began to arrive at Betsy's lodgings. On 25 November 1790 Edward Peach and Elizabeth Leathes were married at the church of St George the Martyr, Queen Square, London. On their return from church, Edward wrote to Mrs Reading to tell her he had at last made her daughter his wife. Betsy had finally married her first love, and a new life in Kent beckoned.

8   Mrs Peach

News of Betsy's marriage to Edward Peach spread quickly, and letters of congratulation from friends and relatives poured in during the following weeks, varying in tone from the slightly censorious to the happily complacent. Betsy's former sister-in-law Elizabeth Leathes offered somewhat brief congratulations, followed by the tart comment that she herself was happy to remain a widow for the rest of her life, despite having received advantageous offers of marriage – a rather cheap shot from a woman whose husband had left her extremely well provided for. Francis Bowness sent his hearty congratulations and best wishes for the couple's future happiness. The rest of Betsy's friends were genuinely pleased that she seemed to have found happiness again.

The relationship between Betsy and her new husband was, however, by no means as straightforward as it might at first seem. It appeared to be a love match, the reunion of childhood sweethearts, and it did seem to operate on that level for much of the time. Betsy had found life very difficult in almost every respect after her first husband's premature death, and was certainly looking for emotional as well as financial security in her second marriage. Edward Peach's reappearance in her life must have seemed a heaven-sent opportunity to escape the loneliness and the social and financial restrictions of widowhood. It is more difficult to evaluate Edward's feelings and motivation because Betsy destroyed many of the letters he sent her during and after their courtship. He seems genuinely to have loved her and wished to make her happy, although in the light of later events it is easy to believe that he was not altogether honest with her.

Edward had had at least one relationship prior to meeting with Betsy again in 1789, as he had three children. He might well have married, but there is no mention of a previous wife. Some of Betsy's letters to him indicate that she did not altogether trust him, and this may explain why she hesitated before they finally married. The image that Betsy and Edward Peach presented to the outside world was that of a companionable middle-aged married couple who were comfortable in each other's company and at ease with the world. The couple exchanged letters regularly when they were apart for more than a few days, and these offer very brief glimpses behind the emotional scenery.

Two days after their wedding, the couple left London for Edward's house at Sundridge in Kent. The pleasant village of Sundridge is situated on what was then the high road between Sevenoaks and Oxted (now the busy A25), sandwiched between the North Downs and the ridge of hills that form the northern limit of the Weald of Kent. It is surrounded by the villages of Brasted, Westerham and Chipstead, and the great houses of Chevening, Combebank and Knole. Edward Peach had inherited his Sundridge estate from Thomas Mompesson, to whom he was related through his mother. The Old Hall at Sundridge was an impressive hall

The Old Hall, Sundridge, Kent

house of late 15th or early 16th-century date, reputed to be the oldest house in the village; it contained seven bedrooms, a great hall, a parlour, drawing room, study, kitchen, scullery, a coach house and stabling for eight horses. Betsy described it as 'a little Paradise', a description echoed by her daughter, who called it 'a charming enchanting place'.[1] Peach also owned the nearby White Horse public house, the two adjacent cottages, 12 more cottages and the workhouse in Sundridge, as well as Washner's Farm in Chelsfield.[2]

Betsy's departure from London to take up residence at Sundridge made it more difficult for her to supervise her children and support her mother. Following their departure from Reedham at the end of September 1790, Betsy and her mother had taken lodgings at Miss Dordoy's lodging house in Norwich. Mrs Reading remained there until Betsy visited Norwich in April 1791, when she moved into new lodgings with Mr Webster on Tombland, near the cathedral gates. Mr Webster was a cabinet maker and upholsterer, and he used the ground floor of his house as his shop, workshop and storage area, obliging his lodgers to access their rooms through the commercial premises. This could have been seen as a disadvantage, but it did not seem to bother Mrs Reading, and Betsy seemed happy enough to lodge there when she visited her mother.

Edward and George continued as boarders at Norwich Grammar School, but George left Norwich for St Paul's School, London in September 1791, perhaps as the result of pressure from Elizabeth Leathes, who continued to treat him as her favourite nephew. Edward remained in Norwich as a boarder at the Grammar School, where apart from regular contact with his grandmother, his mother's occasional visits to Norwich and summer holidays spent at Sundridge, he was left to his own devices.

Elizabeth junior stayed on at Miss Olier's school in Bloomsbury, an expensive option for Betsy as her tuition, board, clothes and other expenses cost £89.2s.2d for the first half of 1791 alone, very nearly all of the £90 available each year to cover the cost of her education.[3] Elizabeth Leathes thought she should stay there for another year, but Betsy agreed with Francis Bowness that the expense could not be justified at her age (she was 16 in August 1791) and that her social education could be continued just as well at Sundridge. So she left school in the summer of 1791, and her yearly allowance for dresses, shoes and other accessories was increased to £20. She was then launched into local society under her mother's supervision. Betsy bought a pianoforte for Elizabeth and George to play with money left to them by their late father, principally so Elizabeth could achieve the level of proficiency necessary for her to perform in polite society.

Betsy had little to say about Elizabeth's looks in her correspondence, but it is probably safe to assume that she was attractive. She was certainly well-drilled in the social niceties, knew how to dress and converse well, and how best to present herself in public. Aunt Leathes invited Elizabeth to join her at Tunbridge Wells for a week in July 1791, a pleasant introduction to the elaborate social protocols that governed life in all fashionable watering holes. Since Sundridge was quite near to London, the family could make fairly frequent visits, and Elizabeth took advantage of any offer to accompany her mother and stepfather on their business trips to the capital. She was an enthusiastic participant in the theatre attendances, balls, parties, social and cultural visits and shopping trips that were a feature of London social life.

Her sister Mary enjoyed few such treats. Betsy had decided she should continue as a boarder at Mrs Ramsay's school in Lowestoft, where Francis Bowness could visit and take her out on occasions. She was a firm favourite with him, so much so that he increased her pocket money to 3d a week in August 1791. She was also a favourite with Mrs Ramsay, who told Betsy her youngest daughter not only had a happy disposition that made her very popular, she was a very able pupil who learned quickly. Mrs Ramsay took good care of Mary when she suffered from chilblains, a condition in which the skin of the fingers, toes, nose or ears become red, swollen and itchy because of exposure to the cold – a common complaint before the days of central heating – and told Betsy how she had dealt with them:

> It is now more than six weeks since her hands and feet appear'd like chilblains, and I immediately made some brandy hot, and bathed them frequently; put flannel socks on her feet, and have had her wear gloves constantly; a little gentle physic I thought necessary, which was of great use; her feet and fingers still look red, but are perfectly easy and are not likely to break or be troublesome.[4]

Mary visited her mother and stepfather at Sundridge during the school's summer break in 1791, and soon settled into the routine of making morning and tea visits with her mother, helping to entertain daytime visitors at the Old Hall and playing in the house and grounds. She returned to Lowestoft in late July with some friends of Betsy's who were travelling there to enjoy the sea bathing.

Despite all these careful arrangements for the education and care of her children and her mother, Betsy soon found that she needed to visit Norwich at least twice a year in order to check on Edward, George (until he left Norwich in the summer of 1791), Mary and Mrs Reading, and to attend to any unfinished or outstanding financial business. On 10 April 1791 she travelled to London with Edward Peach and Mrs Reading, who had been visiting them at Sundridge. They stayed in lodgings for ten days before Betsy and her mother set out for Norwich, leaving Peach to return to Sundridge on his own.

Betsy had yet to pack up all of the crockery, glass, sundries and small items of furniture she had left behind at Reedham parsonage, and to make arrangements for them to be sent to Sundridge. She also had a pressing need to discuss finances with Mr Wilkinson, so he could start to make the agreed contribution from his livings as soon as possible, so she visited Reedham in early May 1791. Eventually a diocesan official made a formal inspection, following which the value of the livings was estimated at £587.6s.11d a year.[5] Mr Wilkinson's payments to Betsy usually amounted to £200 a year.

Betsy was also still keen to get her hands on John Leathes' £1,500 legacy. Major Leathes had indicated on 10 March 1791 that he hoped to be able to give her a banker's draft, and Betsy planned to collect it from him soon after her arrival at Norwich in April. But her departure from Sundridge was delayed by several days, and George Leathes meanwhile deposited the money with a banker friend of his in Bungay. This meant Betsy would have to get a stamped legacy receipt at a cost of around £28 and then travel to Bungay before she could collect the legacy and the back interest. However she did not give up easily, and finally persuaded the Major to deliver the draft to her in person when he visited Norwich on 28 April. She immediately paid the draft into Kerrison's bank. Francis Bowness was keen that she should invest the money as soon as possible, and she might have done so when she met him in London on 25 May. Later she loaned £1,500 to Edward Peach in the form of a mortgage secured on his estate.

After her return from Norwich, Betsy spent most of the rest of 1791 with her husband and eldest daughter at Sundridge. But on 12 December she again left Kent to spend Christmas and New Year with her mother, son Edward and Mary in Norwich. Elizabeth junior was on holiday with Aunt Leathes, so Edward Peach was left to spend the Christmas holiday period at Sundridge with his stepson George.

By December 1791 interest payments on the children's legacies were again six months in arrears, and one of Betsy's objectives for this visit was to ensure they were paid in full. Yet again Major Leathes made life awkward for her by lodging the money with his banker at Bungay. This time she had to make a difficult round trip in order to collect the banker's draft for £86.10s, which she deposited at Kerrison's bank on 29 December.

After a pleasant time socializing with her family and friends in Norwich, Betsy set out for London from the Angel Inn on the market place on the evening of 17 January 1792. The coach stopped at an Ipswich inn for fresh horses during the overnight journey, and Betsy fell backwards through an open trapdoor in the yard while trying to avoid the horses. She tumbled down 14 steps into the wine cellar and hit the back of her head on a bottle on the floor. Despite her injuries, she managed to continue the journey, and arrived at her friend Mrs Loggin's house the next day battered, bruised, severely shaken and suffering from a recurrence of the palpitations that had plagued her for several weeks previously.

Edward Peach rushed from Sundridge to his wife's bedside. Medical help was soon at hand but it took her several days to recover sufficiently to resume her journey to London, transact her business and return to Sundridge on 26 January.

Several factors had come together to cause a new financial crisis for her: late payments of the interest on the Leathes legacies, her apparent inability to control the spending habits of her children, and her chaotic accounting system. Francis Bowness repeatedly encouraged her to be more methodical, and offered to help her organize the welter of bills generated by her children, but his advice fell on deaf ears. He also tried hard to emphasize the need to economize and to put money aside for increased expenditure on education in the future. Betsy knew she should be more prudent and more organized, but it was simply not in her nature, and the extravagance of her older children was already out of control.

She had become very conscious of the need to get her affairs in some sort of order when she heard of the death of her nephew Billy Nelson, on 10 December 1791 at the age of 22, leaving a young wife and baby daughter. The fall at Ipswich reinforced her inclination to think very seriously about her own position, and shortly afterwards she made a will.

Back at Sundridge Betsy quickly integrated herself into the round of morning visits, tea visits, card parties, routs, parties, assemblies and balls that constituted polite social life for the élite of Sevenoaks and district. The upper rank of society in her new neighbourhood was somewhat more exalted than anything she had encountered at Norwich, Reedham, Bury St Edmunds or Woodstock, although she had been well prepared by her youthful contact with the duke of Marlborough and his family. Her voluminous knowledge of social protocol, coupled with her instinctive ability to mix with society at any level, soon saw her on visiting terms with the great and good of the neighbourhood.

Lord Charles Stanhope, third Earl Stanhope of Chevening, was a near neighbour. He had three daughters, the Ladies Hester, Griselda and Lucy, by his first wife Lady Hester Pitt (who had died in 1780), daughter of Lord Chatham and sister of William Pitt the younger.[6] By his second wife Louisa he had four sons, of whom the eldest, Philip, succeeded to the earldom. Lord Frederick Campbell, brother to the fifth duke of Argyll, lived at Combebank near Sevenoaks, a Campbell family estate property. His wife Mary had previously been married to Earl Ferrers, who had murdered her lover and was the last English nobleman to be hanged at Tyburn. The Campbells were childless, although Lord Frederick had two daughters, both of whom were said to have been illegitimate.

The duke of Dorset and his wife Arabella lived at nearby Knole House, close to Sevenoaks. Prior to his marriage the duke had been an unrepentant womanizer, notorious for a string of mistresses and his very public affair with the countess of Derby. He was proficient at both tennis and billiards but was best known for his love of cricket; he was a good player and a generous patron of the game, and had presented the Vine Cricket Ground at Knole to the town of Sevenoaks in 1773. Other eminent neighbours on Betsy's visiting list were Beilby Porteus, bishop of London, who had a summer residence in Sundridge; Lord and Lady Amherst of Montreal Park, Sevenoaks; and Field Marshall Sir George Howard.[7] Edward Peach also had many friends among less exalted but nevertheless important local families, including the Wigsells of Sanderstead Court, the Novailles (or Noailles) of Great Ness, Sevenoaks, the Polhills of Chipstead, and the Lewis family of Westerham. Many of the local clergymen and their families were also on good terms with him, notably Dr William Vyse (rector of Sundridge and St Mary's, Lambeth) and his sister Mary, and the Reverend John Bodicote, vicar of Westerham and his wife Harriet, who became Betsy's faithful friend.

Betsy's diary entries were soon littered with references to visits, dinners, parties and balls involving Lord and Lady Frederick Campbell, Lord and Lady Stanhope and their family, the duke and duchess of Dorset, and the titled or well-known people she met while she was socializing with them and all the notable local families. Her son Edward told his grandmother that cricket matches had been added to their social calendar: 'Tomorrow there is to be a great cricket match and it is expected there will be much company there & you may be sure Mama will figure off [make a good impression] & I shall make an attempt.'[8] Betsy duly recorded the 'Cricketting' at the Vine Ground in her diary, while Elizabeth junior, who was a full-time Sundridge resident by July 1791, told her grandmother she had attended a cricket match at Sevenoaks, 'where we were much entertained with the sight of the company but we did not get out of the carriage', indicating that the game itself proved rather less of an attraction than people-watching.[9]

Its proximity to London made Sundridge a convenient and desirable location for the country residences of politicians, merchants, financial traders, lawyers and business people, which made the social life of the area particularly rich and varied. Betsy revelled in the summer months when the London visitors descended on their country homes for a longer period, but her husband not only failed to share her enthusiasm for the social hurly burly, he actively disliked it. He described his sentiments in a letter to Betsy's mother:

Our neighbours are all down in the Country for the Summer … we have so
much damn'd Tea Drinking & morning visits that I am heartily sick of them;
they seem to defer giving dinners 'till Dark Evenings commence that [they]
may touch your Pocketts at Cards, which you know I hate, they call, grin,
smile, chat scandal a little while & then bow, make a curtesy & then goe away,
that is the fashion with us – well Benedict must submit & do all as they do &
learn to be as Hollow & as hypocritical as they are & eat his own good fare at
Home with his Dame.[10]

Betsy however was in her element, and kept her two eldest children informed of
the local comings, goings, entertainments and marriages:

We return home the beginning of the Week as we expect Lord & Lady Frederick
Campbell, M[r] & M[rs] Noaille & their Son & their new married Daughter with
her Cara Spousa who is reported to have three thousand a Year – a great Match
– on Wed[y] The 5th of Oct[r] we go with them all to the Sevenoaks Assembly – I
forget whether I have written to You since we had a visit from the Duchess of
Dorset – Mr. Peach dined with his Grace last Monday Sennight with a large
Party of Gentlemen – last Monday M[rs] Porteus call'd on us & invited us to Tea
that Afternoon – we had a very pleasant Visit & play'd a Pool at Quadrille – the
Bishop & M[rs] Porteus are both extremely agreeable – On Sunday last we din'd
at M[r] Noailles with the Bride & Bride Groom.[11]

Elizabeth junior found some of the local social functions not quite to her taste.
One single visit to the Sevenoaks Assembly made her reluctant to repeat the
experience, as she wrote to her brother Edward:

On Wednesday next there is to be an assembly at Sevenoaks I hear a very good
one, good or bad they may go to the Old Gentleman [the Devil] for me for
the d[e]uce a bit will I stir out of the door, I have been to one that was enough
to give me a surfeit of it. There were only five couple two of which were L[d] &
Lady Frederick Campbell & Lord & Lady Amherst the Latter of which is about
the size of M[rs] Cross senior at the Bear Woodstock & who slided about like a
ship in full Sail. The Assembly Room is enough to make me melancholy & as
for the stair case O Lord, I'd better hold my tongue.[12]

Her letter was very cynical, but some allowance has to be made for a 16-year-old
girl showing off to her 15-year-old brother.

Elizabeth and Edward became more and more of a drain on their mother's
available income as they grew older. Edward, who celebrated his 16th birthday in
April 1793, was a bright boy academically and had a great love of and aptitude
for music. He learned to play the piano, the cello and the oboe in the space

of two years, all to a high standard. His love of fine clothes had also become evident by the time he was 15, another expensive habit for which his mother was expected to foot the bill. Francis Bowness had already told Betsy that her eldest son was spending far too much money on clothes and shoes, and advised her to supervise his expenditure more closely. But Edward simply ignored all instructions to economize and ordered even more clothes from Norwich tradespeople. Betsy remonstrated with him when his spending on clothes, shoes, sundries, sheet music and music lessons came to £50 for the first six months of 1792. She paid his tailor's bill herself because she knew Francis Bowness would be furious if she presented it to him for payment, and pleaded with Edward not to be so extravagant. He paid no attention and in September she was again berating him for ordering still more clothes, warning him that if he did not curb his extravagance he would have very real financial problems in the future.

Elizabeth junior, who had styled herself Eliza since she left school, was as good at spending her mother's money as her brother. Her Aunt Elizabeth, the wealthy widow of her late uncle John Leathes, planned to travel on the continent for a year or so, and in 1791 she invited Elizabeth to join her. The continental tour was an essential part of the fashionable 18th-century woman's search for improvement of the mind through travel, and Betsy must have seen the invitation as a glorious opportunity for her daughter to finish her social education in style. Aunt Leathes had persuaded Francis Bowness to join them on their travels, and this additional supervisory element must have reassured Betsy that her daughter would be in good hands. So after hasty arrangements had been made and the packing completed, the travellers – Elizabeth, Francis Bowness and his manservant, Aunt Leathes and her maid – left Sundridge for Dover on 4 December 1791.

The party arrived in Brussels on 11 December, and realized almost immediately that the political situation in the Austrian Netherlands (most of present-day Belgium), where invasion by the French was an imminent possibility, could radically

Fashionable gntleman's day dress, 1790s

affect their plans. Nevertheless they settled into rented apartments and prepared to wait for the situation to improve. Elizabeth began to take French lessons and to move amongst the cream of Brussels society, and Aunt Leathes cherished plans for both of them to be presented at court. Fortunately for Betsy this plan came to nothing: they would have needed full court dress for the occasion, and this would have been prohibitively expensive thanks to the inflation of demand on local dressmakers by the tourists and French refugees who had congregated in Brussels.

Aunt Leathes planned to stay in Brussels for five or six weeks before travelling first to France and then to Aix la Chapelle and on to the German resort of Spa. Events dictated otherwise, however, and the difficulties led inevitably to a modification of their travel plans, which would mean travelling through the Austrian Netherlands and Germany by coach to Switzerland for the summer and then on to Italy for the winter.

Francis Bowness lost patience with Aunt Leathes at this point, and told Betsy he intended to leave the ladies and pursue his own travel plans. He warned her that Elizabeth's expenses were mounting, and were likely to increase dramatically if her aunt had her way. He stressed the need for fairness where the children's expenses were concerned, and told her she must be sure in her own mind that she could afford to pay Elizabeth's bills and her travel costs. His warnings were prophetic: although Elizabeth's allowance had been increased from £40 to £60 for the year, Aunt Leathes was soon protesting to Betsy that this was inadequate to cover Elizabeth's share of the expenses for the rest of their tour. She then went on to tell Betsy how much Elizabeth had benefited from her travels, and that she now had a better grasp not only of arithmetic but also of the value of money!

The little group of travellers split up in mid-March 1792. On 20 April 1792 France declared war on the Austrian Netherlands and prepared to invade the country. Betsy must have breathed a sigh of relief when Aunt Leathes was then forced to abandon her plans to travel to Switzerland. The two women went instead to Aix la Chapelle, where they planned to stay for a while before travelling on to Spa in Germany. Aix was awash with frightened and desperate French refugees. They stayed for just over a month before moving on to the Hôtel de la Glacière at Spa. Elizabeth loved Spa, where she and Aunt Leathes again moved in high society. This meant she spent yet more of her mother's money on a riding habit and other articles of clothing. Betsy must have longed for her to return home before she brought them to financial ruin. Elizabeth's share of the travelling expenses was £45, for which Betsy was expected to foot the bill. This meant the cost of the continental tour was around £100 even before incidental bills were taken into account.

The long journey back to England began in early November, and by 8 November the party had reached Maastricht. Many of the roads in the Austrian Netherlands had been destroyed to halt the French advance, and the two women, like many other British travellers, risked being captured and interned by the French. They were delayed at Maastricht for about four weeks before they were able to travel to Ostend and board a boat for England. They arrived safely back at Dover on 17 December 1792, and reached Sundridge on 19 December. Elizabeth told her brother Edward that although she had enjoyed her adventures abroad, she was not sorry to be back in England, free from the fear and worry they had felt in Maastricht while they waited to get a safe passage back home.

9   Separation

Politics, national and international events, and wars were not major topics in Betsy's correspondence, but the years 1792 and 1793 were exceptions. The terrible war that was to dominate life in Europe and much of the wider world until 1815 was just beginning during the 12-month grand tour undertaken by Aunt Leathes and Elizabeth, and the two women were caught up in the early action that preceded Britain's involvement. Elizabeth's letters to her mother were full of references to the pathetic situation of the French refugees who had flooded into the adjacent countries, pushing up the price of food, clothes and accommodation everywhere they travelled.

French refugees also found their way to England. Francis Bowness told Betsy that a number of them had arrived in Lowestoft in December 1792: 'We have had a great importation of Emigrants. On the 4th ins^{t}. 105 landed here & yesterday a great many more, most of them seemingly people of consequence, & much to be pitied. Among those that landed yesterday was our Lord Plymouth & under his protection it is said a Sister of the Marquis of Fayotes.'[1] Like the marquis's sister, some of the families were lucky enough to find patronage, and were able to move on with the assistance of local magistrates such as Bowness: 'Yesterday I gave a passport to a Marchioness & her Suite consisting in all of twelve to insure them to Winchester where the Marquis has hir'd a house. We have yet remaining a Duke, Duchess & several others of some distinction who merit much pity.'[2]

It was against this backdrop of continental upheaval that political unrest inspired by French revolutionary ideology broke out at home. Revolt was in the air, and the threatening atmosphere soon gave rise to panic among the British landowning classes. This feverish atmosphere was heightened by the execution of Louis XVII on 23 January 1793 and the French declaration of war on England and Holland on 1 February.

Not surprisingly, many people felt it necessary to demonstrate their loyalty to both Crown and state in public. Betsy told Francis Bowness about a patriotic meeting that had been held at Sevenoaks, and Bowness responded with details of similar activity in Lowestoft: 'Meetings expressive of their attachment to Government are held everywhere & Tomorrow at this Town I expect that we shall have a very numerous one. Such laudable exertions, I trust, will entirely extinguish that spirit of discontent infus'd into the minds of the common people.'[3] Elizabeth junior demonstrated her patriotism too: she ended a letter to her grandmother, 'God save the King & bless the reader', and one to her brother, 'I hope you are very loyal. God save the King.'[4]

Betsy's two youngest children were by and large much less trouble than their older siblings. George, who was 13 in February 1792, had settled in well at St Paul's School and was making good academic progress. He had had measles late in 1791, but he was well looked after by the headmaster's sister and had not suffered any of the potentially lethal after-effects. Like younger children every-where, George inherited most of Edward's outgrown clothes, redundant school books and other school equipment. He was still Aunt Leathes' favourite, and even though she had ensured that he was taken away from Norwich Grammar School and sent to a school that she considered more appropriate (at an increased cost to Betsy), she continued to take a particular interest in him and he was invited to stay at Herringfleet Hall whenever possible. During one stay she thought his shoes were shabby, so she ordered three pairs of shoes from a local shoemaker and had the bill sent to Francis Bowness for onward transmission to Betsy. Bowness realized this was a considerable liberty, but felt Betsy had better pay up rather than upset her son's wealthy patroness.

Nine-year-old Mary eventually tired of being cut off from the rest of her family in Lowestoft, and during her long summer school holiday at Sundridge in 1792 she managed to persuade her mother to find her a school nearby. Betsy consulted her local friends. Mrs Miller's school at nearby West Malling was selected, and despite Bowness's disapproval, Mary began there as a boarder on 1 October 1792.

Mary must have been an appealing child, for she seems to have attracted adult interest wherever she went. She became a firm favourite with several of Betsy's friends, including the bishop of London, Beilby Porteus and his wife, who made much of the little girl. They visited her at school in West Malling, where the bishop gave her 2s.6d, and when Betsy and Edward visited the bishop's palace in Fulham Mary sometimes accompanied them.

George was still living within his annual legacy income, and any end of year surplus was invested, but Francis Bowness feared his expenses would also outstrip his income as he grew older. Mary's expenses were still comparatively small, and in November 1792 Bowness was able to send £100 of her surplus legacy income to Betsy so she and her husband could invest it. Bowness was sad to see the little girl leave Lowestoft, not simply because he had grown fond of her but because he feared her expenses would rise dramatically once she was outside his direct sphere of influence.

Betsy was conscientious about investing any surplus from the family income in government stock and bank annuities. She kept a close eye on the value of the investments, and when she thought it would be prudent to switch into stock offering better value she consulted Bowness. If he approved of the change, she either employed a stockbroker, or if she was in London and Edward Peach or a male friend was with her, carried out the transaction herself. But sometimes things went awry, as she told her mother in May 1792:

I went to the Bank yesterday & transacted your business tho' the Stocks were two p^r Cent lower than they had been, I bought with the 900$^£$ 3 p^r Cents 700$^£$ into the fives which will produce five & thirty Pounds a Year instead of twenty seven, so I hope you will think I have not made a very bad bargain – Mr.

Bowness went with me intending to do the same with that Stock in his name & Mr. Wigsells, but by a blunder it had not been accepted by the latter & is oblig'd to be postponed a few days which I fear will be a loss to us.[5]

They had to wait for four days before the necessary signature was obtained, and they were then able to effect the change without the loss they had feared.

It became obvious early in 1792 that Mrs Reading's income was inadequate for her to live on independently. At first Betsy ascribed her mother's shortage of cash to absent-mindedness and an increasing inability to manage money, but she quickly realized that Edward's presence so close to his grandmother's lodgings in Norwich might well be a factor. He had probably asked his grandmother for loans that he never repaid. Whatever the reason, Mrs Reading sold one of her Oxford properties, an inn known as The Goats, at the end of October 1792, and Betsy promptly had the money invested for her in 5 per cent government stocks. The only problem was that these stocks paid interest only twice a year, so Mrs Reading had to wait for another six months for any return, and suffered an acute cash shortage in the meantime. Betsy was also short of money, partly because of Edward and Elizabeth's extravagance and partly because she had reinvested a large portion of her own assets when she invested her mother's money, changing the date on which her own interest payments were due.

Although the part of Betsy's income dedicated to the children's education allowed for spending about £90 a year on each of them, Francis Bowness tried to ensure that Betsy kept to £60 a year so the surplus could be invested to cover rising costs as they grew up. The two boys would need every penny she could save for their university education. But Elizabeth and Edward soon made nonsense of the notional £90 allowance by overspending it substantially, in Edward's case usually without any reference to his mother or his trustees. The situation was not helped by Betsy's failure to be sufficiently strict with her children about money. She had actually encouraged Elizabeth's spending habits by allowing her to travel abroad with her wealthy aunt, although both Betsy and Francis Bowness had probably assumed Aunt Leathes would foot much of the bill – a sad miscalculation! Betsy's chaotic accounting infuriated Bowness. She paid the children's bills haphazardly then failed to submit properly itemized half-yearly accounts to him, so he had no idea of the true amount he should reimburse to her. He began to fear that the extent of overspending on Elizabeth and Edward's accounts meant they were eroding their capital, and he told Betsy that if the muddle and lack of spending discipline continued there would be very little left for them to inherit when they came of age.

The final cost of Elizabeth's continental tour was considerably more than it had appeared to be in December 1792, because much of the clothing she had taken with her was worn or damaged and had subsequently to be replaced, adding a further £20 or so to the bill. But Betsy saw this as money well spent, for by January 1793 her daughter had been well and truly launched into Kent society, and it was imperative that she should look her best if she was to make an advantageous match. Elizabeth's letters to her brother Edward were full of descriptions of the balls, assemblies and parties she had attended, the people she had met, the young men she had danced with (many of whom were officers in the locally stationed Hertfordshire militia) and where and with whom she had taken tea. She became friendly with all of the most prominent local families. She was invited to attend several functions at Chevening, and frequently accompanied the Countess Stanhope and the Ladies Hester, Grizelda and Lucy to other local social events. After her final travel expenses had been repaid to Aunt Leathes, Elizabeth at last managed to live within her £60 allowance, and relied on her mother only for little gifts and presents from time to time.

Meanwhile Edward's spending on clothes, shoes, silk stockings, silver accessories and other luxury goods was increasing alarmingly, as were his demands for money. Betsy was extremely upset, not only by his taste for what seemed to her unnecessary luxuries, but also because Major Leathes was encouraging him. She vented her fury in a letter to her mother.

The Contents of Edwards letter gave me great uneasiness & it is a matter of no small concern that I am obliged so continually to repeat my advice for Economy, it takes off very much from the pleasure I should have in corresponding with him because I never receive a letter from him, but it is to acquaint me with some fresh piece of extravagance – his wanting three Coats in a Year is the highest absurdity & his bespeaking a new one without asking my leave offends me exceedingly …. If Major Leathes thinks three Coats a Year necessary let him make a <u>present</u> of <u>one</u>, it is very unfriendly in him to advise Edward into Expences which he cannot afford, particularly as he knows how small his fortune is & how necessary to observe the strictest economy, what is to carry him thro' the University if a little is not sav'd now.[6]

Edward may have had an ulterior motive for enhancing his appearance with fine clothes, improving his musical proficiency and taking

Lady's day dress, c. 1780–90

dancing lessons in order to keep abreast of the latest trends. He and his sister exchanged confidences about matters they would rather keep from their mother, so Elizabeth learned that during 1793 he had become acquainted with a Miss Custance, presumably a relative of the Custance families of Ringland and Weston Longville. Elizabeth assumed he was seeing this young lady on a regular basis. Edward had inscribed her name in an old Latin dictionary that had been handed down to his brother:

> George is much pleased at having discovered your favourite Lady, you say she has 'inflamed your heart to the utmost degree' and that you know she Loves you; however certain I had been I think I would not have written it in a Latin Dictionary, it is signed 'EL'.[7]

Even his grandmother seems to have known the lady's identity, as she told Betsy that Mr Sharp, Edward's music master, had travelled to Norwich with Miss Custance, who had made enquiries of him about Edward. There was no further mention of her in either Edward's or Elizabeth's letters, but if she was a relative of Parson Woodforde's Squire Custance, he was playing out of his league and was clearly doomed to disappointment.

Betsy was concerned most of all with the change in Edward's behaviour: his cavalier attitude to money; his selfish attitude to his siblings, his grandmother and herself; his rudeness; and his determined pursuit of pleasure to the detriment of his studies – all the hallmarks of an over-indulged adolescent. More worrying still was Edward's growing impatience, and the vindictiveness with which he treated any adult who tried to prevent him from achieving his immediate objectives: Mr Bowness, who restricted his income; Dr Forster, who attempted to restrict his social life outside school; and Mr Wilkinson, the temporary rector of Reedham, whose sin is unknown.[8] Edward's resentment, once incurred, remained for life. His mother was concerned because Edward had no father to promote his interests, so men like Dr Forster and Mr Wilkinson were important to his future, and to offend them now might affect his career progression later.

The domestic, social and cultural life at Sundridge Old Hall seemed on the surface to be comfortable and congenial during 1793, but there were occasional indications that the relationship between Betsy and her husband was changing. As early as March 1792 Betsy had begun to search the house during his absence on business for documents relating to his landholdings and financial affairs. She made a comprehensive list of those she found, with a summary of their contents and a note of their location.[9] We can only speculate what caused this, but she obviously felt the information might prove useful. The next indication that something might be awry came when Betsy wrote to Francis Bowness in September 1793 asking if he had the papers relating to the £1,500 she had loaned her husband, because he had decided to discharge the mortgage secured on his estate. Bowness told her he did not have the papers and thought they had been lodged with her friend Mr Wigsell at his home in Sanderstead. Later that month Betsy assured her mother that all was well between her and her husband.

But this was not true. In December 1793 Betsy wrote to tell Francis Bowness that she and Peach had decided to separate. She gave no reason, but Bowness knew her well enough to realize she would not have taken such a drastic step lightly:

> The subject of your letter rather surprises me. But as I am not acquainted with the whole of the circumstances leading to an event that you think likely to take place between you & Mr. P. I can make no other observation upon it than what follows. When a matrimonial union proceeds with a tolerable degree of mutual happiness & comfort its continuation is most assuredly very desirable. When that ceases to be the case perhaps a separation fairly & deliberately made is preferable.[10]

Beyond advising Betsy to employ a competent and respectable lawyer, Bowness could do little else to help her until her husband had repaid the mortgage and confirmed their intention to separate. When Edward wrote to him that the separation would go ahead once he and his brother had found the £1,500, Bowness started the legal separation arrangements.

Divorce required an act of parliament until 1857, and was therefore open only to the very wealthy and influential. As a result, drawing up a private agreement to separate became the preferred method of ending a failed marriage in the 18th century. The matter-of-fact way in which Francis Bowness advised Betsy to do this if reconciliation was impossible indicates it was not unusual, although it is not clear how often it happened. Bowness wrote to Betsy again on 4 January 1794 and offered to help her with the legal technicalities involved with the termination of the mortgage, the deed of separation and the creation of yet another trust to administer it.

Despite the tensions involved, Betsy and Edward Peach appear to have maintained a civilized social façade during the uneasy period leading up to their formal separation, even though Betsy was making farewell visits to her friends and packing up her belongings. By late January she had fallen ill, and Elizabeth tried to explain this to her brother in Norwich: 'You may perhaps have heard that Mama is going to leave Mr. Peach, indeed she has been persuaded by all her friends to do it, for I am very certain were she to remain with him many months longer it would be the death of her.'[11] She then pleaded with him to stop bothering their mother with demands for money, and asked him to write an affectionate letter to her instead.

On 27 January 1794 Betsy left Sundridge with her husband and eldest daughter. They travelled by coach in heavy snow to London, where they took up lodgings in Lambs Conduit Street. They seem to have lived there in harmony, making the social rounds as usual and being visited by their family and friends. Francis

Bowness arrived in London at the end of January, as did their friend George Wenham Lewis, and with the help of the lawyers they began to negotiate the deed of settlement and to make arrangements for the formation of the separation trust. By 5 February the legal documents were complete and all the trust arrangements were in place. At this point Edward Peach left the lodgings at Lambs Conduit Street and took up residence at the Temple Coffee House.

Although their marriage was effectively over, the couple remained on the best of terms, and continued to meet until he left London for Sundridge on 8 February 1794. The deed of separation allowed Betsy an assured income for life in the form of jewellery, plate and furniture approximately equal to one-third of Peach's assets. In return she indemnified him against the consequences of any debts she might incur in the future. The deed also declared that, where her money and property were concerned, Betsy was free to act as a single woman.[12] These seem to have been key clauses in any deed of separation, and by the end of the 18th century both were enforceable in a court of law.[13]

Betsy had hoped the deed would be executed by mid-February, following which she planned to visit Norwich for an extended stay with her mother before she decided where to settle, but the lawyers took another four weeks, incurring expenses she could ill afford. Edward Peach, who seems to have acted with kindness and good humour throughout the separation proceedings, returned to London to provide her with moral support.

The couple continued to be good, even affectionate, friends, and Edward at least clearly felt sadness and a deep sense of loss. Betsy's close family members were probably aware of the reasons for the separation, although the extant correspondence contains no mention of them. The main one was almost certainly financial. Edward's situation was so bad that he had to put most of his estate up for sale later in the year, although it was not sold until 1798. This explained why Betsy was so keen to reclaim the £1,500 she had loaned him before it was swallowed up by his debts.

At last, on 3 March Edward arrived in London and presented Betsy with £1,300, which she swiftly invested in 5 per cent bank annuities. Quite what happened to the other £200 due to her remains a mystery. Betsy, Edward, the lawyers and the trustees met at the Stock Exchange Coffee House on the following day, and the deed of separation was signed at last. But before she could receive the dividends from the separation trust monies Betsy required a letter containing a power of attorney, and this was not forthcoming for a further four days. After that all the relevant documentation was safely lodged with her London bank.[14]

Edward Peach spent much of his stay in London with Betsy and Elizabeth, but finally on 10 March 1794 he dined with them and then saw them on to the mail coach that set out from Fetter Lane for Norwich. Betsy's second marriage had lasted for a little over three years, but the final separation would come only when one of them died.

10   Coldstream Bridge

After their parting from Edward Peach, Betsy and Elizabeth travelled overnight on one of the several coaches linking designated inns in London and Norwich. This time Betsy chose the post coach that left every evening from the White Horse on London's Fetter Lane and arrived at the King's Head in Norwich the following morning. Post coaches carried only three passengers at £1.1s each, although this relatively high cost included up to14 lb of luggage. They were accompanied by an armed guard on the road into and out of London, another attractive extra at a time when highwaymen were still active.

The King's Head was one of several old inns with frontages on Gentleman's Walk, to the east of Norwich marketplace. The inn yard and buildings ran all the way back to a narrow lane, known as the Back of the Inns, into which all the rubbish and manure from the inns and their stables were swept. From Monday to Saturday the marketplace was busy with coach traffic arriving at and leaving from the King's Head, the Angel and the Rampant Horse on its eastern side, and the White Swan on its western side. Roads into and out of the marketplace were mostly narrow, rutted and muddy, and regular use by horse-drawn traffic rendered them hazardous to pedestrians, who often had to dash into adjacent shops to avoid being mowed down or splattered with mud or worse.

Norwich marketplace had been laid out by the Normans during the 1080s in a part of their new borough of Newport, also known as Mancroft (*Magna Crofta*, or big field), to the west of the newly built castle.[1] The market grew and prospered over the centuries, and is still trading today on the same site. In 1794 packed market stalls were busy with the sale of all sorts of foodstuffs and other goods, while the shops surrounding the market place were thronged with customers from Norwich and the surrounding area for clothes, shoes, haberdashery, hats, hosiery, clocks, watches, jewellery, hardware, drapery, crockery, groceries and exotic trinkets. Norwich was the commercial, administrative, financial, leisure and social centre of East Anglia, and was always bustling with activity. Many people were attracted to the inns and lodging houses to transact business and to attend official and social functions.

The Reverend Joshua Larwood observed in the late 1790s that a cross-section of the wealthier members of society tended to gather at the eastern end of the marketplace on busy Saturday market days:

At the bottom [of the market place] is another space of parade-like appearance, emphatically called Gentleman's Walk: this walk, on the market day, is thronged with a collection of very interesting characters; the merchant, the manufacturer, the magistrate, the provincial yeoman, the militia-officer, the clergy, faculty, barristers, and all the various characters of polished and

Norwich Marketplace, 1800s

professional society. In short, not to run into minute particulars of this proud scene of bustle and business, health and wealth, prosperity and pleasure, proud let me call it, as it is the true criterion of provincial and national glory, which is better ascertained amidst the indiscriminate and collected, than in the separated and selected classes of the community.[2]

But however proud and thriving they were, the marketplace and its surroundings were not entirely salubrious. Gentleman's Walk was paved during 1794, but other streets were entirely unpaved and street cleaning was elementary at best. So when Betsy and Elizabeth walked out of the King's Head yard onto Gentleman's Walk they would have been assailed on all sides by the crowded, noisy, smelly, vibrant spectacle that was Norwich's market. They would also have taken great care to avoid horse-drawn vehicles and the horse dung, mud and rubbish in the streets.

Betsy was then intending to stay in Norwich no more than a few weeks, just long enough to check on her mother's welfare and get Edward settled at university in Cambridge. Then she and Elizabeth would be free to move back to Kent and their circle of friends there. The two women made their way from the King's Head to Mr Webster's premises on Tombland, where Betsy had arranged to take a suite of rooms. This ancient part of Norwich consisted of an area of open ground surrounded by houses, shops and market stalls. Part of the open area was occupied by a brick-lined reservoir, a water tower containing a hydraulic engine, and an aqueduct providing piped water to the houses of those who could pay for it. The reservoir also contained sufficient water to fight the frequent fires that broke out in the old timber houses. Housing in Tombland was typical of many areas of Georgian Norwich; a curious mixture of the old and the new, where commerce rubbed shoulders with industry, where the genteel and polite lived next door to tradespeople and even lodged in their houses, and where the poor lived in run-down old houses, courts and alleys alongside the grand houses of prominent citizens.

Betsy's mother had lodged at Mr Webster's since 1791, and although Edward Leathes junior thought it was demeaning for his grandmother, mother and sister to live over a cabinet maker's shop and workrooms, the three women were prepared to overlook this shortcoming because the position was so convenient and the lodgings were reasonably cheap. Barely a day had passed before Betsy and Elizabeth's old friends and acquaintances were knocking on their door. Within a week of their arrival young Elizabeth was enjoying a full social life, aided by her brother Edward and his school friend James Browne Thompson, the son of a deceased woollen draper. The three young people seem quickly to have become firm friends. Elizabeth often accompanied Edward on his frequent visits to the Thompson household, and Edward and James escorted Elizabeth to parties, balls and the theatre. Mrs Thompson and Betsy also seem to have found that they had much in common and were part of the same social circle, so two families forged strong links of friendship. That Betsy was separated from her husband did not seem to affect her socially, and within a month she had renewed most of her old friendships, made some new acquaintances and relaunched her social life.

The upper echelons of Norwich society consisted of a mixture of people with differing occupational and social origins. Many of them had manufacturing and professional backgrounds, others came from gentry families and a few boasted aristocratic connections. But for the most part Norwich's leading citizens were merchants, manufacturers and bankers, and it was they who built fine modern town houses in the finest contemporary style, some of which still stand today. They also enjoyed a lively cultural life, since some prominent citizens had had the good sense and taste to help provide the necessary buildings and facilities. These included the Assembly House (also known as the Assembly Rooms), which was opened in 1755, and the Theatre Royal, completed in 1758, only the second purpose-built theatre to be opened in England. Late 18th-century Norwich also possessed subscription libraries (so much more exclusive than mere circulating libraries); two provincial newspapers for the dissemination of news and the advertising of goods, services and events; several coffee houses in which gentlemen could mix socially and gossip; four pleasure gardens where polite families and individuals could meet, promenade and watch the spectacles provided; and many clubs and societies for the exchange and dissemination of knowledge of all kinds.

The Assembly House, Norwich, a print by James Sillett, 1828

The city compared very favourably with other English regional capitals, and had much to offer in the way of polite enjoyment and culture.

Despite the ease with which the family had fitted back into Norwich society, Betsy continued to feel it would be better for her and Elizabeth to move back to Kent. Her old friend and separation trustee, Mr Lewis of Westerham, sent her news of houses for rent in the area, as did other ex-neighbours, but none of them met her requirements. Then Louisa, Countess Stanhope sent this reply to a letter:

> Altho' I should certainly be very much pleas'd to have you an Inhabitant of our Vale yet I cannot help thinking that this particular spot would only bring more strongly to your mind painful reflections which it were better for you to forget entirely. Your mind, after having been so deeply wounded must want repose which might occasionally be broken into here in an unpleasant manner, and I am inclined to believe that this is the light in which it would be viewed by others in this part of the World.[3]

Betsy took the hint, and although she was happy to visit Kent to see her friends, she abandoned hope of any permanent return.

After a few weeks Betsy concluded that the lodgings at Mr Webster's did not quite fit her requirements. She viewed properties for sale or rent in Colegate, St Giles, Queen Street, Surrey Street and St Martin's Plain during the late summer and autumn of 1794, but without success. The simple problem was that she could not afford to do what she really wanted: to buy or rent a suitably impressive house in the best part of Norwich.

Unfortunately her plans had to be put on hold when she received some startling news. On 23 October 1794 Robert Brett, a close friend of James Thompson, told her he had received a letter from James and her daughter Elizabeth saying they were on their way to Gretna Green to be married.

Mrs Thompson called on Betsy the following day. Much as the two mothers might have liked to stop the marriage, there was little they could do, because not only did the couple have a good head start, they had laid a false trail. On 26 October 1794 Elizabeth Leathes and James Browne Thompson were married, not at Gretna Green but at Coldstream Bridge, on the eastern side of the border with Scotland.

Over the next few weeks several friends and relatives called to see Betsy, and doubtless expressed their opinion, while those who lived at a greater distance wrote to her. Most reacted favourably, while showing concern about the young couple's devious and imprudent actions, and hoped all the parties would swiftly be reconciled. Francis Bowness was wise after the event, which was not particularly helpful:

> I plainly perceiv'd a strong mutual partiality between the two young people which I imagin'd might one time or another end in a matrimonial union. I hop'd however that they might have had the discretion to wait 'till Mr. T. had acquir'd some establishment in life, but they have thought otherwise.[4]

Betsy was most unhappy, and refused to forgive her daughter. She thought James, aged 18, and Elizabeth, 19, were too young to marry because neither of them had any income other than the interest on Elizabeth's legacy. They would have to rely on their relatives for support for the next five years at least, until James had obtained his degree, been ordained and perhaps been presented to a church living. The young couple were living with James's uncle and aunt, Reverend and Mrs Edward Thurlow, at Horseheath near Cambridge, and Betsy insisted that they remain there until they had been married again according to Church of England rites. The wedding was quickly organized, and by 11 November she had been reconciled with the errant teenagers.

Mrs Thompson, however, resisted all her son's conciliatory overtures. The young couple had clearly not anticipated this, which rendered Betsy's cooperation doubly necessary if they were to live in any sort of style when James took up his place at Caius College, Cambridge the following year.

A more immediate problem was accommodation, as they would not be able to stay for long with the Thurlows. So James Thompson sent a letter filled with flowery expressions of gratitude and promises of snow-white future conduct to Betsy, attributing his actions to 'the irresistible charms of your beloved Daughter'.

Lady's day dress, c. 1795

He followed this saccharine flattery by telling her they had financial difficulties because Mr Bowness had not advanced them the full sum they had asked for, and requested the details of Elizabeth's legacy income.[5]

Either Betsy managed to talk Mrs Thompson into accepting her wayward son and daughter-in-law at the family home, or the lady relented of her own accord. The couple returned to Norwich two days after their marriage at Horse-heath, on 24 November 1794, and were greeted by Betsy at the Thompson home. Now that James and Elizabeth were 'properly' married, the social niceties could be observed and they could settle into their new role as a married couple. They threw themselves into the social round with gusto over the Christmas period and into the early months of 1795.

The two mothers must have reached an agreement on how to support James and Elizabeth until they both came of age, although no documentation has survived. Mrs Thompson was probably not prepared to release any money to James other than what was immediately necessary for his education, although she seems to have offered the couple a home in Norwich for part of the year. In June 1795 Elizabeth Thompson told Francis Bowness it had been agreed they would live with her mother for an unspecified part of the year. If this was true, the financial implications for Betsy were serious, and added to the problems her other children were causing. Edward was an irresponsible spendthrift whose behaviour towards her had deteriorated to such an extent that she had been forced to ask his headmaster, Dr Forster, to reprimand him. George was also showing signs of becoming as extravagant as his brother. Mary was growing up fast, and her expenses could only increase in the future. Already overstretched, she would find it difficult to help maintain the young couple too, particularly since accounting was not exactly her strongest point.

At the end of November 1794 Francis Bowness took Betsy to task for her failure to submit proper and timely accounts to him, and warned her that in the future she must either leave it all to him or manage her affairs herself. She was duly penitent and promised to do better in the future. Her financial investments, from which she derived the bulk of her income, were not helped by sudden adverse movements in the stock market, triggered by the progress of the war with France. Bowness was similarly affected, and shrewdly observed that these were the sorts of risk that investors ran in wartime.

In spite of the difficulties Betsy seems to have assumed responsibility for Elizabeth and James, and she agreed to accompany them to Cambridge, where James was to begin his university studies in April, and to stay with them there. The financial storm clouds were gathering around her, and she would probably regret her generous attitude in the future.

In January 1795 the war against the French began to bite into trade with Europe. On 1 January 1795 Betsy donated £1.1s to a subscription for the relief of the poor in Norwich. The winter of 1794–95 was particularly cold, one of several harsh wartime winters between 1793 and 1815, and the growing numbers of unemployed poor and destitute in the city were suffering extreme hardship. Norwich's wealth and prosperity were based mainly on the manufacture of luxury textiles, the famous 'Norwich stuffs' that were exported all over mainland Europe. The city's worsted industry was already in decline by the 1770s, squeezed by a combination of competition from the increasingly mechanized factories of the north of England, changes in fashion and the effects of war. Textile exports from Norwich were then virtually extinguished when France declared war in 1793, a blow from which there was no complete recovery, despite the best efforts of manufacturers and entrepreneurs.

The city's manufacturers and merchants complained about the sudden fall in their incomes, but the production workers and weavers who found themselves without jobs, income or the means of subsistence were much worse off. The inevitable fall in purchasing power fed through to the rest of the city's economy, and the whole area suffered from the loss of trade to a greater or lesser extent. Many workers were quickly reduced to poverty, workhouses were filled to capacity and public subscriptions became necessary in order to supplement the poor rate and relieve the terrible suffering of the city's poor. The busy social life of the moneyed classes, however, continued almost unabated, and Betsy, her children and their friends attended parties, balls and assemblies with few apparent cares.

Having at last taken the decision to settle in Norwich, Betsy realized it was no longer practical for Mary to remain at school in Kent, so she arranged for her to attend a school run by the Misses Costerton at Ipswich. Betsy took Mary and her friend Sophy Wells there by post chaise on 18 January 1795, and took tea with the Misses Costerton before leaving the two girls. After spending the night at Ipswich she boarded the London coach and set out on her travels, determined to enjoy herself before she joined Elizabeth and James in Cambridge at Easter. From London she took a coach to Westerham in Kent, where she met up with her youngest son George, and stayed for a few days at Mr Lewis's house. There she was visited, wined and dined by her friends, including Edward Peach. On 27 January Betsy used her own coach, which had been temporarily stored for her by Mr Lewis at Westerham, and hired horses to take George back to St Paul's School in London. During her two-day stay in the capital she transacted financial business, put her coach into storage again, visited her old friend Mrs Man and generally enjoyed herself.

Her obligations in London having been fulfilled, Betsy set out on 29 January for Salisbury, where her old friend Mrs Cuthbertson (formerly Mrs Goldwyer) was then living. The two friends had corresponded regularly, but this was the first time they had succeeded in meeting up, so they had a good deal to catch up on. Betsy thrived in this new social environment, and she soon found her way around Mrs Cuthbertson's circle of friends, quickly making them her own and joining in all the entertainments that Salisbury and district had to offer. She stayed with Mrs Cuthbertson until 17 March, when she moved on to Bath with friends she had made in Salisbury.

Betsy had never visited Bath before, although she had intended to do so on several occasions. She wasted no time in launching herself into enjoyment of the sights, the shops, the Pump Rooms, the theatre, and above all the genteel socializing. But time ran out, and on 24 March she returned to London, where she met up with George, who was again on vacation from school, and spent three days there. She took her coach out of storage once more, hired some post horses and set off with George for Cambridge. There they were met by Mr and Mrs James Thompson, and they all took up residence in the lodgings she had reserved some weeks previously.

Their lodgings were on Trumpington Street, and it was not long before Betsy's maidservant Betty and her manservant Michael arrived there to look after them all. James had begun his studies at nearby Caius College, and the young people led a social life of their own with James's college friends. Betsy was frequently called upon to provide a venue, food and drink for the necessary socializing, hospitality which was occasionally returned by some of the young men or their relatives in the vicinity. Not surprisingly she quickly involved herself in Cambridge life, renewed old acquaintances and made new ones, made and received visits, attended church on Sundays, attended tea parties, dinner parties and very frequently the card parties that were a prominent feature of college social life.

Betting and gaming were fashionable vices in the late 18th century. Both men and women gambled, some of them to excess, but upper-class women usually confined themselves to card games. Betsy loved card parties and played several times a week, sometimes winning or losing as much as 21s at a sitting, although the sums involved were usually much lower. She always recorded in her diary the type of card game played and how much she had won or lost.

Early in May 1795 Betsy began to hunt for new lodgings because Elizabeth had announced she was pregnant, so they would need larger and better accommodation after the summer vacation. She eventually settled on a suitable house and reserved it for ten months from 10 October, at a cost of £50. On 28 May the university term ended and Betsy, Elizabeth, James, Betty the maid and Michael the manservant travelled to London, where they were scheduled to stay for two weeks or so before they moved on to the seaside for a holiday. A few days later they were joined by Edward Leathes, and the three teenagers embarked on a hectic round of theatre-going and parties, much of it at Betsy's expense.

Despite the presence of Francis Bowness in London between 29 May and 10 June, the unholy trinity of Edward, James and Elizabeth seemed to be as inconsiderate, unruly and rude towards Betsy as they possibly could. She was devastated by their behaviour, and began to suffer from headaches, sickness and general debility. She complained bitterly to her mother about the way the trio behaved, the late hours they kept and their attitude towards her, and asked her to tell Mrs Thompson what was happening, in the vain hope that a reprimand from this redoubtable lady would improve James's manners.

They chose Margate for a summer break, and the family party arrived there on 16 June. The sea air did not improve the behaviour of the three teenagers, which deteriorated still further. At one point they moved out of their lodgings for a short time before being reconciled once more with Betsy, who was after all footing the bill, and in August the party moved to a new address. The reconciliation involved Betsy in even more expense: £50 to Elizabeth for clothes and other essentials, and £90 to Edward to pay his debts, 'loans' which she knew would never be repaid. James Thompson informed Mrs Reading in a fulsome letter that all was now well.

A perfect reconciliation has taken place. I am happy to inform you that Mrs. Peach has behaved in a manner so liberal as must eternally blot out the remembrance of what is past, & will I trust be the means of preventing any disagreement in future .... Elizabeth continues better than could reasonably be expected: & it is not a small addition to my enjoyment that she is capable of partaking of every amusement except dancing, which decency tells her not to attempt, her size being not a little increas'd by the incumbrance of her new Visitor: she says – he kicks very much, & dances so often that there wants no addition to the Party: all circumstances consider'd I begin to think there must be two if not three Imps to occasion so great a bustle.[6]

Despite all the emotional and physical upheaval of their early weeks at Margate, Betsy managed to relax and enjoyed a reasonably full social life, partly because her old friend Mrs Man was there for much of the time, with her children and her mother, Mrs Loggin. They ensured that Betsy did at least have someone to confide in, and that she did not have to venture into Margate society alone. Her subscriptions to at least three Margate libraries meant she had a ready supply of reading materials, while exchanging her books provided the opportunity for meeting other people, as did regular church attendance. Friends from Kent, Salisbury, Cambridge and Norwich also made short visits to the town, so there was no shortage of diversion and distraction. When the fashionable autumn season began at the end of the third week in August, Betsy was able to subscribe to the Assembly Rooms, and access all the polite entertainment on offer there. Her social horizons were further enlarged when the Playhouse opened at the same time. The last six weeks of their stay at Margate passed quietly, and Betsy gave herself up to the sort of polite socializing and sightseeing that she enjoyed so much.

During her stay at Margate she maintained a steady flow of correspondence with friends and relatives. In June she received news from Kent that her friend Harriet Bodicote, a widow since 1792, had married Edward Turnour, fourth Earl of Winterton, a widowed and none too wealthy Irish peer with seven children. After the briefest of honeymoons the couple had returned to Shillinglee Park in Sussex, the Winterton family seat. Betsy quickly wrote to congratulate her friend, who replied indicating that her new life as stepmother to three girls and four boys, the youngest only 3 years old, was not easy. Her first task was to cure the family of their extravagance and to find ways of cutting back on expenditure. How that must have resonated with Betsy! Someone else who embarked on matrimony for the second time in 1795 was her uncle by marriage, 67-year-old William Nelson, rector of Strumpshaw. He wrote in August that he had married Susanna Panchen, widow of William Panchen, who had been rector of nearby Burlingham St Peter. His new wife was 22 years his junior, and Francis Bowness told Betsy he would not be surprised if the venerable gentleman acquired a belated second family.

Not all the news and opinion that Betsy received was welcome. By the end of June her financial situation was considerably overstretched, a situation that gave Bowness cause for concern:

> If you find Margate very expensive, your prudence will direct you to leave it as soon as the object of your journey is at all answer'd, and it will further guide you to some place or other where you may live more snugly. Such caution as this is necessary for us all, for I never knew a time when money slipt away from one with more ease or when it was with more difficulty acquir'd.[7]

As if the burden of supporting the Thompsons was not heavy enough, Edward's extravagance continued to spiral out of control, and Betsy made ever larger 'loans' to him from her own money, on the understanding that he would repay her when he received his legacy. She was forced to tell her mother, who was also asking her for a loan, that she did not know whether she would be able to hold out until she received the dividends on her investments at Christmas. She sent her mother

£2.16s, the proceeds from the sale of her horse harness, and told her she intended to raffle her coach at Margate to bring in some extra cash.

Bowness offered his assistance, but Betsy was beyond help by this time. She confessed to her mother that she had given Edward £94 to repay his debts during the previous eight months. She had also given Elizabeth Thompson £70 since her marriage, plus clothes and presents, as well as covering the young couple's accommodation and living expenses. She could not continue subsidizing the Thompsons from a fixed income that had also to support her mother, her younger children and her servants.

In order to avoid the disgrace of legal proceedings against Edward for debt, and to keep Elizabeth and James afloat, Betsy had borrowed £148 from friends and family members during the previous few months, all of which would have to be repaid at the earliest opportunity. She had been unable to raffle or sell her coach, and admitted she was at her wits' end for ready money. All her Christmas investment income had already been earmarked to pay off her debts. Both she and Bowness were desperately worried about how Edward would cope once he went up to Cambridge in the autumn, as he had already spent all the money Bowness had held in reserve for him, as well as the money Betsy had given him. It seemed inevitable that financial problems would dominate Betsy's life for years to come.

From Margate Betsy went to London and then on to Cambridge, where she took up the lodgings she had booked back in May, and awaited the arrival of Edward and the Thompsons. She contacted Edward's tutor, Mr Porter, who had taken furnished rooms in Cambridge for Edward until rooms at Trinity College became available. He told Betsy it would be possible for Edward to maintain a gentlemanly appearance at Cambridge on £120 a year (unlikely, given his track record), and that he might be eligible for a scholarship worth £24 a year. Betsy was relieved, and resolved to work with Francis Bowness on a plan to pay off Edward's debts, although she explained her reservations to her mother.

I hope to God he will consider how necessary it is for him to keep his £1000 [legacy] untouch'd that he may have something to furnish his House with & to begin the World or his Living will be under Sequestration & he will be poor & wretched all his lifetime .... I wish Edward could be made sensible how very necessary it is for me to keep my fortune whole & entire that I may have it in my power to afford him & his Brother & Sisters a comfortable home at the Vacations – which I cannot do if he contracts debts more than his Income is sufficient to discharge, & hope his Pride will whisper to him that all respectability must be lost when once people go beyond their Income, nothing can make respect <u>lasting</u> but being prudent & economical.[8]

His debts were eventually paid, because he left Norwich for Cambridge on 3 November.

The Thompsons' return to Cambridge on 19 October 1795 was far from happy. A chronic shortage of money forced Betsy to greet them with the news that she could no longer afford to support them as she had during the previous six months, and intended to return to Norwich. The youngsters were furious because they had been left with little alternative but to seek help from Mrs Thompson. Poor Betsy packed her belongings and left Cambridge for Thetford with her maid Betty. They caught the Expedition coach there early on 23 October, and arrived at the Maid's Head in Norwich later that morning.

No sooner had they arrived at her mother's lodgings than Betsy hurried round to call on Mrs Thompson. They must have had an interesting meeting. Betsy did not record the outcome, but Mrs Thompson must have been forced at last to take a major role in providing for her errant son, his wife and the child they were expecting. As a result Betsy seems to have been excluded from the birth of her first grandchild. There is no mention whatsoever in her diary of the baby boy who was born in November 1795 and named James after his father.

During Betsy's absence Mrs Reading had moved to new lodgings at 3 Queen Street, the house of James Nosworthy, a hairdresser, perfumer, dealer in toys, jewellery and trinkets. He was known to Parson Woodforde and his niece, who had stayed at the house on 1 April 1793 when there were no beds to be had at the King's Head.[9] The lodgings may well have been adequate for an overnight stay, but Mrs Reading, Betsy and Betty the maid found them cramped and far from ideal. It became increasingly clear they would need more spacious lodgings to house Edward, George and Mary over the Christmas vacation, so Betsy began to look for alternative accommodation. Her search was short but successful, and she rented a house, also on Queen Street, for 26 guineas a year. By 28 November workmen were putting up new shelves and making modifications to the internal fittings, and on 3 December 1795 the two women moved in, accompanied by the faithful Betty. Mary arrived back from school at Ipswich on 13 December, then on 17 December they were joined by Edward and by George, who had stayed for a few days with his aunt at Herringfleet Hall.

All this drama had taken its toll on Betsy's health. She was taken ill during the night of 7 December and took to her bed for several days, relying for medical attention and medicines on her friend Mr Leath, the surgeon apothecary from Acle. She did not spell out in her letters what her illness was, but it seems to have been severe, and it may well have prompted Mrs Thompson senior's call at the Queen Street house on 13 December. This was followed by another visit from her on 19 December, accompanied by Elizabeth and James. A truce of sorts seems to have been declared, although the relationship between Betsy and her daughter and son-in-law was never again close.

Betsy left her bedroom for the first time on Christmas Day to enjoy the festivities with her mother, Edward and Mary, but without George, who had returned to Herringfleet Hall to spend Christmas with his Aunt Leathes. The last few days of the year passed quietly enough – a calm end to another turbulent year for Betsy and her family, disfigured by filial dissent and an increasingly pressing shortage of money. That shortage was emphasized by further borrowing from her friends and even from her servant Betty during November and December.[10] The outlook for 1796 was not promising.

11   Trials and tribulations

Betsy and her children never saw a shortage of ready cash as a barrier to their involvement in the social life of Norwich, Cambridge, Ipswich, Salisbury, London, or wherever they happened to find themselves. On the contrary, it seems to have given them an incentive to extend the range of their social contacts (their 'acquaintance'), not simply because they were naturally gregarious, but because there was always the possibility that a new contact might prove an influential patron. All three young men would need patrons when they graduated, James Thompson more so than Edward or George Leathes because he had no guaranteed church living to look forward to. Edward was already assured of presentation to the livings of Reedham and Freethorpe after his ordination as priest, but his taste for the good things in life meant he would always need to increase his income by seeking more and better preferments. George's future was also assured: once he was ordained he would be presented to the modest livings of Wickhampton and Limpenhoe with Southwood. As Aunt Leathes' favourite nephew, he could also hope for one of the other livings in her gift, or one in the gift of the numerous friends with whom she had influence.

There can be little doubt that Elizabeth's elopement with James Thompson had been a great disappointment to Betsy. He had no prospects of earning a living for some years to come. A considerable amount of money had been invested in Elizabeth's education and her continental travels, and financially her marriage had yielded little return. Mary had yet to be launched fully into society, and it would undoubtedly be necessary to spend more money on her. Betsy must have hoped Mary would find a more affluent husband, although she would have to do so without some of the financial advantages her sister had enjoyed.

The Leathes children, like their mother, were particularly adept at using their considerable social skills to ingratiate themselves with members of prominent local families. Both Edward Leathes and James Thompson had made such friends during their years at Norwich Grammar School, where many wealthy and well-connected Norwich families sent their sons. The process continued at university, which was often considered to be an appropriate conclusion to the education of young gentlemen even if they were not destined for the priesthood. Edward's undergraduate friends often called at his home during the university vacation, and came into contact with his mother, younger brother and sister. Prominent among these contacts were Edward Donne and Augustus Beevor. Edward was the son of Dr William Donne, a Norwich surgeon. He eventually married his cousin Anne, daughter of the Reverend Castres Donne, who was well known to Parson Woodforde. Augustus was the third son of James Beevor, a Norwich brewer, and his wife Mary. He was later renowned as an outrageously flamboyant cleric and one of the best amateur boxers of the age.

Contact with the Beevor family was particularly advantageous. James Beevor was the youngest brother of Sir Thomas Beevor of Hethel Hall and of Dr John Beevor, one of the first physicians at the Norfolk and Norwich Hospital. A wealthy and successful businessman, he had had the great good fortune to win a £20,000 prize (around £1 million in today's money) in the State Lottery in 1794.[1] The Beevor clan was both large and influential, linked by marriage with many other prominent local families, so that Edward and Augustus were on friendly terms was potentially valuable. Betsy herself had been busy making new contacts and strengthening old ones, and by 1796 she was on visiting terms with ladies (and a few gentlemen) from the wealthy and socially prominent Stannard, Freemoult, Kerrison, Morphew, Ives and Harvey families. She was particularly friendly with Jane Branthwayt, another Beevor relative.

Maintaining her correspondence with friends who did not live locally kept her in contact with people who might be able to exercise some influence on behalf of her children, kept her supplied with news of and gossip about old friends, and reminded her of familiar places. Lady Winterton invited Betsy to come and stay with her at Shillinglee Park near Guildford, although she first warned her about the household's straitened circumstances:

> You are not to expect any finery or magnificence because it is a Lord's House for you'll see no other than plain M^rs. Bodicoate and her house at Westerham all we aim at is comfort not extravagance or ridiculous shew which would be the height of folly when we have seven Children to educate & provide for.[2]

Betsy missed her old friend and confidante and would dearly have loved to visit her, but letters would have to suffice until she was able to make the journey to Shillinglee.

Mary Vyse, sister of the Reverend William Vyse (rector of Lambeth, Sundridge and Brasted and later archdeacon of Coventry), wrote to Betsy in April 1796 to tell her that 16-year-old Lucy Stanhope, the youngest daughter of Earl and Countess Stanhope of Chevening, was engaged to marry a local surgeon, Thomas Taylor. Earl Stanhope, a radical politician who had for some years enjoyed the nickname of 'Citizen Stanhope', was popularly thought to disapprove of the match, which provoked a great deal of public amusement. Miss Vyse, however, told Betsy that the earl was having a house prepared for the couple, and had declared he intended to refer to his daughter as 'Citizen Taylor's Wife' after her marriage, which would seem to indicate that he tolerated the situation with equanimity and a degree of humour.[3] Miss Vyse, who was not in the first flush of youth, wrote to Betsy again in August 1796, this time to inform her that she had married Dr Spencer Madan, the bishop of Peterborough. Betsy was delighted for her friend, and the two women maintained a fairly regular correspondence until Betsy's death.

Outwardly Betsy and her family managed to maintain the illusion that they led a comfortable upper-class existence, but the reality was rather different. Betsy was forced to borrow money occasionally from a few close friends, and found it necessary to beg advances from the children's agreed income from the Reedham and Freethorpe livings far too often for the Reverend Wilkinson's own financial comfort. Francis Bowness recognized that most of her financial problems stemmed from her children's often unreasonable demands, a situation that threatened to destabilize the family unit for several years to come. He advised her to put aside part of her income for her own use, but it is doubtful whether this was feasible. Edward managed regularly to overspend his £40 quarterly allowance at Cambridge, and he continually bombarded both Betsy and Bowness with requests for more money, so much so that in July 1796 Bowness was forced to remark that the well would soon be dry, and advised Betsy to restrict him to his allowance.

In July 1796 the whole Leathes family was stunned by the news that Leathes Johnstone, cousin to Major George Leathes and Betsy's first husband Edward Leathes, had filed a bill in Chancery contesting the will of their great uncle William Leathes, who had died in 1700.[4] This was a potential disaster for the whole Leathes family, including Betsy and her children, because a successful challenge to William Leathes' will would invalidate the wills made subsequently by Hill, Carteret and John Leathes. Chancery procedures could be lengthy and expensive, and even if the challenge was unsuccessful it would inevitably delay the payment of any further legacies. The news was extremely unpopular with Elizabeth Thompson, who reached her 21st birthday on 28 August 1796 and had expected prompt payment of the legacies of £100 from her father and £1,000 from her uncle. Now the legacies were all in jeopardy, and could not be paid until the Chancery case was resolved.

James Thompson had become a zealous manager of his wife's money, and kept a very careful eye on payments due from Betsy or from Francis Bowness, such as the interest on her legacy from John Leathes, the interest on the money Betsy had invested for her when she was much younger, and her share of the payments from the Reedham living. He was swift to protest when any of the payments was late, and equally swift to ask for an advance if he was short of cash. So when Elizabeth's 21st birthday came and went with no legacies paid, he pressed Betsy to liquidate some of her stock and give them the amount they had been expecting. But the war with France was exerting downward pressure on stock prices, and Betsy was unwilling to sell out when prices were low, so she asked him to wait a few months in the hope the market would improve.

Betsy's efforts to curtail the family's financial outgoings prompted her to negotiate with her landlord for a reduction in her rent of £33.12s a year. Bowness sympathized, but thought she could save even more money. 'I cannot say that I wou'd advise you to hire a house in Norwich at this time at such a price as you speak of, if you can any way avoid it. Rates, taxes & the mode of living are so extravagant that a lodging wou'd be preferable if it cou'd be obtain'd to your mind.'[5] Whatever the reason, Betsy found herself hunting for new lodgings yet again, a search that led her back to her old landlord, Mr Nosworthy, at 3 Queen Street. After haggling with him, she hired all the lodging rooms available in his house, presumably at a lower rent than her previous lodgings.[6]

As soon as the arrangements were complete, Betsy moved back to 3 Queen Street with her mother and her maid on 10 May. Mrs Reading seems to have been as desperate for money as her daughter, because Betsy opened negotiations on her behalf for the sale of the former family home at Woodstock. After negotiations the house was sold in August 1796 to Charles Heynes of Woodstock for £400.[7] Betsy did not record any purchases of stock with the money, so it was doubtless used to pay off debts and to satisfy her mother's immediate financial needs. Luck at the card table seems also to have been elusive, because she made an overall loss of 10s.8½d in 1796. This was money she could ill afford to lose, but gambling in general and card playing in particular were so firmly embedded in the mores of polite society that it was not something she could easily avoid.

Men in the upper ranks of society took a great interest in national, and to a lesser extent local, politics, and while it was considered inappropriate for women to involve themselves in political affairs or debate, Betsy was happy to provide her male friends and relations with news of elections held in her own backyard. Norwich, the 'Jacobin City', had a reputation for hard-fought and turbulent election campaigns. Pitt called a general election in 1796, a year that had opened with a shortage of wheat in both city and county and the highest bread prices in living memory, much to the dismay of the poor and the ever-growing numbers of unemployed. The better-off families in Norwich tried to restrict their household consumption of bread and flour as much as possible, but despite their best efforts and the limited release of government stocks of grain onto the market, wheat became even scarcer in the city and prices rose still further in April. The poor of the city became desperate and mounted fierce protests, accompanied by attacks on millers, bakers and bread shops, culminating in a riot that was eventually quelled by the mayor, the sheriffs and a group of citizens without recourse to military help.

The distress was so great that the mayor and 12 aldermen subscribed £100 each to buy meal and flour to be sold cheaply to the poor under the supervision of a committee. Many citizens of Norwich blamed the war on France for all their economic woes, and wanted to see an end to it so that trade, and therefore employment, could return to normal. So they did not want to see Pitt return to power, although he had made tentative moves towards peace negotiations with France in February. These moves were swiftly rejected by the French.

Norwich returned two members to parliament, and there were three candidates at the election on 25 May 1796: the sitting Tory members, Henry Hobart and William Windham (Minister for War), and the Whig candidate, Bartlett Gurney, a Norwich banker. Feelings ran high, and there was considerable public disorder and some violence before the poll was completed. Although Gurney had polled

The Guildhall, Norwich, a print by James Sillett, 1828

the most Norwich votes, Hobart and Windham retained their seats thanks to their mobilization of non-resident voters – a most unpopular conclusion to a bad-tempered campaign.

The parliamentary election for the county was scheduled for 2 June 1796, and Parson Woodforde, like many other people, feared a repetition of the disturbances seen at the city election: 'I am sadly afraid that the Peace of the County at the approaching election for Members ... will be disturbed by some designing, artful & republican People.'[8] There was a considerable amount of jockeying for position, with six individuals vying for nomination, but in the event only the sitting candidates, Sir John Wodehouse and Thomas William Coke (later earl of Leicester) were nominated. They were returned unopposed without any of the public disorder that had marred the city elections. Nationally the election returned Pitt and his colleagues to power, increasing their already unassailable majority and vindicating Pitt's decision to hold the election 12 months before the expiry of his mandate.[9]

But despite this electoral coup, the failure of substantive peace talks with France late in 1796 quenched even Pitt's usual optimism. By January 1797 Britain was the only European power left standing against the French Revolutionary armies and their continental allies. Napoleon's star was on the rise and his victories during 1796 had encouraged Spain to invade Portugal, sign a defensive alliance with France and then to declare war on Britain. The mood of the British people was uneasy, fuelled by unrest at home and lack of military success abroad. It was lifted only partially by the failure in February 1797 of an attempted landing by a small

French force in Pembrokeshire. At sea, Britain's navy was much more successful, although celebration of the defeat of the Spanish fleet at Cape St Vincent by Admiral Jervis and Commodore Horatio Nelson in February 1797 was quickly marred by the mutiny of sailors from the Channel fleet at Spithead in April, followed by a similar uprising among men of the North Sea fleet at the Nore in May. Both mutinies were successfully repressed, although the harsh measures taken against the mutineers at the Nore provoked apprehension and uncertainty among the population in general. People worried what might happen should the French be more successful than they had yet been in their attempt to invade Britain.

Pitt's government again tried to broker peace with France in April 1797, but negotiations ended abruptly in September, when the Directory appointed Napoleon Bonaparte as commander-in-chief of the French armies. The public mood in Britain was temporarily assuaged by the comprehensive destruction of the Dutch fleet off Camperdown by the North Sea fleet under Admiral Duncan on 11 October 1797. The Dutch ships captured there were taken to Great Yarmouth, where Edward Leathes and a friend went to see them soon after their arrival.[10]

The war was by this time having a disastrous effect on public finances, forcing Pitt to borrow very heavily in a short space of time, a course of action that sent government stock into free fall. Panic was in the air and a run on the banks became likely, so in order to avoid a financial catastrophe the Bank of England instructed all banks to suspend cash payments as a temporary measure on 27 February 1797. The crisis was averted and the banking system eventually recovered, but Pitt realized that in future he would have to look to taxation, perhaps even direct taxation, as a more reliable means of raising money for the future conduct of the war than the combination of borrowing and indirect taxation he had used up till then. This change of direction was embodied in the Finance Bill of November 1797, which provided for a substantial increase in assessed taxes in 1798 and led ultimately to the introduction of income tax in 1799.

It is a fact of life that taxation leads those who are taxed to complain. Often the people who suffer the least complain the most, and the well-off of late 18th-century Britain were no exception. No matter how great the justification, those liable to pay the new and increased taxes began to grumble more loudly than was customary, and the tenor of those complaints changed noticeably during 1797. Even the patriotic Francis Bowness grumbled, although he observed that taxation had had little real effect on the lifestyle of the well-to-do in Lowestoft: 'We all of us complain of the oppression of taxes & poverty, & indeed very justly. And yet I never remember so much feasting as we have had here for many years past. For these last ten days we have had a series of eating drinking and cards.'[11]

Taxpayers became increasingly apprehensive about the length and cost of the war because they realized that the longer it went on, the greater the burden of taxation was likely to become. The failure of peace negotiations in September combined with economic distress, consistently low stock prices and the impending arrival of increased taxation to create a negative atmosphere for many people. Lady Winterton was among those who were apprehensive about the potential effects of the new tax: 'Upon my word these severe Taxes will oblige us to keep at home, I must not think of them if I do I shall be as melancholy as a Cat.'[12]

Betsy's financial situation remained desperate throughout 1797. In February she instructed her bank to sell some of her stocks, because Elizabeth and James Thompson were no longer prepared to wait for payment of the overdue legacy from her father. Francis Bowness warned her it was not a good time to sell, and urged domestic economy as an alternative, but both he and his fellow trustee, John Love, realised there was little else she could do if the Thompsons were pushing for payment. On 27 February 1797 Betsy went to Kerrison's bank to receive the money she needed to pay the £100 legacy and the £2.10s interest owing on it, only to find that the bank had suspended payment on the instructions of the Bank of England, courtesy of the national financial crisis. So the Thompsons had to wait until the banks reopened for business on 2 March.[13]

This payment seems to have prompted Elizabeth and James to also demand payment of Elizabeth's legacy from John Leathes, although the legal challenge to his will had not been resolved. James Thompson wrote to Francis Bowness and threatened legal action of his own to force immediate payment of the £1,000, plus interest of course. Major Leathes was incandescent with rage, and although he assured Betsy that she could not be held responsible for their actions, he made it very clear to her that if the Thompsons were to pursue their claim in this manner it could prejudice the eventual outcome of the case, as well as exposing to public view the limitations that it had imposed upon him and the estate. If the case went against him, he said, then Betsy's children would lose their legacies and Edward and George would lose their church livings, so it was essential not to rock the boat or leak information that could potentially be used by Johnstone until the case was decided.

The impatient, thoughtless and irresponsible attitude of the Thompsons had clearly done nothing to endear them to one of their two rich and influential relatives, and this sort of behaviour was to characterize much of their social and familial interaction in the future. Fortunately the case was finally settled in favour of the Leathes family in December 1797, and Major Leathes was then free to put some of the estate lands up for sale in order to pay the legacies that had become due.

The two young Leathes brothers continued to spend money regardless of whether or not it was theirs to spend, although in fairness to George, his debts seem to have been considerably less than Edward's, and the funds available to him were just about adequate to cover them. By March 1797 Edward had moved into rooms at Trinity College, Cambridge and was busy furnishing them to his exacting taste, so Betsy constantly received requests for more money to pay for the furniture, soft furnishings, plate and cutlery he had either acquired or wished to acquire. Meanwhile his appetite for fashionable clothes had not diminished and he continued to commission items he had no intention of paying for, confident that his mother would eventually subsidize him. His total yearly allowance was around £160 a year, which was more than generous in the circumstances, but during 1797 he received well in excess of that sum from Betsy and Francis Bowness. Such was Edward's desire for money and his mother's inability to say no that she paid him £2.2s for giving music lessons to his brother and a further £2.2s for teaching her to play chess.[14]

Given all these trials and tribulations, it was not surprising that in April 1797 she decided to take up some of the offers of hospitality extended by her friends and get away from it all. She travelled from Norwich to London by the Expedition coach on 2 April, and took up lodgings at 15 Kirby Street, Hatton Gardens while she transacted some financial business and tried (unsuccessfully) to sell her coach, which was still in storage there. After two weeks or so she moved on to stay with her friend Mrs Whately at 12 Dover Place. Her principal occupations were visiting friends and acquaintances, taking tea, dining out whenever she was invited to do so and playing cards, mainly because she was so short of money that she could not afford to do anything else. But she did manage visits to Covent Garden to see a performance of the *Messiah* and to the theatre on a few occasions, as well as attending several churches to hear the sermons and visiting the Magdalen, which was considered to be a fashionably 'improving' experience for the mind and spirit.[15]

Her business in London finally completed, Betsy set out for Salisbury by coach from the Bell Savage Inn on Ludgate Hill. In Salisbury she was reunited with her old friend Mrs Cuthbertson at her house on St Anne's Street, where she spent four happy weeks renewing the acquaintances made two years previously. Keen not to overstay her welcome, she then moved on to Woodstock, where she stayed at Charlbury Place with Mrs Holloway, an old friend of her parents. She revisited many old friends and acquaintances, saw the familiar haunts of her youth, and not surprisingly soon became very nostalgic and began to wish that she and her mother had not sold the old Woodstock house. Unfortunately reality was never far away, and towards the end of June she was brought back to earth by a letter from her elderly mother, who had begun to feel insecure about managing both the Norwich household and her grandson Edward.

Betsy's reply to her mother's letter is indicative of the frustration and resent-ment she felt about this summons back to Norwich and reality, despite the fact that she was well aware of the old lady's frailty:

With respect to my returning home I will endeavour to do so as soon as possible as You seem so desirous of it, but surely the housekeeping cannot be so very fatiguing to You as there is only yourself & Edward to provide for & you must consider that I am living here very pleasantly & without any expence, why therefore cannot you let me enjoy a little happiness uninterrupted? You know how uncomfortable the greatest part of my life has been, why then cannot you suffer me to spend a few weeks pleasantly? [16]

Realistically Betsy could not afford to return to Norwich until she had received her half-year dividends in July, because most of her available cash had already been sent to Edward. She eventually left Charlbury on 15 July for London, where she stayed for two nights before moving on to Shillinglee Park for her long-awaited visit to Lord and Lady Winterton. She greatly enjoyed the company of her friend and her new family, but realized after a few days that her return to Norwich could be postponed no longer. On 25 July she regretfully set out for Norwich, where she arrived on the morning of 27 July, very hot and extremely tired.

As soon as she arrived home Betsy realized the extent to which she had missed her family. She was glad to see Edward, Mary and her mother, for whom she had brought a present of some of her favourite snuff. George was home from school, but was of course dancing attendance on his aunt at Herringfleet Hall. At the beginning of April, a few weeks before Betsy's departure for London, Elizabeth Thompson had given birth to a baby daughter, yet another Elizabeth, a sister for 2-year-old James. Betsy had missed her grandchildren and was delighted to be reunited with them. Baby Elizabeth had been inoculated against smallpox a few weeks earlier, and Betsy was relieved that the procedure had gone smoothly and the child was healthy and strong. Within a few days of her return she had picked up the threads of her social life, caught up with all the local news and gossip, and adjusted to her familiar surroundings once more.

Betsy travelled to Ipswich in early November 1797 to visit Mary and the Misses Costerton. She took up residence at Mrs Hammond's boarding house in St Clements, where she quickly made friends amongst the other residents and settled into a routine of visiting, taking tea, playing cards and dining out. One of her fellow lodgers was the authoress Clara Reeve, who had published several novels as well as a volume of poetry and some more serious work. Her *The Old English Baron: A Gothic story* (published in 1778) and *The Memoirs of Sir Roger de Clarendon* (published in 1793) had been reprinted several times. Miss Reeve freely admitted that her novels were bread and butter work, providing an income that permitted her to indulge her interest in more serious subjects, such as the debate on the French Revolution and the role of women in social improvement through educational reform.

Betsy was delighted to make the acquaintance of a literary celebrity, and quickly set about acquiring and reading some of her books. Clara Reeve also had something of a reputation as a conchologist, and Betsy took Mary to see an exhibition of her shell collection in mid-November.[17] The two women were both the daughters of none too affluent clergymen. They seem to have struck up an immediate friendship, and they corresponded until Clara's death in 1807. Betsy enjoyed her stay at Ipswich but was unable to prolong it for more than four weeks, so after entertaining Mary and 16 of her friends to tea on 23 November she regretfully returned to Norwich on 24 November 1797. She resumed her social life as if she had never been away, and settled down to enjoy the Christmas and New Year celebrations at home.

12   Coldstream Bridge revisited

The war with France was a constant background to much of Betsy's correspondence. Fear of invasion by the French amounted almost to paranoia during 1798, and did much to unify public opinion in Britain. Plans for augmenting the country's defences had to be implemented immediately, and raising taxation was the quickest and easiest way for the government to pay for them, although it was predictably unpopular. The recruiting of volunteers was intensified, temporary barracks and fortifications were built, particularly in the southern and eastern areas of the country, and troops were mobilized. Mrs Novaille of Great Ness, Sevenoaks, told Betsy that an artillery camp had been built at nearby Gallows Common: 'It is placed here as a reserve in case of invasion to be ready to fly to different great Roads leading from the Coasts of Kent & Sussex. It is the Horse Artillery so much prais'd for its swiftness & Effects. The manoeuvres will be a very pleasing sight.'[1]

Although they accepted the need to be prepared for an invasion, several of Betsy's friends doubted the French would actually invade. Francis Bowness was among them. Mrs Man, one of Betsy's London friends, agreed with him: 'It is my Opinion, tho' not built upon any Foundation whatever, that it will not take place, notwithstanding all the preparations made for it, or rather perhaps I should say against it.'[2] She also commented on the surprising effect that the militarization of the population had had on fashion. Women, it seems, had adapted military dress and converted it into fashionable items such as short jackets embellished with frogging and gilt buttons, and hats trimmed with feathers and fringes.

Despite the feverish preparations, imminent invasion had come to seem much less likely by the end of May 1798, following the departure of Napoleon and his Army of the Orient for Egypt. The arrival there of the French army was followed in August by the destruction of the French fleet by the British under Horatio Nelson, in the Battle of the Nile at Aboukir Bay.

The British victory forced Napoleon to abandon his plans to invade Syria, and he returned to France, leaving his army in Egypt. With the Mediterranean once more safely under British control, Pitt's government was able to concentrate on the land war in Europe. A second coalition of European powers including Britain, Austria and Russia was formed to combat the French, and a new military initiative was launched, one element of which involved the recapture of Holland from the French. A joint Anglo-Russian force of around 30,000 men, with British troops under the command of Sir Ralph Abercromby and the duke of York, landed in Holland in August 1799. But despite some early successes elsewhere in Europe, a combination of military defeats and the withdrawal of the more fragile 'allies' saw the whole enterprise collapse into chaos and confusion. By mid-October the duke of York was forced to negotiate with the French in order to secure a safe but ignominious withdrawal of his troops.

The war affected every corner of England. In Norwich, volunteers continued to be recruited to the growing number of patriotic military corps throughout the summer of 1799, and the city's population became increasingly militarized. In late October dispirited and war-weary British troops were landed in Great Yarmouth over a ten-day period after their defeat in Holland, and from there they began the long march back to their bases. Their route took them through Norwich, setting a continuous stream of tired and resentful men against residents who were both apprehensive and defensive. Fortunately the mayor, John Herring (one of Betsy's friends), was equal to the challenge, and thanks to his leadership and organization the city authorities maintained control. Herring became the hero of the hour, and was thanked by the government for his achievement.

The war also continued to exert a downward pressure on textile manufacturing and its associated industries in Norwich. It was unlikely the situation would improve until peace was restored in Europe and normal trading conditions returned. The poor and destitute continued to bear the brunt of the hardship and suffering, which was exacerbated by the wet summer and poor harvest of 1799, and the first of several harsh winters that followed. Shortages of grain, flour, bread and coal pushed prices way beyond the means of many people, and distress became widespread and acute. Voluntary subscriptions were again raised in both Norwich and Norfolk in order to provide clothes, bread, soup and coal for the poor, many of whom would otherwise have died of starvation and hypothermia. Wealthier citizens were urged to restrict the consumption of bread and flour by their families and servants, and to use only Norwich-made fabrics when clothing them, a gesture seen as both pragmatic and patriotic.

War on such a massive scale was cripplingly expensive, and Pitt was left with little alternative other than to raise taxation yet again, making himself even more unpopular with the tax-paying classes. Tax evasion became rife, and in 1799 he introduced legislation permitting the taxation of individual incomes. Both the method and level of taxation (10 per cent) provoked a great flurry of protest, although many people recognized the need. Lady Winterton's mixed feelings on the subject were typical of many:

> I do think that if Billy Pitt would not lay on Tax upon Tax, I should be very comfortable, as you know it is not right intirely to eat the bread of idleness, but pray what does your Ladyship say to this Income Tax, I think you will pay handsomely, as well as the rest of us, but we must all do as well as we can, as grumbling will not relieve us.[3]

Increasing taxation was the least of Betsy's money worries. She continued to live on a financial knife edge, borrowing from one person to repay another until her next half-yearly interest payments enabled her to repay her outstanding debts and loans. So when her former brother-in-law Major Leathes offered to buy her unwanted coach for a nominal sum, and pay the backdated storage charges and the cost of cleaning and transporting the vehicle from London, she jumped at the chance. At least the sale meant some cash in her pocket and a welcome release from a status symbol that had become a financial liability.

But by far the greatest threat to Betsy's financial stability and well-being was her eldest son. Edward came of age on 10 April 1798 and received his £1,000 legacy on 9 May. He had long before earmarked at least £100 to pay his outstanding debts, and there can be little doubt that the £100 from his father had already gone the same way. Instead of investing the remainder to provide for the future, he seems to have spent part of it on 26 September 1798, when he put on a ball in Norwich for his friends. It was a grand occasion, according to Elizabeth Thompson, who described it to her mother in great detail:

> Edward's Ball has been a subject of conversation ever since it took place. I believe it was allow'd with justice by all who were present to be the most elegant and well plann'd thing of the kind ever given in Norwich, the Company were receiv'd and drank Tea in Mr⁵ Hare's & Miss Smith's rooms, where the Ladies & gentlemen drew for partners, George handed the Ladies numbers & James the gentlemens, Edward of course took number one being master of the ceremonies and Miss Thurlow drew number one of the Ladies Tickets, after which Edward introduced each gentleman to his partner, there being many strangers to each other, particularly the Barrack officers all of whom he invited, the Company being all arriv'd and Tea over each Gentleman handed his partner into the dancing room, those who were not dancers were handed down by other gentlemen & as he contriv'd on purpose to have more men than women, the former being much sooner tired of dancing than the latter, the passage to your parlour where we danced had a temporary door put up at the entrance which inclos'd it entirely and made it very comfortable as it was most brilliantly lighted up, cover'd with Carpet and Miss Gostlings Sopha and Chairs set down one side, the Band which consisted of three Violins a Violincello pipe & Tabor & Bassoon were likewise there, a harp he could not procure in Norwich, there were three Card tables in Miss Jones's room, and the refreshments were made in the room that was Mr⁵ Freemantles bed room, the door of which as well as the parlour were taken off the hinges and a large screen put before the Table and fire to hide preparations & Servants, the Supper was as elegant as anything could be, was set out in Miss Gostlings room down the two sides and across one end of the room in the form of a Gallows …. we sat down about fifty four to supper with very great ease and had seven servants in the room to wait and one at the side board in the passage, so that there was no confusion whatever. Birch sent down the … Cakes and rais'd pies, and a London fishmonger Sturgeon, prawns, & Crawfish, & Covent Garden furnish'd the Pines, Grapes & Peaches, we danc'd till about four o Clock in the morning and everybody seem'd to

enjoy their evening very much and went away highly delighted; really without the least flattery I cannot do justice to it in the account, what Captain Talbot told James the other day will give you a better idea than I am able, that if the Prince himself gave one at Carlton house it could not have been more splendid or elegant.[4]

The only adverse reaction to Edward's extravagant gesture came from his uncle, Major Leathes. Even Francis Bowness was mild in his reaction: 'It might have been as well to save his money; but I can see no great harm in a young man shewing his respect to families from whom he had receiv'd civilities.'[5] Although it would have been much more prudent for him to invest the money, such parsimony was anathema to a young man who wished to cut a dash in the world and to attract a patron with church livings at his disposal. For the rest of his life Edward aspired to a lifestyle that exceeded his income, so he was always a financial albatross around his mother's neck. Betsy's younger son George was also showing worrying signs of following in his brother's footsteps.

James Thompson hoped to graduate from Cambridge at Easter 1798, and planned to be ordained deacon in August. Elizabeth's £1,000 legacy from her uncle John Leathes was eventually paid on 9 May, so she and her husband were at least solvent for the time being, although much depended upon James acquiring a lucrative living after his ordination as a priest. His first step was to make a favourable impression on Lord and Lady Winterton when they visited Cambridge during the summer of 1798. His efforts were obviously successful because Lord Winterton promised to appoint James as his chaplain as soon as he had been ordained deacon. Lady Winterton was swift to point out to Betsy that this would not actually do James any good if he intended to use the appointment as a justification for holding more than one living in England, as the Winterton peerage was Irish.

Fortunately for James, the Wintertons did not find out about his apparent involvement in an incident in Yarmouth in August 1798. Elizabeth seems also to have been kept in the dark about her husband's part, because she wrote to Betsy, who was staying in Yarmouth with George Leathes and his family at the time, and asked her to make enquiries:

I shall be particularly oblig'd to you if you will discover what scrape James has gotten himself into at Yarmouth ... and let me know as I am kept in a continual state of uneasiness and anxiety owing to the letters that are arriving daily from Beevor and the great care that is preserv'd in keeping <u>a something</u> from me, both by James and all his friends here. I shall feel myself much hurt if you are not honest and tell me, and you may depend upon it that I shall leave no means untried of discovering the real affair.[6]

It later transpired that James had quarrelled with a Mr Cole, and that his conduct both during and after the quarrel had been despicable, so much so, said George Leathes, that 'it must ever disgrace him in the Eyes of every Man of Honor'.[7] Betsy must have begun to wonder whether Elizabeth had made a major error in her choice of husband.

Mary seemed to be the one child who caused her mother no trouble. Betsy would have preferred to send her to a finishing school in London in order to give her the same advantages that Elizabeth had enjoyed, but she was unable to afford the fees, so Mary returned to Ipswich to finish her education with the Misses Costerton. She was obviously a good-looking girl with a pleasant nature, and Betsy's friend Mrs Man predicted that she would not remain single for long after she had been launched into society. Even though Mary was still at school she seems already to have been launched into Norwich society, for she accompanied her brothers, sister and brother-in-law on numerous visits, excursions and even parties during the school holidays. She met many of their friends, including Horace (sometimes known as Horatio) Beevor, the youngest son of James Beevor the brewer, who was a particular friend of James Thompson and her brother Edward. Horace accompanied the young Leathes family group on many social occasions; he was an occasional caller on Betsy herself and seems to have become a family friend.

Mary returned to school on 25 July 1798 to complete her final half-year, accompanied by her brother Edward and James Thompson. Less than two weeks later Betsy was stunned to receive a letter telling her that 15-year-old Mary and 24-year-old Horace had eloped. They were married at Coldstream Bridge on 4 August 1798.

Despite her obvious youth, the family did not meet this news with the same angry reaction as had greeted Elizabeth's elopement. Betsy was positively noncommittal in her diary entries, while the reaction of the Leathes family and her friends was almost benign. Most commented on Mary's youth, but Horace Beevor was generally regarded with approval. Major Leathes was able to shed some light on the background to the elopement, and could not, of course, resist giving Betsy the benefit of his opinion:

> Tho' I by no means approve the Step Mary has taken and am very far from wishing to encourage Disobedience to parental Authority yet since my Niece was so imprudent as to marry at so early an Age I am happy to think She has taken for her Protector a Man who has had some experience in the World and whose general Character gives her a right to expect Happiness & Contentment, which I most sincerely wish them Both and am ready to do everything in my power to promote .... On Wednesday last Horace Beevor call'd upon us here, appear'd to me a good deal confused & seemed as if there was something upon his mind which he wished to disclose to me, upon my asking him to dine with us he said he was immediately going off by the Coach call'd the Telegraph, you

are then going to London I suppose said I, <u>only Part of the Way</u> was his reply & that he shou'd soon return to Yarmouth to make some stay, & off he went, but little did I suspect upon what Errand.[8]

Horace Beevor was an extremely presentable young man who had good family connections and excellent career prospects. In other words, he was much better husband material than James Thompson had been when he married Elizabeth. The reaction of the Beevor family was probably a lot less philosophical. Mary was undoubtedly charming and paternally well connected but she was far from rich, and they might well have thought her an unsuitable match for a Beevor.

Horace had entered the East India Company Marine as a midshipman in 1787 at 13. He was successful in his chosen career, and by 1798 he had risen to second mate. There was every reason to suppose he would continue up the promotion ladder until he was awarded the captaincy of an East Indiaman, a position that guaranteed very profitable personal trading opportunities.[9]

The couple might have been lawfully married in Scotland but the social and ecclesiastical proprieties had to be observed, and they were married for a second time on 10 September 1798 at St Saviour's Church in Norwich by Horace's brother, the Reverend Augustus Beevor. The service was attended by Betsy, Edward Leathes and James Thompson, and although Betsy did not mention whether any of the Beevor family had attended it, the rest of the day was spent at the Beevor family home in Magdalen Street.

The day after the wedding Horace travelled to London to report back to his ship. Mary and Betsy followed him on 17 September and took up residence in lodgings at 15 Lower Brook Street, near Chancery Lane. He spent most nights with them and reported to his ship in the daytime, while the two ladies passed their time shopping, visiting friends and attending plays at the Covent Garden and Drury Lane theatres. On 26 September Horace was sworn in as first mate of the *Carnatic*, an East Indiaman of 1,169 tons built in 1785, one of the élite class of ships over 1,000 tons built originally for the China trade.[10] He boarded the *Carnatic* at Deptford the following day, and on 29 September Mary and Betsy boarded the ship, met Captain and Mrs Jackson and sailed as far as Deptford. They disembarked the following morning and returned to Lower Brook Street, where they stayed for several more weeks. On 2 October they were fortunate enough to see the fireworks and join in the general rejoicing that greeted the news of Admiral Nelson's great victory at the Battle of the Nile, news that had taken two months to reach Britain.

October and early November passed in a welter of socializing, theatre visits, exhibitions and 'improving' activities, while Horace, who celebrated his 25th birthday on 6 October, spent much of his time on board ship, taking Mary with him on occasions. Before his ship sailed he commissioned a miniature portrait of Mary from William Grimaldi, miniature painter to George III and the prince of

Wales. It was presumably set in a small frame for to him to keep as a reminder of his pretty young wife during the long voyage to India.[11] On 11 October 1798 the *Carnatic* prepared to sail on to Portsmouth, and Betsy and Mary left London for Norwich the following morning. Horace travelled from Portsmouth to make an unexpected reappearance at Norwich on 16 December, but had to leave before Christmas. It was the last Mary would see of her husband for many months.

From Betsy's point of view, Mary's marriage opened up the possibility of new friendships and new social vistas. James Beevor's family was connected by blood and marriage with many other prominent local families, including the Branthwayts, Buxtons, Hares, Russells, Lubbocks, Blatches, Fosters, Batchelors, Rigbys, Harveys, Crowes and Partridges, an eclectic mix of gentry, merchants, bankers, manufacturers and professionals. Betsy and her children were already acquainted with some of these people, but the marriage promised a much wider and more influential social environment. Betsy also remained faithful to her old friends in Norwich and elsewhere through her correspondence. Sadly one of her oldest friends, Ann Cuthbertson (formerly Goldwyer), died from 'an Apoplectic Seizure' early in January 1798.[12] During one of several frequent and sometimes over-enthusiastic culls of her voluminous correspondence Betsy inadvertently burned all but two of Mrs Cuthbertson's letters. The surviving letters are scorched, so she obviously retrieved them from the flames.[13]

This ever-increasing circle of acquaintances meant that Betsy's social life became a crowded round of visits, tea drinking, dinners, suppers, parties, routs, balls, concerts and theatre-going. She rarely stayed at home alone unless she was ill or had to look after a sick family member. In her diaries she most commonly mentioned drinking tea and playing cards in the afternoon, often with sandwiches for refreshment. Betsy first began to mention sandwich parties in her diary while she was staying at Cambridge with James and Elizabeth Thompson in 1794. They made their first appearance in London high society during the 1760s, when they became popular as a means of eating without leaving the gaming table. Provincial society was slower to take up the sandwich habit, but within three decades it had become the tea party snack of choice. A typical diary entry read: 'I drank Tea & stay'd Sandwiches at Miss Smith's with a Party. Won at cards 4s. 6d.'[14]

Betsy played cards almost every day of every week, either in society or at home with family members and friends. In March 1798 she held a card party for 29 people at her lodgings in Queen Street, combining cards, tea and sandwiches in the fashionable manner. Sometimes her gambling losses were quite high (she lost 13s on 26 February 1798), and sometimes her winnings were equally high (14s on 7 March), but more usually they ranged from 1s to 5s. They most commonly played whist, but also loo and picquet, and occasionally faro, a variation on roulette.

Like many people of all classes, Betsy loved the theatre and attended performances as often as possible during the season, wherever she happened to be.

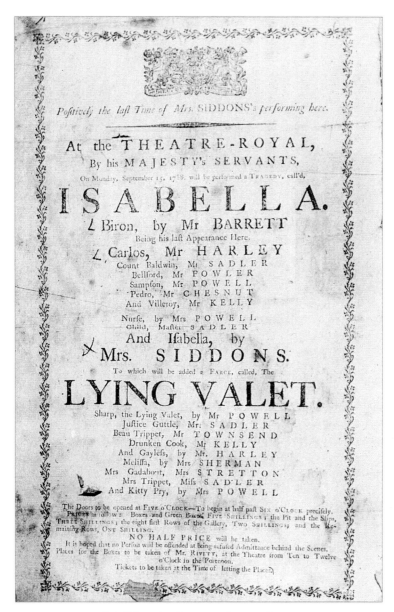

Playbill from the Theatre Royal, Norwich, 1788

Theatres outside London were not legalized until 1767, when the Edinburgh theatre was licensed to perform stage plays by the Lord Chamberlain. It was closely followed in 1768 by Bath and a few days later, Norwich. The Norwich licence permitted the theatre company based at the Theatre Royal (the Norwich Company of Comedians) to perform plays between 1 November and 31 May,

The Theatre Royal, Norwich, a print by T. Woodfall, 1805

plus a three-week period in the summer. In practice plays were performed at the Theatre Royal on Monday, Wednesday, Thursday and Saturday evenings from December until early or mid-May. Evening performances were much longer than they are today. A performance in the 1790s began with the main play at 6.30 pm, followed by an interlude of either music or dance or both, or perhaps a short play, before the final offering of a light play or a melodrama. There were no intervals, and it was common for people to get up and walk around, seek out their friends for a chat, and buy refreshments (usually oranges) during the performance.

The Norwich Theatre Royal was damp before its renovation in 1799, partly because the roof was not fit for purpose and partly because it was in use for only five months of the year. When in use the building was heated by coal fires and lit by oil lamps and candles, so it must have been very dark, smoky, smelly and not particularly warm. Both the quality of the plays performed and the expertise of the actors were variable, and this was often reflected in the behaviour of audiences, who were noisy, frequently vociferous and demonstrative, with a tendency to be unruly if the performance was particularly poor. Between May and October each year the Norwich Company of Comedians toured the larger centres of population in East Anglia, including Kings Lynn, Great Yarmouth, Dereham, Beccles, Bungay and Cambridge, giving performances at inns and other venues that could be adapted as theatres.[15]

The Assembly House was another prime social centre for Norwich's great and good. This venue offered the most polite forms of entertainment (card assemblies, public assemblies, subscription assemblies, dances and balls) to the great and good of the city and county. Betsy was an enthusiastic participant in many of the events there, particularly the subscription dances and card assemblies. In fact her life was a succession of attendances at and participation in many of the events that made up the polite social calendar of Norwich in the 1790s and early 1800s.

Betsy and her mother were still lodging at 3 Queen Street, and both thought they could save money by downsizing their accommodation. So Betsy gave her landlord, Mr Nosworthy, notice to give up the tenancy of two rooms, reducing her rent by £10.10s a year. Edward took a dim view of this because he thought that retaining the whole of Nosworthy's available lodging area increased his mother's respectability and status in the eyes of her peers. His opinion must have struck a chord with Betsy, because she then discussed the matter with Nosworthy and agreed to keep the rooms on condition that he made some improvements.

In Edward's eyes, it was impossible to contemplate saving money if it affected the social credibility of the family in general, and himself in particular. This was really the crux of Betsy's problem. Any active attempt to retrench financially might well affect her social standing in the city, a most undesirable outcome, to be avoided if at all possible. But she was actually unable to save money on any scale because her eldest son had an extraordinary ability to spend not only his own money, but hers as well. In January 1789 Edward graduated from Cambridge, but instead of applying himself to seeking ordination he spent the next 18 months in idleness. She must by this time have been very concerned that he would eventually bankrupt her, as well as ruining himself.

Elizabeth and James Thompson were expecting the birth of their third child in early 1799, a brother or sister for 4-year-old Elizabeth and 2-year-old James. On 23 March 1799 Elizabeth drank tea with her mother and stayed on for supper, then suddenly went into labour. Realizing it would be impossible to get her home without mishap, Betsy summoned Dr Martineau, who delivered a still-born baby girl at 6 am the following morning.[16] Elizabeth was able to return home later in the day, but Betsy was so 'fatigued' that she had to put off her afternoon tea-drinking session with her friend Mrs Harrington.[17]

Elizabeth apparently recovered quickly from her ordeal, and was churched on 28 April. Betsy passed on news of the stillbirth to Lady Winterton, who expressed her concern for Elizabeth's welfare: 'Tell her with my Love, she must be more careful, or she will I am afraid injure her health & strength …. those frequent mishaps are very prejudicial to the Ladies constitution.'[18]

James Thompson graduated from Cambridge at Lent 1799 and wasted no time in seeking ordination. He was ordained deacon on 12 May and priest on 31 August, but had not managed to secure the promise of a living. He asked Francis Bowness for help, but Bowness was either unable or unwilling to do so, and advised James to cultivate his acquaintance with Prebendary Edward Thurlow, who might be able to secure him a living in the gift of the dean and Chapter of Norwich Cathedral.[19] Lord Winterton kept the promise he had made earlier, and James was formally appointed as his chaplain in June. While this position carried no salary, it did confer a certain amount of status and might help him to secure presentation to a living in the future. Lady Winterton, who was much smitten with the young man, had no doubt about his ability to do so: 'He is so much the Gentleman, and <u>every</u> thing that can be desired by <u>Mortal Woman</u>, if I was a young woman Mrs. Thompson would have <u>great</u> reason for jealousy.'[20] James was clearly an accomplished charmer. Betsy's relationship with the Thompsons continued to be somewhat volatile, and on 28 June she and Elizabeth had a serious argument, most probably about money. The atmosphere became distinctly frosty, and mother and daughter met infrequently thereafter.

Fortunately for Betsy, she and Mary Beevor enjoyed a close and happy relationship. They saw each other nearly every day and undertook many social engagements together. It is not clear whether Mary was still living with her parents-in-law in Magdalen Street or whether Horace had rented a nearby house. Mary celebrated her 16th birthday on 13 April 1799, and would remain a minor until her 21st birthday in 1804, even though she was a married woman. Her trust income was paid by Major Leathes via Francis Bowness to her father-in-law James Beevor, who received it on her husband's behalf during his absence.

It was a lonely life for Mary. Since their marriage she had spent only three months with her husband before he sailed off on a hazardous voyage to India, and she had heard very little from him during his absence. Horace wrote to her when he was able, but he could post his letters only when his ship made landfall, and they took months to get to England, if they arrived at all. Betsy recorded the arrival of letters on 1 January and 16 July 1799, the latter sent from the Cape of Good Hope some months previously.[21] Mary might well have had other letters whose arrival went unrecorded. She had to wait until half way through the following year before she could be certain her husband would arrive home safe and sound.

Family problems, however bad they were, did not greatly affect Betsy's social life. Her circle of acquaintance continued to expand, partly as a result of her relationship with the influential Beevor clan and partly through her own social networking. It was James Beevor, Mary's father-in-law, who introduced her to his relative Sir Edmund Lacon of Ormesby St Margaret near Great Yarmouth, another wealthy brewer.[22] Betsy was more than happy to meet the Lacon family, and over time she grew to know them well. She had been introduced to John Herring and his mother in 1798, and by 1799 they were on such friendly terms that Betsy was invited to the feast at St Andrew's Hall that marked the beginning of Herring's term as mayor of Norwich, although unfortunately she had to plead a prior commitment. Herring was a wool-comber and wool merchant who had his house and his work rooms at Gilden Gate. At a tea party during 1799 Betsy also met Mrs Maltby, the wife of surgeon Charles Maltby, and the two went on to become firm friends.[23]

But it was in clerical circles that Betsy moved with the greatest ease, and this segment of her acquaintance grew most during the first decade after her move back to Norwich in 1794. By the end of 1799 she was on friendly terms with Thomas Wigg Hancock, rector of St Michael at Plea, and his wife, and through them she was introduced to a few more clerical families. Thanks to invitations to tea and card parties at various houses in the Cathedral Close, she was gradually beginning to gain access to the upper echelons of the cathedral's social circle. In 1799 she recorded in her diary engagements at the houses of Prebendary Dr John Pretyman, Prebendary Edward South Thurlow, Canon Charles Wodehouse and the dean of Norwich, Joseph Turner. These were the people she most wished to cultivate, not only to benefit her own social standing but because her sons would need powerful sponsors to ever stand a chance of presentation to some of the wealthier livings in the gift of the dean and chapter. Another recent acquaintance was the diocesan official and 'ecclesiastical lawyer' John Morphew of 24 Lower Close, and he too became Betsy's valued friend, as did his wife and family.

Postal contact was Betsy's lifeline when it came to maintaining links with her old friends in Oxfordshire and Kent. She may not have been able to visit them on a regular basis, but their letters enabled her to keep abreast of their births, deaths, marriages and gossip, as well as keeping them up to date with her own news and views. She stayed in direct contact with friends and relatives who lived sufficiently close to Norwich for her to make fairly regular visits. She never neglected Reedham, or Acle and Strumpshaw. In fact she frequently combined the three villages into a round trip that linked visits to many of the friends she had made during her 14-year marriage to Edward Leathes. Betsy's friends sometimes represented a lifeline during those periods when some close family members made her life very difficult.

13 A mixed blessing

In January 1800 the war between Britain and France entered its eighth year. Britain may have enjoyed supremacy at sea, but Napoleon reigned supreme on land. In northern Italy he smashed the Austrians at the Battle of Marengo in June 1800, and again at Hohenlinden in December. Not surprisingly, the Austrians decided that they had taken enough punishment and withdrew from the ailing second coalition of allies. The Russians had also suffered a few reverses at the hands of French forces by the end of 1800, and decided to sue for peace, leaving Britain standing alone against the growing power of Napoleon. Pitt and his cabinet colleagues had bickered about the conduct of the war for most of the year, and their failure to arrive at any sort of meaningful strategy was undoubtedly a significant factor in the woeful performance of the allies.

Few British families were unaffected by the war in some way, and Betsy's friends and relatives were no exception. Her nephew, another George Leathes, her brother-in-law's eldest son, was an army captain and had seen active service. Lady Winterton's 13-year-old stepson Arthur Turnour was serving as a midshipman on the *Caesar*, an 80-gun ship in the Channel Fleet under the command of Sir James Saumarez, who had been Nelson's second-in-command at the Battle of the Nile. 'I thought him almost too young,' Lady Winterton told Betsy, 'but all the Navy Gentlemen told us [he was] full old enough to go.'[1] Betsy's diary entries are peppered with references to male friends and relatives who had acquired the rank of lieutenant, captain, major or colonel, some of them in the regular army but many in the local militias and the volunteer regiments that came into being between 1793 and 1815 as the nation responded to the call to arms.

The nation also responded, albeit unwillingly, to the government's need for money to pay and equip the army, navy, militias and volunteers. This was provided by additional taxation, including the new tax on incomes. Pitt had anticipated that the income tax would raise £6.5 million in 1799–1800 but it raised less than £2 million. He attempted to increase the amount raised but was thwarted by the House of Commons, and forced to borrow and to take more moderate measures as a result.[2] Despite this setback, the money collected through taxation in this period greatly exceeded the amounts raised by any previous government. People on relatively modest incomes noticed the loss. Mrs Holloway of Woodstock complained to Betsy that she did not have sufficient ready money to travel to London because she had paid out over £64 in taxes over the previous two weeks, including £33.6s.8d in income tax, and she expected another tax bill the following month. Francis Bowness regretted that the tax was to be continued for longer than was originally anticipated, but during a stay in London he observed that, although people of modest means in the provinces were feeling the pinch, 'in this great Town one wou'd be led to suppose that the kingdom in general was rolling in riches'.[3]

The suffering of the Norwich poor continued unabated in 1800, exacerbated by a bad harvest, another freezing winter and record high prices for corn, flour and bread in February. 'The price of Wheat being so very dear at present occasions very great grumbling amongst the Poor at this time, and makes them talk loudly,' Parson Woodforde observed.[4] By March the very real danger of starvation amongst the unemployed and the destitute had become so great that the mayor, Betsy's friend John Herring, opened a subscription for soup kitchens to help feed them. Betsy immediately subscribed one guinea, and a total of over £1,100 was raised, money that enabled Herring to open six soup shops in the city where poor families could buy one pint of soup for each family member at ½d a pint. By April about 16,000 of the very poorest people in the city were receiving two meals a week from the soup kitchens.

Bread riots were narrowly avoided in May, after which prices began to ease a little and the summer months passed without great incident. But in early September supplies of flour and meal again failed to meet demand and civil unrest flared up once more, although the city authorities were able to deal with it without calling out the militia. Small-scale remedial measures were taken but again they failed to alleviate distress in the city. The mayor who succeeded John Herring, Robert Harvey, called a meeting of citizens in November to discuss how best to provide relief for the poor. It resulted in an agreement to raise another voluntary subscription, a solution that was popular with the less wealthy ratepayers because it meant that a further increase in poor rates was unnecessary.[5]

In addition to her charitable donations Betsy also helped to support a poor Norwich family by the name of Healde, which consisted of mother, father and two grown-up children. She had employed Mrs Healde as a children's nurse when she lived at Reedham. Her help took the form of occasional employment for the family members, a weekly meal for Mrs Healde, and when she could no longer work, a small 'allowance' of 6d a week. By January 1799 the family were clearly suffering, and Betsy gave them 'Tickets for Soup'. In June she asked Mr Kerrison to try to get Mrs Healde admitted to the Norfolk and Norwich Hospital, but he was unable to help. Mrs Healde struggled on into the following year, when John Herring was so moved by her plight that he gave Betsy 5s to pass on to her. Unfortunately it was too little too late, and Mrs Healde died in April 1800, another victim of the life of hard work, crushing poverty, malnutrition and disease that was the lot of the poorest classes.[6]

As in London, in Norwich the wartime economic situation seems to have been only a minor irritation to the better off. Some of Betsy's friends might have experienced a degree of financial inconvenience, but few if any suffered real distress, and the social life of the city continued much as it had during peacetime. The pages of Betsy's diary mentioned new social contacts, notably Mr and Mrs William Foster, Mr and Mrs Bartlett Gurney and Mr and Mrs Paul Colombine, all of them

A print from Heideloff's Gallery of Fashion, *1794, showing a day dress made of chintz in the 'nightgown style' (left) and two day dresses made of lawn in the 'round gown' style (middle and right)*

prominent Norwich names. William Foster was an attorney who later acted for her on several occasions; Bartlett Gurney was a member of the Norwich banking family; Paul Colombine, a doctor, was a member of a well-known and respected Norwich family of merchants, manufacturers and clergymen.

Betsy also remained faithful to her old friends, although her visits to them were becoming more infrequent. Death continued to thin their ranks, and in July 1800 Mrs Holloway of Charlbury Place near Woodstock, with whom Betsy had stayed in June 1797, died suddenly. Betsy must have experienced a pang of conscience, as the old lady had repeatedly asked her to visit Charlbury again but she had pleaded ill-health in the family, when the truth was that she could not afford the cost of the

A print from Heideloff's Gallery of Fashion, *1795, showing two evening dresses made of white satin (left and centre) and one made of white spotted muslin (right)*

journey. Thankfully none of Betsy's other correspondents died, but their letters began to dwindle in both length and number.

Betsy's social life demanded that she should dress appropriately and fashionably for each and every occasion. She might have been in her early 50s in 1800, but she tried to keep abreast of fashion. At least once a year she visited a fashionable mantua maker to see the latest book of fashion plates. In 1799 she went to Mrs Godfrey's establishment in Norwich, where she must have seen a volume of fashion plates such as Heideloff's *Gallery of Fashion,* which would have helped her to decide which dresses to have made up by her dressmaker.[7]

Provincial ladies were well acquainted with the fashions of the day thanks
fashion plates and regular visits to London. Fashion had undergone a radical chan
by the 1790s: the rich fabrics, corsets, bustles and panniers of the 1770s and 178(
were out, and ankle-length, low-necked gowns with tight bodices gathered und
the bust and worn without stays were in. Dresses in the new fashion were mad
from cambric, calico or muslin, but plain or spotted thin Indian muslin was th
fabric most commonly used for fashionable day and evening wear by the lat
1790s. A short jacket known as a spencer, usually made from a warmer fabric suc
as velvet, was often worn with the 'empire' dress. Warm, soft shawls came int
fashion, and quickly became an essential part of the female wardrobe. The fines
shawls were imported from Kashmir, but English manufacturers were swift to se
a business opportunity and began to manufacture their own. Because fashionabl
gowns were so flimsy, pockets became impractical and small handbags, or reticule
came into use. Hairstyles also changed; wigs were relegated to history and ladie
wore their hair curly and unpowdered, crowned by ostrich plumes, turbans o
bonnets.

It was no longer appropriate for Betsy to dress like a young girl, but like othe
more mature ladies she adapted the latest designs to suit her own situation. Sh
bought a 'Cambrick Muslin Gown' in 1799 and had a yellow muslin gown made
by a local dressmaker in 1800; she does not mention the style but it was presumably a flattering adaptation of the fashionable empire style.[8] The new fashion for
shawls gave the ailing Norwich textile industry a much-needed boost in the 1790s,
providing a modicum of work for some of the city's factories. Shawls had been
made in the city in the 1780s, but they were cheap goods aimed at the American
market. By the early 1790s Norwich manufacturers aimed at the luxury end of the
market, taking their inspiration from the best Kashmiri shawls.

Alderman John Harvey and his partner P. J. Knights devised a technique for
weaving shawls of a 12-foot width without a seam, using a worsted yarn with
a silk warp. Harvey's shawls were hand-embroidered, but in 1802 the process
was mechanized and the design was woven in on the loom. The Norwich
shawl industry had been born.[9] John Herring was also experimenting with
the manufacture of shawls in the early 1800s, and it is possible that the white
silk shawl given to Betsy by John Herring in 1800 was a prototype of his own
manufacture.[10]

Life had not always been straightforward or easy for Betsy in the past, but in
1800 it became considerably more problematic, not least because her three eldest
children all created social or financial difficulties for her. Her relationship with
Elizabeth and James Thompson had been distinctly cool since July 1799, and on
25 June 1800 it became cooler still when Betsy found out that James intended to
file a bill in Chancery alleging mismanagement of Elizabeth's trust funds when she
was a minor.[11] Betsy immediately wrote to Edward seeking his help, but received
only a brusque initial response in which her son deplored the fact that she had

nothing better to do than sit at home and worry about such trifles. This was followed two days later by a rather lukewarm endorsement of her efforts to manage his financial affairs:

> With respect to my becoming a party in any suit which may be instituted to compel you to produce your executor's accounts ... having no reason to be dissatisfied with the disposal of your affairs hitherto, & judging of the future from the past, I have consequently no reason to distrust your management on the whole.[12]

This offhand response must have cut Betsy to the quick, coming as it did on the back of his endless requests for more cash. His letter would certainly have been of little use to her in a lawsuit. It was Major Leathes who rushed to his sister-in-law's defence when he heard the news, fully prepared to believe the worst of anything that James Thompson did or said after his disgraceful behaviour during the Chancery suit Leathes Johnstone had brought against the Leathes estate in 1797. Francis Bowness, who had first-hand knowledge of the facts, was convinced that Betsy had nothing to fear. He introduced her to the Norwich attorney William Foster, who scrutinized her accounts and represented her against Thompson's claims. Despite his mother-in-law's obvious innocence of any financial misdemeanour Thompson would not let go of the matter, and it dragged on until the end of the year. Thereafter Betsy's contact with her eldest daughter and her husband seems to

Lady in a muslin day dress wearing a spencer nd carrying a shawl, early 1800s.

have been minimal or nonexistent until Elizabeth visited her on 21 February 1801. By 5 March their relationship had been patched up, but if Betsy's diary for that year is to be believed social contact between mother and daughter was still sparse, although Elizabeth continued to visit her grandmother.

It is difficult to know whose behaviour was the most reprehensible, the Thompsons' or Edward's. The Thompsons' behaviour was malicious, while Edward's was selfish, arrogant and thoughtless. The only common characteristic was that both were extremely difficult for Betsy to cope with. In March 1800 Edward declared categorically that he would not contemplate ordination unless one or two lucrative curacies fell into his lap. He continued to live a life of leisure at Cambridge, pestering his mother for 'loans' of money, but Betsy now consistently refused to meet his demands. By June he had become so desperate that he was forced to ask Francis Bowness to arrange for his ordination as soon as possible, doubtless with the intention of accessing the income from the church livings that were reserved for him rather than from any sense of vocation.

By January 1801 Edward was on the threshold of ordination, but before Mr Wilkinson could resign diocesan officials had to initiate the process of assessing the value of the livings of Reedham, Freethorpe, Southwood and Limpenhoe, and the extent of dilapidations at Reedham parsonage.[13] Edward was constantly in need of money and must therefore have been keen to secure a favourable decision on the dilapidations, which meant that the negotiations were likely to be both lengthy and contentious. His extravagance and his requests for loans to pay his debts and fund his lifestyle were never-ending, and Betsy must have begun to wonder whether she would ever be free of this drain on her capital.

Edward hoped the bishop of Norwich would ordain him as both deacon and priest at the same ceremony, so he could take over his livings at the earliest possible date. In the event he was ordained deacon by the bishop of Norwich at the Chapel Royal, St James's in London on 3 May 1801, followed by ordination as priest by the bishop of Ely at Ely on 31 May. Unfortunately there was an administrative hiccup in his presentation to the livings, attributed by Edward to the outgoing Mr Wilkinson, and he had to wait until 6 June before he was presented. He took services at Reedham on a few Sundays in late June and July, but thereafter he must have delegated the responsibility to a deputy, because Mr Wilkinson and his family were unable to move out of the parsonage until they had made other living arrangements. A very bad-tempered and resentful Edward took up temporary residence at North Walsham, where he stayed until the Wilkinson family vacated the Reedham house. Edward finally took possession of the parsonage and the glebe farm on 3 October, although the internal renovations were incomplete.

George continued to be the more amiable of Betsy's sons, even if their relationship was conducted at a distance. He visited his mother and grandmother in Norwich from time to time, and his letters to them seem to have been reasonably frequent. Francis Bowness told Betsy that George was permanently short of money, and he certainly had outstanding debts, some of which were paid by his mother, although settlement of his remaining debts was left until he attained his majority on 2 April 1800, when he could expect to receive £1,100. The £100 legacy from his late father was paid promptly by his mother, and the £1,000 left to him by John Leathes was paid in mid-May. When the money was safely in his bank account George paid off his debts and invested the residue, although neither Betsy nor Francis Bowness ever found out exactly how much was left.[14]

George was awarded his Batchelor of Arts degree in 1801, but like his brother he was in no great hurry to be ordained, and spent the rest of the year commuting between Cambridge and Herringfleet, making occasional visits to Betsy in

Norwich. Herringfleet had been George's second home since childhood; he had always been the favourite of his widowed and childless aunt, and both women must have had great expectations for his future. Francis Bowness's only criticism of George was that he had a tendency to spend money without any thought for the consequences, but the amounts involved cannot have been too excessive as his complaints were never very loud or frequent.

The close and happy relationship between Betsy and her youngest daughter must have been a source of great comfort to each of them at this stressful time. Mary's long wait for her husband's safe return from his hazardous sea voyage finally ended on 24 June 1800 when she heard that the *Carnatic* had reached Weymouth. Two days later she dined with her parents-in-law at their Magdalen Street house, where the family had gathered to await Horace. Horace wasted no time after the ship docked at Gravesend: he caught the first available coach to Norwich, arrived the following day, and was greeted with great enthusiasm by his wife and his relatives. He was careful to include his mother-in-law in the celebrations because he called on her on 28 June and presented her with two fans he had brought back from India. A veritable orgy of visiting, tea partying, dining and supping followed, as the young couple greeted and were greeted by all their friends and relations in Norwich and the surrounding district.

Finally they were free to leave the city for London on 9 July to spend some time enjoying each other's company free of well-wishers, although Horace would almost certainly have had to put in some time on Company business at East India House in Leadenhall Street. They stayed in London for a month or so before moving on to stay with George Leathes and his family at their house in Great Yarmouth, where they were joined by Betsy and another bout of socializing ensued. Horace and Mary finally returned to Norwich on 3 September, although Horace made at least two journeys to London on business during their holiday.

While they were staying with George Leathes and his family at Bury St Edmunds in early October, Horace heard that he had been promoted to captain in the East India Company. He had recently turned 27, a comparatively young age at which to shoulder such a great responsibility, albeit one that promised significant rewards in the years to come.

Horace was assigned the command of the *Carnatic*, the East Indiaman that had already made seven voyages to the east since she was launched in 1785, and on whose previous voyage he had been first mate. Ships of this size were mostly used by the Company after 1784 to carry greatly increased tea cargoes from China, but the *Carnatic* seems to have been the exception to the rule, because her last two voyages had been to Bombay (now Mumbai). The Company had lost its monopoly of trade with India in 1793, a setback that prompted the use of smaller ships of varying sizes that were more suited to the type of freight they were carrying, so larger ships like the *Carnatic* were eventually phased out. Ships of around 800 tons tended increasingly to be used for the India trade in luxury goods such as chintzes, calicoes, silks, spices and tea, while smaller ships of between 500 and 600 tons were used to carry 'gruff' or inferior goods such as sugar, saltpetre, cowries, pepper, lacquer and chinaware.[15]

Towards the end of October 1800 Horace, Mary and Betsy travelled to London, where they took lodgings at 32 Craven Street. Mary was pregnant, although her morning sickness did not seem to prevent the trio from enjoying a full social life and making the most of the facilities and entertainment in the capital. Horace was sworn in as captain of the *Carnatic* on 19 November, and congratulations on his promotion came thick and fast. Lady Winterton's reaction was particularly favourable: 'I understand from those who are more conversant than myself in Tracking to India, that Cap[t]. Beevor's Station is a more advantageous appointment than any to India, and that all the Commanders consider themselves very fortunate in getting the Carnatic's station.'[16] Horace and Mary continued to enjoy their extended holiday until 10 December, when Horace finally boarded his ship at Gravesend and another long separation began. Mary faced the prospect of giving birth while her husband was away on a dangerous voyage from which he might never return, while Horace faced the prospect that, given the considerable hazards of childbirth, he might never see his young wife again.

Mary did not allow her pregnancy to stand in the way of visiting Betsy on a regular basis and socializing in the normal way, even though her rapidly increasing girth gave rise to speculation that she was carrying twins. She was devastated by the arrival on 20 March 1801 of a letter from the East India Company's offices in London, telling her that her husband's ship had been damaged in a storm.[17] At this time Mary was about six months pregnant, and she must have wondered whether her husband would ever see the child she was carrying. Fortunately the rest of her pregnancy passed without mishap and on 9 June she gave birth to a fine healthy daughter, who was baptised Mary Leathes Beevor on 10 June by her uncle, the Reverend Augustus Beevor. On the same day Mary received a letter from her husband, ending the months of anxiety she had suffered.

A delighted Betsy took her mother to visit Mary and the new baby on 14 June, no doubt thanking God that at last her daughter could look forward to her husband's homecoming. The Beevors employed two nurses, one to look after Mary during her lying-in month and the other to look after the baby. Mary was churched on 5 July, and four days later she took the baby and the nurses to visit Betsy and Mrs Reading at their Queen Street lodgings, where they stayed for both tea and dinner. She then resumed her normal social life, waiting only for her husband's return to complete the happy family.

Since her first husband's untimely death in 1788 Betsy had been guided and assisted in the management of her financial affairs by Francis Bowness, who together with John Love of Somerley (or Somerleyton, as it was later known) had been appointed a trustee of the children's trusts under the term of John Leathes' will. Although he was not one of Betsy's oldest friends, Bowness became one of her staunchest allies. Because he was a good friend and trustworthy she had appointed him as a trustee of her own separation trust, in which capacity he continued to look after her financial interests. But by 1801 he was not in the best of health, having suffered a bout of St Anthony's fire (erysipelas) early in 1800 which had left him weak. In January 1801 he contracted influenza, and was confined to his house for three weeks.

For a little while it seemed that Bowness had made a good recovery, but in February he became ill once more, and this time his doctor diagnosed an obstruction in his biliary duct, for which he prescribed medicine. He remained unwell and by late March had begun to take laudanum (opium dissolved in alcohol) to relieve his pain. Betsy visited him at his house in Lowestoft at the end of March because the old man was confined to bed and unable to travel. This was the last time Betsy saw her friend, for on 30 April 1801 Francis Bowness died. His death was a sad loss for Betsy in many ways, and in the years to come she would sorely miss his advice and support. In the shorter term his death meant Betsy would have to embark on the tedious and lengthy process of looking for a new trustee for the various family trusts.

Perhaps it was because Bowness was no longer there to counsel financial prudence that she decided to leave her Queen Street lodgings and move to a rented house, a more expensive option and one that Bowness had encouraged her to avoid. But she may well have felt that, with her sons having entered into their inheritance and her daughters married, the time had come for her to mark a new era in her own life. On 29 September 1801 she and her mother moved to 5 St George's Court (also known as Old Chapel Court), Colegate, near the Octagon Chapel, an area much favoured by the merchant families of the city. Betsy lost no time in making herself at home and putting her own stamp on the house in an orgy of painting and decorating, making interior alterations, ordering new soft furnishings and purchasing new furniture. Francis Bowness would definitely not have approved of either the removal or the expense.

The British political scene underwent something of a transformation in February 1801 when William Pitt, who had been prime minister for 17 years, resigned over the refusal of King George III to consider emancipation for Roman Catholics. Henry Addington formed an administration which in essence was more of a reshuffle than a change of government, as Pitt did not leave office immediately, but stayed on long enough to present his budget and to soothe anxiety in the financial sector. Although this budget included steep increases in both taxes and government borrowing, it was accepted relatively quietly by the Commons, the Lords and the king. Pitt remained a powerful force in British political life, even though he was no longer at the forefront of government.[18]

The war with France rolled on irrespective of political change. At the end of 1800 Britain had been deserted by most of the countries in northern Europe. Russia had allied herself with France, while Sweden, Denmark and Prussia had signed a treaty of armed neutrality which was tantamount to a declaration of war on Britain. So a fleet of 18 ships of the line under the command of Sir Hyde Parker and Admiral Nelson was despatched over the North Sea with the intention of encouraging Denmark's withdrawal from the alliance. On 2 April 1801 Nelson engaged the shore defences at Copenhagen, and by the following day his fleet had destroyed both the defences and the Danish fleet, albeit at a heavy cost to Britain in both men and ships. As a result, the alliance of Baltic states was weakened and the threat to British trade in the Baltic was diminished. Britain and France recognized that the war had reached a temporary stalemate, so peace negotiations were opened and preliminary terms were agreed with France in October.

The news was received with almost universal joy throughout the country. Betsy recorded the arrival of the news in Norwich in her diary on 3 October, and on Wednesday 21 October the city celebrated with 'Illuminations for Peace'. Unfortunately the chosen day was wet and miserable, but the celebrations took place nonetheless:

> At night the Volunteer Corps were drawn up in the market and fired a 'feu de joie'. The bells were rung, flags displayed, and the customary demonstrations of joy renewed. At six o'clock, the illuminations generally commenced, an immence bonfire was lighted in the market, and at seven the Mayor and Sheriff attended by the Court of Aldermen and City council walked round it in procession, amid the acclamations of the populace. They afterwards returned to the Hall in the market, and partook of the refreshments provided …. Joy, sincere and unalloyed, pervaded all, and all were studious to display the satisfaction which they felt.[19]

Many of the citizens of Norwich must have felt very joyful indeed, for peace meant the resumption of trading and the prospect of better times to come.

14   Scandal and rumour

The preliminaries of peace with France were signed in October 1801, and the treaty was finally ratified at Amiens in March 1802. The terms were less than generous to the British, who gave up most of their territorial gains, while the French retained nearly all of theirs, with the exception of Trinidad and Ceylon. The fact that these terms were acceptable to Britain demonstrates just how desperate for peace both government and people were.

Peace may have been popular, but these terms meant it was unlikely to last for any length of time, which made for a very tense atmosphere in political circles. The new administration, headed by Henry Addington, Viscount Sidmouth, struggled to govern with any degree of competence on the diplomatic and foreign policy fronts, where all their attempts to thwart French international ambitions proved totally ineffective. Fortunately some of Addington's domestic policies were more successful. Income tax was revised to make it simpler to collect and more difficult to evade, and the amount of revenue it yielded rose significantly. The government also took measures to gag increasing internal dissent before it spilled over into action. Meanwhile Napoleon used the opportunity to build up the French fleet, and continued to pursue his empire-building activities in Italy, Switzerland and Holland, contravening the terms of the Treaty of Amiens. Britain was left with little alternative but reopen hostilities against France on 16 May 1803.[1]

The French responded to Britain's renewal of hostilities by interning the 10,000 or so British tourists who had mistakenly assumed it would be safe to travel in France following the 1802 treaty. Napoleon then began serious preparations for the invasion of Britain, gathering together a large army and commissioning a fleet of barges to carry it over the Channel. Addington's response was to mobilize the population for the defence of the realm. Legislation combined with patriotic zeal to recruit more than 800,000 men of all classes aged between 17 and 55, mainly for the militias. Patriotism was stimulated to a quite remarkable extent by the fear of invasion, and political dissent subsided throughout Britain as most of the population temporarily buried their opposition to government policies and united behind the war effort.

The Norfolk militias had been disbanded in 1801–2, but they were re-embodied in 1803 and provision was made for more men to be recruited. Both city and county responded magnificently, and by the end of November 40 infantry units and 22 cavalry troops had been formed in Norfolk, although the new units could not have been described as ready for action, since few men had received any instruction and most had neither uniforms nor arms. Sea fencibles were recruited to help with coastal defence, and the Navy Office drew up plans for a system of signal stations and warning beacons on or near the coast.[2]

Conditions for the poor and the unemployed remained grim in Norwich and in rural areas all over Norfolk despite the short-lived peace. Regular subscriptions were raised by the better-off throughout the war years in order to provide clothing, coal, soup, bread and flour for the poor and unfortunate. Deaths from hypothermia, malnutrition and disease might otherwise have been more numerous. In Reedham, the ratification of the peace treaty in 1802 was seen by some parishioners as a good reason for raising money by subscription in order to give a meal and entertainment to the poor of the parish so they too could celebrate.[3] Poor relief was always a reliable indicator of economic health, and in 1803 one in seven Norwich residents was either in receipt of poor relief or resident in the workhouse.[4]

Unfortunately the renewal of hostilities with France in 1803 guaranteed that the trade in Norwich-produced textiles would never regain its former vigour. There was a post-war recovery of a sort, but growing competition from mechanized manufacturing in the north of England meant the glory days of the mid-18th century were well and truly gone.

Norwich had other profitable industries, but major diversification was imperative if the city was to regain its former prosperity and importance. Some of the more astute local magnates, notably members of the Ives, Harvey, Patteson, Day and Gurney families, had been quick to appreciate the difficulties the Norwich textile industry would face after the outbreak of war in 1793, and following the example of their predecessors in earlier recessions, they moved substantial amounts of capital from the worsted industry into banking, brewing and other industries. An adventurous newcomer to the city, Samuel Bignold, set up an insurance company known as the Norwich Union Fire Society in 1797, which grew and prospered during the war period. By the time the French were finally defeated in 1815 the Norwich financial sector was in reasonable health, a green shoot of regeneration among the decay of the old staple industries.[5]

Betsy's investments and the trusts through which they were administered underwent substantial change during 1802. John Herring had agreed to take the place of Francis Bowness as one of the two trustees of the Leathes and Reading trusts, and the legal process of replacement had already begun when John Love, the other trustee, decided to resign. William Foster, Betsy's lawyer, agreed to take Love's place, but the replacement process had to begin afresh, and this delayed the completion of the legal formalities until 1803. The Leathes trust held £2,700 (the residue of Edward Leathes' estate, plus interest), while the Reading trust held £2,261.14s, derived from James Reading's residual estate plus sales of property and interest. Betsy drew part of her income from the Leathes trust, while the half-yearly interest from the Reading trust constituted her mother's only income.

The rest of Betsy's income came from the Peach separation trust, and Bowness's death meant it also required a new trustee who would meet with the approval of Edward Peach. Betsy nominated another of her Norwich friends, the Reverend Thomas Wigg Hancock, and the deed of separation was duly amended by the firm of Foster and Unthank and signed by her on 17 March 1802.[6] However the long-winded nature of trust fund law meant it was July 1803 before all the necessary signatures were in place. Most of the separation trust money, some £3,809.10s.6d, was invested in 3 per cent government consolidated stock, or consols, but the amendments to the deed permitted the liquidation of £2,009.10s.6d.[7] Betsy seems to have taken this opportunity to liberate some of the money for her own use, a move that would explain her spending spree refurbishing her new house. But she was usually quite shrewd with her investments and kept a record of any share transactions in her diary, so it would have been a surprising departure from her usual practice to divert capital in this way. It is more likely at least half the money was reinvested, though not certain because her diary for 1803 has not survived.

What is certain is that she furnished the house at St George's Court, Colegate in some style. She first indulged in new beds and bedding – a considerable expense because beds were the most costly items of furniture.[8] She bought a four-poster mahogany bedstead with fashionable glazed chintz hangings and drapery, together with feather bedding, plus a more modest 4-foot bedstead and feather bedding, from the cabinet and upholstery warehouse of John Freeman at 12 Upper Market Street, near St Peter Mancroft. Among other items she bought there were a mahogany night table, a mahogany pot cupboard, a painted table, 16 black bamboo japanned chairs, a pair of mahogany card tables and a mahogany voider, or butler's tray. She bought an additional four-post bedstead and a tent bedstead, plus feather bedding, from Nathaniel Knights, another Norwich furniture maker, who also supplied her with two dining tables and a chest of drawers.[9] Betsy sourced some items of furniture from family contacts: she bought two elbow chairs, a dining table and a tray from Ann Beevor on 2 September 1801, and paid for them on 4 September – much more promptly than she would ever have dreamed of paying a tradesperson.

Betsy's spending on furniture, plate, linen, curtains, carpets and redecoration amounted to more than £300 between September 1801 and the end of 1802.[10] She also paid off debts to friends, family and Kerrison's bank amounting to £455, so it is unlikely that more than £1,200 was left of the money released. A reasonable proportion of her annual income from her investments went on household expenses. During the year from Michaelmas 1801 to Michaelmas 1802 they amounted to £173.2s.2d, including payments to the grocer, coal merchant, tradespeople, baker, brewer and two wine merchants; market purchases of meat, fish, eggs and vegetables and so on; house rent and taxes, and servants' wages.[11] Taken together, these figures represent a very comfortable standard of living for two ladies of independent means.

The newly furnished house fulfilled Betsy's need to entertain her ever-expanding circle of friends and acquaintances in appropriate style. Some of the people she entertained were already known to her socially, acquaintances who had become friends over the years. A few individuals and their families, such as Robert Harvey (mayor in 1770 and 1800) and Jeremiah Ives Harvey (mayor in 1783), became near neighbours when Betsy moved to St George's Court. These two men had country houses in Catton, and Betsy's diaries indicate that she visited them there quite regularly, often accompanied by Mary, who was equally well acquainted with most of the rich Norwich merchant families through her Beevor relatives by marriage. The list of Betsy's Norwich friends and acquaintances was impressive by 1802, and there were few drawing rooms in the city in which she would not have been welcome.

Clerical connections continued to figure strongly in her social life. Charles Millard, who lived at 18 Lower Close, was a minor canon of Norwich Cathedral and held the livings of Trowse Newton with Whitlingham, Lakenham and Taverham. The family were clearly well connected in cathedral circles because their son, Charles Freeman Millard, inherited his father's livings as well as his cathedral post. W. F. Wilkinson, who had held the Leathes living of Reedham with Freethorpe until Edward Leathes took over in October 1801, moved to Norwich with his wife and family, although he continued to serve the other Leathes living of Limpenhoe with Southwood until George Reading Leathes was fully ordained. The Wilkinsons, who were already well acquainted with the Leathes family in general and Betsy and her children in particular, quickly became Betsy's valued friends and were absorbed into her social circle.

Not all of Betsy's friends were rich merchants, bankers, brewers, lawyers and clerics. She was also a great fan of contemporary literature and the performing arts, and relished any contact with what, to her, was the exotic world of celebrity. Her acquaintance with the author Clara Reeve was maintained through an erratic correspondence until Reeve's death in 1807. Another acquaintance with a claim to fame was Francis (Frank) Lathom, reputedly the illegitimate son of an English peer, who was born in Norwich in 1777. As a teenager he wrote plays for the Theatre Royal, and may well have acted there. Betsy first became acquainted with his mother in 1796, a year after Francis had published his first novel, *The Castle of Ollada*, and by 1800 the Lathoms were part of her theatre-going and partying circuit. Francis Lathom wrote a large number of formulaic but highly successful novels in the Gothic style, and one of them, *The Midnight Bell* (1798), merited inclusion in the list of 'horrid' books recommended by Isabella Thorpe to Catherine Morland in Jane Austen's *Northanger Abbey*.[12] Betsy occasionally attended the Theatre Royal with his mother, probably to see some of his plays performed. Largely light comedies and satires, they were extremely popular and were frequently performed all over the country. He was a colourful and flamboyant character who divided his time after 1801 between Norwich and Scotland, where he may have pursued a long-term homosexual relationship, perhaps unknown to his family and friends.[13] Betsy read all of his novels as soon they were published, and seems to have enjoyed them immensely.

Lady Winterton was the most faithful of Betsy's correspondents. Her letters were infrequent but she managed to keep her friend up to date with the lives of her aristocratic step-family at Shillinglee Park. Arthur Turnour, Lord Winterton's second son, was still a midshipman aboard the 80-gun *Caesar*, the flagship of Rear-Admiral Sir James Saumarez, and at 14 had already seen action. His first taste of naval engagement came during the first of the two actions that comprised the battle of Algeciras Bay, near Gibraltar, in July 1801. Twenty-two of Arthur's shipmates were wounded and nine killed in the first action, and the ship itself sustained serious damage. After undergoing some running repairs during the four-day gap between the two encounters, the *Caesar* was able to rejoin the squadron, and was one of only eight British ships that gained a victory on 12 July against a combined Franco-Spanish fleet of 13 ships. Lady Winterton told Betsy in March 1802 that Arthur had been wounded in the battle and sent home to recuperate for two months. Lord Winterton had received a flattering account of his son's conduct from Sir James Saumarez.[14] In 1802 young Arthur was transferred to the 44-gun frigate *Argo* under the captaincy of Benjamin Hollowell, whose orders were to organize and control British patrols of African coastal waters off Guinea.[15] After completing her tour of duty the *Argo* called at Barbados on her homeward voyage, where she was commandeered by Sir Samuel Hood and sailed with his fleet on the successful expedition to liberate St Lucia and Tobago from the French. She finally arrived back at Portsmouth in August 1803. At 17 Arthur was an experienced naval officer and the veteran of at least one sea battle and one assault on land.

Back home in Norwich, Betsy was somewhat dismayed by the news that her former sister-in-law, Elizabeth Leathes of Herringfleet Hall, was to marry for the second time. Both Betsy and George had long assumed that his career would sooner or later be boosted by one or more of the church livings in her gift, since his aunt had doted on him and spoiled him from his early childhood. A new husband could well restrict her liberality.

Mrs Leathes had met Anthony Merry, a career diplomat, in Paris early in 1802. He was serving there as temporary British minister following a stint as secretary to the embassy that had negotiated the Peace of Amiens. After a short courtship the couple were married in London on 21 January 1803. A few days after his marriage to the 'brisk widow', as she was known to some of Betsy's Kent friends, Merry was named the British minister to America. So after a few months' stay at Herringfleet the newly married couple left for Washington in September, and remained there until he was recalled in 1806.

Elizabeth Merry was a lively and independent woman, a good conversationalist and an excellent hostess – all the qualifications required of a diplomatic wife. Unfortunately Washington was a difficult posting at this time, even for an experienced diplomat like Merry, and his time there was soured by a row over protocol and strained to the limit by issues arising out of the war in Europe.[16] Despite his three uncomfortable years in the United States, Merry seems to have regretted

*Herringfleet Hall, 1970, reproduced by permission of Mrs Helen Sandon
and Suffolk Record Office (HG 402/3/83)*

that his recall to England left his work in Washington unfinished. Mrs Merry, however, seems to have been neither comfortable nor happy in Washington, and was certainly not sorry to see the end of her stay, a feeling that was reciprocated by President Jefferson, who waspishly and unjustly described her as a virago, and publicly stated that she had disrupted Washington society during her husband's term of office.[17] Merry retired from the diplomatic service in 1809, when he and his wife settled down to comfortable domesticity at Herringfleet Hall.

Closer to home, the four Leathes children continued to provide their mother with equal measures of pleasure, pain, pride and exasperation. Still subsidized by his mother, George divided his time in 1802 between Cambridge, where he prepared for his ordination; Herringfleet, where he danced attendance on his aunt at her expense when she was not in Paris or London; and Bury St Edmunds, where he made himself comfortable at his Uncle George's expense. But the good times had to end, and George was eventually ordained deacon at Norwich on 27 April 1803. He was then ordained priest, also at Norwich, on 25 September 1803, following which he was swiftly presented to the two small livings of Limpenhoe with Southwood and Wickhampton. Neither living had a parsonage attached, so after his presentation George divided most of his time between the parsonage at Reedham, where he stayed with his brother, and Herringfleet Hall, where his aunt seems to have given him carte blanche to come and go as he pleased during her absence in the United States.

Edward Leathes continued to make requests for loans or gifts of money from his mother, mainly to furnish his parsonage and stock the glebe farm. His farming efforts were not entirely successful, although he always had a plausible explanation for his failures. Special seed wheat ordered from Cambridgeshire went missing in Norwich, some of his animals died, his cheeses failed to sell, and he never had enough money to pay his taxes – all good reasons why he needed more money from his mother and could not repay what he already owed her.[18] He expected her to do all his food and household shopping for him and to send it on to Reedham; to run all his errands in Norwich; and to procure servants for him regularly, because few of them stayed with him for long. He also expected her to oversee the marketing of his produce at Norwich market, keep a thorough account of any sales, and forward the money to him. Betsy's reward for all this inconvenience was the occasional gift of glebe farm produce or game shot on his land. Edward's visits to Norwich seem to have been largely recreational, although he usually made time to visit his mother and sometimes stayed at her house overnight.

After an absence of 18 months, Captain Horace Beevor and the *Carnatic* finally docked at Greenhithe in early June 1802. Mary, together with her mother and her brother George, travelled to London to meet him as soon as they received the news. The party took rooms at Lothians Hotel and began to enjoy a full social life. In London they met up with several Kent friends, including the Countess Stanhope and the Dowager Countess Stanhope, Lady Frederick Campbell, Dr Vyse, Mr and Mrs Noailles, Wenham Lewis and Betsy's estranged husband Edward Peach, as well as a few Norfolk relatives and friends, including Mrs Forster and her daughter Kitty, Lord and Lady Gordon, Captain Robert Beevor and the Reverend Augustus Beevor. They enjoyed the usual cultural and social events and activities, and notably a balloon ascent by the French aeronaut André Jacques Garnerin from Lords cricket ground.[19]

Betsy, Mary and Horace broke their holiday in London to spend a week at the White Hart at Sevenoaks Common. From here they visited their Kent friends and introduced Horace Beevor to those who had not yet met him. They arrived back in Norwich on 6 August, where Horace was finally introduced to his one-year-old daughter.

At home in Norwich, Horace and Mary settled back into their family and social life. The only interruption came when little Mary had an attack of measles on 31 August. This was a potentially life-threatening disease, but she seems not to have been too badly affected, and her parents resumed their social life two days later, leaving her nurse to cope with her recovery. Horace and his brother-in-law George went off on occasional fishing expeditions; Mary accompanied them on one occasion, but despite the company of Kitty Forster she probably found the pastime rather tedious, and shunned subsequent outings in favour of visiting and tea parties. But towards the end of September 1802 Mary and Horace's comfortable existence was shattered by an event that threatened the security of their marriage and divided the Leathes family for many years.

The pages of Betsy's diary were reserved more for recording daily chatter relating to her social life than for family events of any great substance. On 22 September she recorded that she had written to Major Leathes, and on 24 September she recorded visits from her eldest daughter and grandchild to drink tea in the afternoon, and from her lawyer on the evening, although she did not mention the reason for either the visits or the letter. Instead it was revealed in George Leathes' indignant and forthright reply. It seems that James Thompson had unsuccessfully attempted to seduce his sister-in-law, Mary Beevor, who had repulsed him. No date was ever given for the assault but it must have occurred during Horace's absence at sea earlier in 1802, when Mary was living alone and unchaperoned except for servants and nurses. In a fit of pique provoked by the failed seduction, Thompson decided to ruin Mary's reputation by publicly bragging that far from failing in his seduction attempt, he had succeeded.

Elizabeth Thompson had clearly visited her mother to try to convince her of the truth of the allegations against Mary. At this stage Betsy was unwilling to have the incident become public, and had reacted sympathetically by opting for concealment. Major Leathes, uncle to both girls and no friend of James Thompson's, roundly condemned her attitude:

> I am very sorry poor Elizabeth should suffer for the rascality of her husband but no punishment can be too severe for such infamous Conduct both as a Man, a relative and a Divine. I am ready to acknowledge family Quarrels ought not to be exposed to public View, but I will never confess it as my opinion that the actions of a Villain who has taken every Opportunity of publickly traducing & falsely exposing the Character of a virtuous Woman ought to be concealed or forgiven on account of his Wife, whose own Sister he attempted to debauch. You should recollect that She is also your Daughter as well as Elizabeth and then ask yourself what ought to be your Conduct towards that man who married to the One and attempts the Chastity of the Other, Nature, Virtue and Religion recoil at the Idea. Then what does he do, instead of admiring that Purity and Innocence he was unable to undermine publicly boasts of having debauched her and takes every Opportunity of turning her Foibles into Vice & Guilt, for Shame! For Shame! He is a disgrace to the Name of Man and deserves to be banished [from] Society.[20]

Mary found herself in the spotlight overnight, the subject of tittle-tattle and malicious gossip. We can only conjecture about the 'foibles' her uncle had referred to. Possibly Mary had naively allowed Thompson, who was after all her brother-in-law, to visit her at home when she was unchaperoned, although servants would certainly have been present. This might have been an error of judgement, but it hardly constituted an admission of guilt. The unravelling events created unbearable tensions within the family, and Betsy found she could not remain neutral for long. Elizabeth made occasional visits to her mother, while Horace and Mary tried to carry on normally. Mary began to feel unwell in October, although her sickness probably had as much to do with the early stages of pregnancy as with the strain imposed by Thompson's allegations.

The young couple attempted to ease the situation by making week-long visits to friends and relatives outside Norwich. They struggled on valiantly until 10 November, when it was decided it was advisable for Horace and Mary to part for a while, pending legal advice. At this point Betsy, who had been torn between her daughters, decided Mary had been grievously wronged by James Thompson, who should not be allowed to escape the consequences. Mary moved in with her mother while her husband and their families tried to sort out the mess. George Leathes also decided his mother and sister needed his support, and moved temporarily into St George's Court. Edward, completely self-absorbed at the time, chose not to become involved at all, and did not even mention the affair in his many letters to his mother.

Meanwhile the gossip-mongers were busy, and many of Betsy's friends and acquaintances did not know what to believe. It may have been legal advice that prompted Mary to take the sacrament and swear an oath of her innocence on 20 November.[21] This was a serious move, and it seems to have convinced at least some of the doubters.[22] It certainly convinced Horace, if he needed to be convinced, that his wife was totally blameless, and he and his legal adviser agreed he should be reconciled with her as soon as possible. Mary was escorted by her brother George to her uncle's house at Bury St Edmunds, and the couple were reunited there on 29 November.

Betsy lost no time in writing to several of her friends on 30 November to tell them this news.[23] She was doubtless highly gratified when several responded by promptly calling on her, no doubt eager to hear further details. Horace and Mary stayed at the Leathes house in Bury St Edmunds until 10 December, when they returned to Norwich. They must have been relieved and gratified to receive a steady stream of visitors, indicating that their social credibility had not been seriously compromised by the drama of the previous weeks.

Unfortunately this was not quite the end of the affair. Elizabeth Thompson had espoused her husband's cause enthusiastically from the outset, which was not surprising since to do otherwise would probably have ended her marriage. After Mary had sworn her innocence on the sacrament most people of any consequence in Norwich chose to believe her, which implied that James Thompson was a liar as well as a blackguard. James and Elizabeth responded by continuing to fuel the Norwich gossip machine with further malicious allegations. James even went so far as to challenge Major Leathes to a duel – a challenge that the older man sensibly declined. The major then condemned both James and Elizabeth in no uncertain terms, and urged the family to stand firm in the face of the rumours that were still flying around:

> I find Norwich & It's Vicinity are in general thoroughly convinced of her [Mary's] Innocence and of the Villainy of her Accusers, this is sufficient and here let Matters rest. A Rascal's daring to vindicate his Conduct by fighting is no proof of Innocence, it only shews he is not afraid or ashamed to defend one crime by committing another, a fellow of this Stamp is so conscious of the Baseness of his Character that he cares not how soon or in what Cause he falls. Such Men are unworthy the Notice of the Just and honourable. But what must we say of the Baseness of a Woman who not content with making every attempt to ruin the Character of her own Sister sends a Bully to take away the Life of her own Father's Brother because he thought it proper to step forth in the Vindication of injured Innocence, in Vindication of her own Sister, if such Characters do not meet from the World [with] the Contempt they deserve the good Opinion of mankind is but of little Value.[24]

This traumatic episode convinced Horace that Mary needed different living arrangements during his long absences at sea, so on the day following their return to Norwich from Bury St Edmunds the couple began house-hunting. They quickly arranged to rent a house on Colegate, close by St Clement's Church. Betsy and her mother agreed to leave their house in St George's Court in order to move in with the young couple, so on Christmas Eve 1802 Horace, Mary, Mary junior, Betsy, Mrs Reading and all their servants moved in to St Clements House. Horace had no intention of leaving either Mary's safety or her reputation to chance after the terrible events of the previous months. The move must have represented a considerable financial loss to Betsy because she had lived in her expensively decorated and furnished house at St George's Court for a mere 15 months. The episode created a permanent rift in the family. Betsy had no further contact with James Thompson during her lifetime, and several years were to pass before she spoke to Elizabeth again. The Thompsons had also alienated Elizabeth's siblings, her brother-in-law Horace, and by implication the whole powerful and well-connected Beevor clan – a foolish move for a clergyman on the lookout for further preferment.

The repercussions of these events were felt well into 1803. Given the nature of gossip, it must have been several months before the affair was superseded by more current topics and began to fade from public memory. Betsy's friends in other parts of the country were largely shocked and upset by the news, although it is noticeable that their reactions depended on their personal preferences. Mrs Man, Betsy's friend from childhood, was not only astonished but indignant:

> Good Heavens what a critical situation for so young a person as M[rs] B! and it will ever be a critical Situation with such diabolical Enemies ... but to what

can be attributed her brother in Law's conduct? I felt very much for M^rs: T's unhappy connection with such a Being till I found by M^r G: L: that her own conduct respecting the affair did not appear to deserve it.[25]

Lady Winterton, a great fan of James Thompson, was somewhat brusque in her response and not at all sympathetic towards Mary: 'I shall have much pleasure in being acquainted with the unpleasant difference between M^r and M^rs. Thompson &^c. &^c. having entirely subsided, as all Family disputes are extremely distressing to all parties.'[26] She should have known that a 'difference' of this kind would not subside but would instead leave wounds that were unlikely to heal.

For Horace and Mary the distress of the previous year was dissipated to a great extent by the birth of their son Horatio Clarke Beevor on 10 May 1803. Horace had been away at sea when his daughter was born in 1801, so her official christening had been postponed until his return. The events of September to December 1802 and the birth of Horace delayed their plans even further, so Mary Leathes Beevor was eventually christened at the same time as her baby brother on 5 January 1804. The christening was the cause of great celebration, marked by parties for adults and children, followed by a ball attended by more than 100 people.[27]

15   Release

British political activity and the progress of the war with France met with varying degrees of success and failure between 1804 and 1807. Addington's government fell in May 1804 and Pitt returned to power, albeit with limited Commons support. The mobilization of the male population and the strengthening of homeland defences against the threat of invasion by French forces continued apace in 1804 and 1805, especially in southern and south-eastern coastal areas of England. Anti-French feeling spread rapidly; bullish patriotism reached fever pitch and nationalism was expressed with enthusiasm in prose, poetry, newspapers, pamphlets, cartoons, plays, opera and popular songs. People became increasingly willing to commit their money, skills and labour to the war effort.

Another attempt was made to curb French expansionism in 1805 when Britain, Russia and Austria combined in a third coalition. The coalition was successful in deflecting Napoleon's attention from the invasion of Britain, but was otherwise ineffective. Napoleon brushed aside the coalition's military efforts, and crushed the Austrians at Ulm on 20 October and the combined Russian and Austrian forces at Austerlitz on 2 December. His victories established French supremacy on land and shattered the coalition, for neither the Austrians nor the Russians had the will to carry on the fight.

At sea, however, it was another story. British morale was massively strengthened by the victory of Admiral Lord Nelson's fleet against the combined French and Spanish fleets at Trafalgar on 21 October 1805, an emphatic victory that guaranteed long-term British naval supremacy. On the minus side it cost many lives, including that of Nelson himself. The nation rejoiced when news of the resounding French defeat at Trafalgar reached Britain, but mourned the heroic death of Nelson. The outpouring of national grief that accompanied his burial in St Paul's Cathedral on 9 January 1806 was almost hysterical in its intensity. His death was felt particularly keenly in his native county, for Nelson had always been proud to call himself a Norfolk man and Norfolk was equally proud of him.

A grand ball and supper to celebrate Nelson's life and his last great achievement was held at the Assembly House in Norwich on 17 December 1805. The Norfolk Society took charge of the arrangements, and 476 of the great and good of city and county attended. The common anteroom of the Assembly House was converted into an octagonal 'saloon' by the use of large paintings created for the occasion, and was appropriately decorated with representations of all Nelson's great victories, together with 'emblematical naval devices, and other suitable embellishments'.[1] The ballroom was divided by ropes into four sets, each designed to cope with up to 25 couples dancing to music provided by the band of the Norwich Volunteer Regiment. The music room contained three long tables laden with delicacies which were consumed with great relish at midnight. Dancing was resumed

A lady in evening dress (left)
and a lady in a day dress wearing a shawl(right), both early 1800s

after a lengthy refreshment break and lasted until the company dispersed at
6 am. One newspaper correspondent told his readers that 'The Rooms exhibited
a brilliant and interesting assemblage of fashion and beauty; some of the married
women looked divine – the dresses were most elegant, and there was a dazzling
display of jewellery and rich bandeaus, with appropriate mottoes and devices.'[2]
Betsy recorded the event in her diary but it is unclear whether she attended.

The war continued to affect families up and down the land. In January 1804
Betsy's recently widowed friend, Lady Gordon, received the news that her eldest
son had died on active service in the West Indies. She bewailed the fact that her
only remaining son, Orford, had been ordered to rejoin his regiment in Barbados,
and prayed he would be safe. Her prayers were granted, because at the end of the
year she wrote to Betsy to say he was still in good health and expected soon to be
posted to the Mediterranean. Lady Gordon wanted him to leave the army and he
had agreed, but had been unable to find suitable employment in civilian life and

therefore decided to continue soldiering. As a result, she had been forced to 'trust him under the Protection of the Almighty, with the hope of restoring him to me before I bid Adieu to this vain World'.[3]

Betsy's circle of friends and acquaintances was already extensive by 1804; new acquaintances were mentioned in her diary each year, while a few of her existing acquaintanceships blossomed into friendships over time. The name of William Dalrymple, for instance, appeared for the first time in her diary on 11 January 1804. He was a surgeon with a large and successful Norwich practice, and it was in his professional capacity that Betsy first met him when she was taken ill at home.[4] He visited her on five occasions between 11 and 14 January and treated her for an unspecified illness which lasted for around two weeks. During the next few months Betsy and the Dalrymples began to visit each other on a social basis, and a friendship gradually developed between Betsy and Mrs Dalrymple.

Other acquaintances gradually became friends too. Betsy had known the Reverend and Mrs Glover and their family since 1794, but in 1804 she began to see a great deal more of them. Mr Glover was the curate at St Clements, where Betsy went to hear him preach on many occasions.[5] Mr and Mrs Starling Day had also been part of Betsy's social circle since 1798, but it was not until 1804 that their paths began to cross on a regular basis. Day was a wool factor and merchant who had wisely used a part of his profits to found a bank in Norwich in 1795. He lived at 103 Pottergate, and like many other successful businessmen had his workrooms next door, at 101 Pottergate. He was active in local politics, and was elected mayor of Norwich in 1782 and 1812.[6]

Betsy's diary also began to mention some female relatives of the cathedral clergy resident in the Close. Sarah Smith, for instance, was the wife of a minor canon who lived at 26 Lower Close; Mrs Pile, wife of the Reverend Pile of 19 Upper Close, was also mentioned, as was Miss Jones, housekeeper at the Deanery. The most important was Mrs Bathurst, wife of Bishop Henry Bathurst, appointed in 1805 following the promotion of Charles Manners Sutton to the archbishopric of Canterbury.[7] Betsy paid a morning visit to Mrs Bathurst on 12 August 1805 and was rewarded with a reciprocal visit on 24 August.

The new bishop threw open the doors of the Bishop's Palace to polite society when he began to hold public tea parties. Naturally the good ladies of Norwich were incapable of resisting such a treat, and Betsy, with her friend Mrs Harrington, attended one such tea party on 10 October 1805 to satisfy their curiosity. These occasions led to much conjecture in clerical circles, and Edward Leathes was swift to ask his mother what the people of Norwich thought.[8] Betsy's reply has unfortunately not survived. During the following two years Betsy and Mrs Bathurst gradually became better acquainted, and Betsy was invited to smaller, more exclusive gatherings at the Bishop's Palace.

Social life amongst the well-to-do continued much as usual in Norwich, despite the effects of war and the downturn in textile manufacturing. Music in one form or another played an important part in the cultural life of the city. Concerts at which amateur and occasionally professional musicians played were often held at private houses. Reverend Glover held well-attended concerts at his home, and some members of his musical family, as well as other talented local musicians doubtless performed on such occasions. Betsy went to two concerts at the Glover house in 1804, one of them on 2 February at which Miss Gurdon sang and Mr Elwin played the harp, and another on 24 April at which Mr Morgan displayed his talents.[9]

Handel's music continued to be popular throughout the country; his oratorios attracted large crowds of middle-class music-goers and helped to create a new concert-going public. Betsy was one of the many people in Norwich who flocked to see a performance of *Judas Maccabeus* on 6 April 1804.[10]

Professional musicians frequently performed at inns that boasted a large room with a stage, such as the White Swan near St Peter Mancroft, the home of the Norwich's theatre company until the Theatre Royal opened in 1758. Betsy went there with the Reverend Thomas Wigg Hancock and his family in February 1804 'to hear M[r] Etonis play the harp'.[11] During the summer of that year Betsy and her friends attended the concerts given in the Cathedral Close by the band of the Norwich Regiment of the Seventh Norfolk Volunteer Infantry. It seems to have become fashionable for well-to-do people to stroll in the Upper Close and listen to the band; Betsy did so on four occasions in June and July, once with Miss Harvey (whose brother Robert commanded the regiment), twice with Mrs Harrington, and once with Mr and Mrs Charles Millard.[12]

The visual arts had been an important part of the cultural life of Norwich for centuries, and many artists and craftspeople continued to live and work in the city. The 18th and early 19th centuries were particularly notable for the talented artists who lived, painted and taught in Norwich, such as John Crome, Robert Ladbroke, John Sell Cotman and Joseph Stannard. Norwich and the surrounding county were also home to a significant number of wealthy merchants and bankers, such as Thomas Harvey of Catton, Dawson Turner of Yarmouth and several members of the Gurney family, who appreciated fine painting and could afford to indulge their collecting habits. The Norwich Society of Artists was founded by Crome and Ladbroke in 1803 to encourage painting, architecture and sculpture in the city. The Society's first exhibition of paintings was held in 1805 at Sir Benjamin Wrench's Court in Norwich, and exhibitions continued to be held there until the building was demolished in 1825 to make way for the new Corn Exchange and Exchange Street. Exhibitions were resumed in 1828, when they were held at the Corn Exchange. The 1806 exhibition took place between 11 and 23 August and was advertised in the *Norwich Mercury*. Tickets were priced at 2s.6d, well beyond the means of those with a small income.[13] Betsy attended the exhibition along with Miss Harvey and a party of friends on 16 August, although she did not confide her verdict on the paintings to her diary.

Painting was considered a particularly suitable cultural pursuit for ladies. Mary

Beevor began to take lessons at home from no less a teacher than John Crome, whom Betsy referred to in her diary as 'old Crome'. He first visited her at St Clement's House on 23 October 1805, and then on five more occasions in October and November.[14] These visits may have been the sum total of Mary's tuition, but it is equally possible that Betsy grew tired of recording the lessons in her diary. Like many artists before and since, Crome relied on teaching for a steady income, and he taught the children of several prominent local families, including those of Dawson Turner, the Yarmouth banker. Mary's brother George was a friend of Turner's, so possibly she was influenced by him in her choice of tutor.

The relative affluence of Betsy, her family and her friends insulated them to a great extent from the poverty, insecurity and desperation that marked the lives of those born into or consigned by circumstances to the lower classes. The better-off salved their consciences with good deeds and charitable giving, but just occasionally the real world intruded into their comfortable existences when the have-nots decided to redress the balance of life's lottery by relieving wealthier people of their money or goods. Before the 1820s the concept of policing by a uniformed body of men patrolling both countryside and town to prevent crime and disorder was completely alien to the vast majority of people, and regular, paid police forces were not introduced until the Police Act of 1839. Until then policing in England was the province of local government, and relied on local men who served as parish constables on a selective or voluntary part-time basis for a limited period of time.

Parish constables performed a variety of functions, notably the collection of county rates. They did not detect or prevent crime, but were obliged only to serve warrants and make arrests when offences were reported to them. They were not paid for their services, but they could claim fees and expenses. Twenty-four parish constables were elected annually in Norwich, two for each of the city's 12 minor wards, and they were supported by a number of watchmen who patrolled the streets at night. During the 18th century most towns and cities in England introduced measures aimed at improving street lighting and providing for a permanent force of reliable watchmen. Street lighting in Norwich was improved in 1794 by the provision of around 1,000 oil lamps, although darkness descended when they were extinguished at 11 pm. The formation of a gas company in 1820 permitted the introduction of gas lighting to the city's streets during the 1820s. The combination of parish constables, better street lighting and watchmen did much to improve the safety of town and city streets by the early 1800s, but more remained to be done.

Travel on the public highway was a risky business, especially at night. Many people, Betsy included, thought nocturnal journeys should be undertaken only in groups, preferably under a full moon to help reduce the chance of surprise attacks by highwaymen and footpads. Many misfortunes could befall the unwary traveller. Edward Leathes told his mother of Philip Browne, one of his Reedham farmer parishioners, who had travelled on horseback to Bungay Fair with two friends. On the return journey Mr Browne unfortunately become separated from his friends somewhere between Bungay and Loddon. He carried on alone, but before he reached Reedham Ferry he was thrown from his horse and knocked unconscious. While he lay at the side of the road he was robbed of everything he had, apart from two cakes that he had bought for his children. He was found dead the following day, either at the hands of the robbers or from injuries sustained in his fall. Edward was greatly alarmed by these events and asked Betsy to make sure his manservant, who had brought his note and had errands to do in Norwich, returned home in daylight.[15]

The public highway was not the only place where danger lurked, for the houses of wealthier members of society were a prime target for burglars. Many house-holders were very security conscious, and used a combination of window shutters, stout doors with good locks and burly servants to act as deterrents. St Clement's House, which was occupied by Betsy and her mother, Horace and Mary Beevor, their children and their servants, was visited by burglars on three occasions during the last five months of 1805. The burglars may well have known Horace was on his way to India, and assumed the house was an easy target. First Betsy and Mary were woken in the middle of the night of 23 August by someone breaking in. Betsy immediately opened her bedroom window and called the watch, but the would-be burglars made their escape through the back kitchen window before the watchman arrived. On 2 November Mary again woke in the middle of the night and was terrified to find a man in her room. Betsy did not elaborate in her diary, but presumably the man disappeared swiftly when Mary began to scream. Finally, on 10 December two men tried to gain access to the house through the back gate but failed, possibly because they were drawing too much attention to themselves.[16] Betsy did not record any further disturbances so it seems that the household got away relatively lightly. It is also possible that Betsy and Mary took steps to tighten household security afterwards.

In Betsy's family group, relationships were still strained by the rift between Horace and Mary Beevor and James and Elizabeth Thompson. Betsy and Elizabeth were barely on speaking terms for much of 1804; Elizabeth occasion-ally visited her grandmother for tea and a chat, but only when Horace was away at sea and Mary was out of the house. A reconciliation of sorts came about when 79-year-old Mrs Reading suffered a devastating stroke in October 1804. Elizabeth pleaded with Betsy to let her visit her grandmother for perhaps the last time, and Betsy let her do so on the following day, when Mary and Horace were in London. Edward rushed to his grandmother's bedside as soon as he received the news, and George came from Bury St Edmunds. Both of them visited at regular intervals over the next few weeks, often staying overnight. Strangely Betsy waited for two days before writing to Mary, who did not return to Norwich for four weeks, having spent a week at Bury on the way back. The devotion of Betsy's three oldest children to their beloved grandmother was truly remarkable, and probably reflected the bonds formed at Woodstock when they were being schooled there by James Reading. Mary, on the other hand, had stayed at Reedham with her parents during her infancy, and so her strongest bond was with her mother.

Mrs Reading's condition was grave. The stroke had left her paralysed and she lay in bed unable to walk or talk. During Horace and Mary's absence, Betsy was responsible for overseeing the running of the house and the care of the two eldest children, as well as caring for her mother. The future looked grim for the old lady. Edward Peach told Betsy he was 'much afraid she may continue a very considerable time in that truly melancholy state and require a good deal of attendance with close confinement to her room', and he feared the effect on Betsy's health.[17] It is not clear whether a nurse was engaged to care for the old lady or whether Betsy undertook all the nursing herself, with some help from the servants. A full-time carer was certainly employed in 1805, relieving Betsy of many of the chores associated with the care of a stroke victim, but her social life was still restricted.

All Betsy's regular correspondents commented on the pathetic position in which the once-active old lady found herself: bed-ridden and helpless, with little or no hope of recovery. Mrs Reading's illness did however bring Betsy and Elizabeth together, even though their relationship could not have been described as close. Elizabeth and her older children visited Mrs Reading on at least eight occasions in 1805, notably when Mary and Horace were not at home, but Betsy still refused to have anything to do with James Thompson.

Fortunately for Betsy, Edward Leathes was somewhat less of a problem to her by 1804. His parsonage had been completed more or less to his satisfaction and he was concentrating on serving his parishes and farming his glebe land. His life was made even busier because he acted as his brother's curate at Southwood, Limpenhoe and Wickhampton on an increasingly frequent basis. Not surprisingly, he continued to rely on Betsy to do his shopping and arrange for the marketing of his produce in Norwich, change his library books and find replacements when servants left him, as they did on a regular basis. He managed his money somewhat better than previously, but still lived on a financial knife-edge and frequently requested loans from Betsy to tide him over until his produce was marketed or his tithes were due. His autocratic manner had clearly not endeared him to some of his farmer parishioners, and he began to have trouble extracting tithe payments from them. This was particularly unfortunate because despite his appeals to the Income Tax Commissioners he had to pay tax on his tithe receipts even when the farmers had not paid their dues.[18]

Clergymen all over England were experiencing difficulties similar to Edward's, and tithes were becoming a hot political issue. Tithe payments represented the largest part of clerical income, and without them many clergymen would be reduced to dependence upon their glebe lands. Clearly it was not in their interests to let any of their farmer parishioners default on the payments. But many farmers regarded the payment of tithes as an anachronism and an unjust tax on the time, money and effort that they had put into improving their land, and their views had considerable support among the laity. So Edward developed an active interest in the law regarding tithes, and began some research on the subject. In June 1805 he asked his mother to keep the newspaper containing the House of Lords debate on tithes, while in August he asked her to book an appointment for him with a Norwich lawyer, preferably Mr Morphew, an ecclesiastical lawyer with no involvement with the farming community. Tithes would become Edward's obsession in the years to come.

His brother George added the elective curacy of the church of St James (later the Cathedral Church of St James) at Bury St Edmunds to his livings of Wickhampton and Limpenhoe with Southwood in 1805. He then made his permanent home in the town and largely ignored his Norfolk livings. Occasionally he took services, but most of the time the three churches were served by his brother Edward, who continued to act as his unofficial curate.

The little church at Southwood, which was already in need of substantial repairs, continued its long-term slide into neglect during George's incumbency, assisted by his tardiness in paying towards repair of the chancel roof.[19] His primary interest lay not in his churches and parishioners, but in his botanical studies. Like his friend Dawson Turner he was an accomplished botanist and a fellow of the Linnaean Society. Turner was four years George's senior, a family man who was rich enough to indulge his passions for botany and collecting art and books. He had a formidable reputation as a botanist by 1805, when he made a two-day trip to Cromer with George.[20] It seems likely the purpose of the trip was to collect seaweed, on which Turner was an acknowledged expert. George's own interest in seaweed might well have been stimulated during this trip. Seaweed continued to be his study of choice for the rest of his life, and a genus of seaweed (*Leathesia*) was named after him.

Mary Beevor had led a more settled existence since the traumatic events of 1802 and the family's removal to St. Clements House. She bore a second daughter, Harriet, on 24 July 1804, and at 21 she was a young matron with three children to care for. Horace spent the years between 1802 and 1805 at home in Norwich, since the *Carnatic* had been taken out of service. He made regular visits to the East India Company's London headquarters to petition for the captaincy of another vessel, but his efforts were not rewarded until 1805, when he was given command of the *Glory*. At 502 tons, the *Glory* was less than half the size of the *Carnatic*, and she represented a considerable demotion for him, although possibly she was a temporary posting until a new *Carnatic* had been built.

In addition to the regular ships used in the China and India trade, the East India Company also used 'extra' ships of between 500 and 600 tons for Indian coastal trade and occasional overseas trade.[21] As an 'extra' ship, the *Glory* was used mainly for transporting inferior goods at a lower rate of freight, and although she had space for passengers, Horace could not have made the same income from her. Nor were lack of size and status the *Glory's* only problems. She had gained a reputation as an unlucky ship because her previous captain had been killed during a duel with one of the passengers at the end of her last voyage. She was also slow, probably because she was poorly built and did not handle well.[22] But to Horace the *Glory* was better than no ship at all, so despite any misgivings he took command and eventually sailed for Madras in late summer 1805, stopping at Southampton, Cork and other ports to pick up passengers.

Although Betsy and Edward Peach had separated formally in 1794, they had remained on friendly, though distant, terms and he had continued to exert a degree of influence over her life through the deed of separation trust. This state of affairs came to an end on 15 January 1805, when she heard through a Mr Sankey of Cheam that Edward had died during the night of 11/12 January: 'He was to all Appearance, perfectly well when he went to Bed, but was found dead & cold, by his Servant, when she went to awake him in the Morning.' The letter asked Betsy to notify a firm of London solicitors by return of post if she wished to nominate a representative to attend the reading of the will, although the writer warned her Peach had died in relative poverty.[23] The warning was not needed, for Betsy was one of the few people aware of her husband's desperate financial position. Edward Peach was buried at Sundridge on 20 January, and a notice of the death appeared in the *Maidstone Journal* on 25 January.

Betsy had never divulged the financial reasons for her separation from Peach to anyone other than her immediate family, not even to her closest friend, Harriet, countess of Winterton. Lady Winterton's letter of condolence expressed the hope that Peach had left her a token of remembrance in his will, so that her still curious friends might be convinced they had parted amicably.[24] Widowhood must have freed Betsy's tongue. Her reply completely satisfied Lady Winterton's curiosity, as the latter's response showed:

> I am much surprised at your [account] of M[r]. Peach's affairs, as I never under-stood that he had so near outlived his fortune, however he is now released from all his sufferings (I hope) and <u>you</u> <u>ought</u> to congratulate yourself on your narrow escape for I agree with you that had you continued to live with him you certainly would have been involved in many difficulties, and therefore be thankful that you separated before it was too late, and bury the circumstance for ever from your own mind.[25]

Another old friend, Mrs Whately, took a more world-weary view. She confessed to Betsy that she had been uncertain whether to send a letter of congratulations or condolence on her friend's final emancipation from the 'thraldom' of matrimony.[26]

Betsy was now a widow for the second time, and went into official mourning. She was not mentioned in Peach's will, but he may well have reasoned that he had more than discharged his obligations to her through the relatively generous deed of separation. Betsy wrote to his daughter Mrs Kelsey, offering to return her father's profile portrait and requesting the reciprocal return of her letters to him and the miniature painting of herself that she had given him before they married. Mrs Kelsey replied that she would appreciate the return of her father's portrait, but his correspondence had been burned on the day after his funeral, in accordance with his will, and she had been unable to find the miniature. The little portrait held sentimental value for Betsy, as it had been painted for her first husband, Edward Leathes. Possibly Peach had destroyed the miniature following the separation, but it was framed in gold, so more likely he sold or pawned it when he was chronically short of money.

Peach's death meant Betsy was finally freed from the financial shackles of the separation trust. Prior to 1802 the trust's assets had comprised £3,809 in 3 per cent bank annuities, plus jewels, plate and household furniture. In 1802 annuities worth £2,009.10s.6d were sold, followed by the sale of a further £400 worth in August 1804, leaving residual trust assets of £1,400 in bank annuities, plus jewellery, plate, furniture and possibly property.[27] The trustees wasted relatively little time in winding up the trust, and on 25 March 1805 the stock was finally transferred into Betsy's name. Her friend, the Norwich clergyman T. W. Hancock, expressed his pleasure that matters had been settled to Betsy's satisfaction, and thanked her for appointing him as her trustee, a duty he had been glad to undertake for 'so amiable a lady as you are'. Mr Hancock had little sympathy for her late husband. 'I am doubtful whether I ought to Condole with you on the Loss of the late M[r] Peach, since he is departed to a happier World, & he was not likely to have much Comfort, any longer, in This – He has paid dearly for his Errors.'[28] When all the formalities had been completed to the satisfaction of the lawyers and the banks, Betsy was once more a free agent and another phase of her life began.

16   Care, sorrow, mortification and disappointment

Pitt's government finally fell early in January 1806, after a number of defeats in the House of Commons and allegations of misuse of public funds. Pitt took it all very much to heart; his already fragile health gave way and he died on 23 January 1806, aged only 46. His administration was succeeded by a coalition including Lord Grenville as prime minister, Charles James Fox as foreign secretary, and Lord Sidmouth. This inaptly named 'Ministry of all the talents' came close to being a disaster both at home and abroad. At home, a steep hike in property taxes and Windham's proposed army reforms proved wildly unpopular. Abroad, Fox's longing for peace caused him to propose ridiculously favourable peace terms to Napoleon. Fortunately Napoleon preferred to consolidate his virtual domination of Europe by crushing the Prussian army at the battles of Jena and Auerstadt in October 1806.

Grenville's short-lived government fell not through incompetence, but because of a collective failure to realize that proposals to allow Roman Catholics to serve in senior commissioned ranks in the army would alarm the king. George III would not tolerate the idea and dismissed Grenville in March 1807, turning to the duke of Portland. The new administration, beefed up by two of Pitt's disciples, Castlereagh and Canning, was prepared to take a more bullish stance on both trade and war. 1807 saw Britain take increasingly aggressive action against French attempts to restrict British trade, using Royal Navy ships to defend commercial interests. The change of attitude was successful and the French exchequer was significantly damaged by the resulting fall in customs revenues. British military and naval tactics were equally aggressive. In September 1807 Copenhagen was bombarded following the Danish government's refusal to surrender its fleet to British forces, an essential part of Britain's plan to mount a military and naval expedition to the Baltic. This was to have been followed by further military aggression in Europe, but it was brought to an abrupt halt when Napoleon attacked Portugal (Britain's most significant remaining ally) and occupied Lisbon in November 1807. Not content with Portugal, Napoleon then prepared to move on Spain at the beginning of 1808.

At home, the war effort increased and few people were totally unaffected. Lady Gordon continued to fret about her surviving son Orford, although his regiment, the 78th, had not been ordered back to the West Indies as she had originally feared. Instead, he had been ordered to take ship for Gibraltar in June 1806 to rejoin his regiment under the command of General Frazer. According to Lady Gordon, the regiment was to rendezvous with the forces already assembled at the British naval base on Sicily. Although she consoled herself that the Mediterranean climate was much more beneficial than that of the West Indies, Lady Gordon was still very anxious about him.[1]

The West Indies was indeed a generally unhealthy posting for those unused to the climate and without immunity to tropical diseases. For instance George Augustus Leathes, the eldest son of Major Leathes and a colonel in the 96th Regiment of Infantry, was posted there in 1808 and succumbed very quickly to yellow fever. Lady Winterton kept Betsy abreast of the wartime postings of her stepson, Lieutenant Arthur Turnour, who had returned home on leave in August 1803. After a few weeks of being pampered he sailed on the 32-gun frigate *Mermaid*, which arrived in Jamaica in 1804, and stayed there for a year or so before being posted to the 'American Station' for a further two years. Naval absences were frequently very lengthy.

Lady Winterton, Lady Gordon and Betsy's other female correspondents wrote about relatives caught up in the war, but they rarely mentioned politics or political affairs. Like most ladies of her class, Betsy too neither involved herself in politics nor expressed political opinions, although she enjoyed the social activities that followed local elections. Registered electors in the city of Norwich and the county of Norfolk elected two MPs for the city and two for the county from a list of nominated candidates, a process that took several days and was wide open to abuse and disruption.[2] Landowners, patrons and other people of influence used every trick in the book to ensure their tenants, dependants, debtors and place seekers voted for their favoured candidates. They plied voters with alcohol, causing such levels of drunkenness that elections were frequently rowdy and boisterous and sometimes erupted into violence, although mostly they stayed good-natured. The polling booths for city and county elections were sited on the castle hill and in the market place. When polling was completed and the votes counted, the victorious candidates were ceremonially enthroned on a special chair and carried around the market place by their supporters. Betsy and her friends and family loved to watch this.

Bribery and 'treating' were commonplace in general elections throughout the country, and challenges were rare, but one occurred after the Norfolk county election of November 1806, when the Whig pairing of William Windham and Thomas William Coke defeated the Tory candidate, Sir John Wodehouse. It was alleged that during the campaign two Norwich prostitutes publicly impersonated two eminently respectable ladies who were supporters of Wodehouse. The ladies' relatives and friends encouraged Wodehouse to avenge the insult by bringing charges of bribery and corruption against Coke and Windham, and the case was heard in February 1807. Although both sides had substantially breached the electoral codes of conduct. Coke and Windham were found guilty and the result was declared null and void. In the rerun election in May 1807 the Whig pairing of Sir Jacob Astley and Edward Coke of Derby (Thomas William Coke's brother) were returned uncontested. But the affair did little to damage the careers of either

Coke or Windham, who soon secured safe seats and returned to the parliamentary fray.[3]

Life at St Clement's House continued very much as usual during Horace Beevor's absence in India between 1805 and 1807, punctuated in 1806 by little Harriet Beevor's successful inoculation against smallpox in February and Mary's short illness in late March. Betsy took up wine-making in 1803 following her move to these more spacious premises, and by 1807 was producing large quantities, although probably the cook and kitchen maid did most of the work. She kept a record of the amounts made and recipes used between 1803 and 1813. In 1805 the household made 214 pints of white currant wine, yielding 115 bottles when it was bottled in 1806. The 1806 vintage yielded 178 bottles of white currant and 21 bottles of elderberry wine, and the 1807 vintage yielded 168 bottles of white currant and 83 bottles of grape wine.[4] These quantities might seem large, but all classes consumed plenty of alcohol in the early 19th century.

During Mary's illness in March 1806 Betsy's son Edward wrote her a letter which suggested all was not as peaceful, even mundane, in the household as it might have appeared. Horace Beevor evidently expected Betsy to ensure Mary had constant company, so she would not suffer further from the kind of stress and unpleasantness that had surrounded the Thompson affair. But Betsy not only had responsibility for Mary and her children in Horace's absence, she had her mother to look after and her own life to live. Edward recognized her problems, but thought she should take precautionary measures:

> I am sorry to hear that Mary is not well. I fear she is left too much alone. I have always thought that you should prevail upon Mrs Beevor [Horace's mother] to be with her, whenever you are unavoidably obliged to leave her; so that she may always have you or Mrs Beevor for her Companion: & this, not only for the sake of her health, which may be hurt by solitude, but for the satisfaction of her husband, whose disposition you know.[5]

During Horace's absence on the *Glory*, his family communicated with him through a postal service run by the East India Company. They could send letters to prearranged destinations via Company ships, while he left letters at the *Glory*'s ports of call to be picked up by other Company vessels. He wrote to his wife, his parents and his mother-in-law as frequently as he was able, and they responded in like manner, but the letters took many months to reach their destination, if they arrived at all. On his outward journey in 1805 Horace wrote to Mary from Madeira, San Salvador, the Cape of Good Hope and finally in May 1806 from Calcutta – a letter she received on 23 November. Betsy and Mary wrote in January, April and May 1806, sending all these letters to St Helena.[6]

Mrs Reading's stroke had left her a permanent invalid with no hope of recovery, and Betsy employed a nurse to help with her care. Elizabeth continued to make clandestine visits to her grandmother at St Clement's House. She was pregnant for the sixth time. Lady Gordon wrote disapprovingly to Betsy, 'I do not rejoice to hear that M^{rs.} J^{s.} Tompson is again in the family way, as from experience, I can say, that large families, are by no means convenient.'[7] Elizabeth gave birth to her second son, Edward, on 27 August 1806, nearly 11 years after the birth of her first son, James.

Betsy was on much better terms with Elizabeth by 1806 and had evidently chosen to disregard her past misdeeds, although she had probably not forgiven or forgotten them. The same was not true, though, of Horace and Mary Beevor. There was no communication between the Beevor and Thompson families, and Elizabeth only visited St Clement's House when Horace was absent at sea and Mary was out of the house. Perhaps Mary, or perhaps a Beevor relative, found out that Elizabeth and her children were secretly visiting and told Horace, since this seems the most likely reason for Betsy's mysterious banishment from St Clement's House in April 1806.[8]

This abrupt change of circumstances was a bitter humiliation for Betsy, and left her in need of a house to rent. Elizabeth accompanied her to view a property on 25 April, and they viewed others in May. The search then flagged somewhat until September 1806, when Betsy had tea with Mrs Forster and the two women went to view 'Dr. Proctor's small House in the Close'.[9] Dr Joseph Proctor had held one of the prebendary stalls at Norwich Cathedral since 1799 and was also master of St Catherine's Hall, Cambridge, where he lived for most of the year. He owned or leased one of six prebendary houses in the Upper Close, almost certainly number 15 (as it was then), the one built on the site of the old bell tower adjacent to the Erpingham Gate. He or a predecessor had divided it in two, and he used the larger and more impressive part himself. Although it is always possible he also owned or leased another house there, most likely it was the smaller part of this prebendary house that Betsy viewed.[10]

Edward Leathes, often hard to please, approved of its location and encouraged his mother to take the house: 'It is small; but the neighbouring society is the principal consideration: & you may afterwards remove into a larger & better. Perhaps however when it is fitted up with neat furniture, it may improve much: that if you like it, upon the whole I think you had much better take it.'[11] This modestly sized property seems to have matched Betsy's requirements and the rent of £14 a year was well within her means. She lost no time in applying for the tenancy, which was equally swiftly granted to her. Unfortunately repairs were needed and Dr Proctor was slow to engage workmen, so she had to continue to rely on Mary's goodwill for a roof over her head for several more months.

It is not clear whether other events also upset Betsy at this time, but she found 1806 a dreadful year, one so upsetting that she destroyed most of her correspondence for this period. In the last entry that she made in her diary for that year she summed up her feelings: 'Thus endeth a Year in which I have endur'd much Care much Sorrow much Mortification & much Disappointment'.

Tombland, Norwich, taken from the cathedral spire by Edward le Grice in 1958. To the left of the Erpingham Gate (bottom middle) is the house occupied by Prebendary Joseph Proctor in the early 1800s; his 'small house' was probably the extension attached to the third gable on the far left of the building.

Betsy hoped 1807 would be a much happier year. But during January her mother's condition began to worsen, and although the old lady valiantly attempted to rally, Betsy was forced to send urgent messages to her children concerning their grandmother's failing health. Edward and Elizabeth arrived in time to see Mrs Reading before she died at 4 pm on 29 January, but George, who had further to travel, did not reach Norwich until 30 January. Friends and relatives were swift to write to Betsy or to call at the house with their condolences. The general tone is probably reflected in the letter sent by William Nelson from the rectory at Strumpshaw. 'M[rs.] Reading labour'd so long under Affliction, we sh[d.] be thankful to Providence for her Removal from a Scene of Sorrow. You have the conscious Satisfaction of having done your Duty to her, & that everything was provided for her to make her as comfortable as possible under her Circumstances.'[12]

Mr Glover, Mr Dalrymple, Mary, George and Betsy travelled together to the funeral, which took place at Reedham on 4 February. The mourning coach was met by Edward Leathes at Reedham church, where the funeral service was performed by Mr Glover of St Clement's church, Norwich. Mrs Reading was interred next to her husband in the Leathes family vault, and the service was followed by a dinner hosted by Edward at the parsonage.[13] Elizabeth and James Thompson were conspicuously absent.

Elizabeth Reading had left £100 in her will to each of her four grandchildren. The remainder of her estate, after payment of funeral expenses and outstanding debts, was bequeathed to Betsy, who was also named as sole executrix.[14] The three eldest Leathes children had all been particularly close to their grandmother, and Betsy made sure that each of them had their choice of her belongings as a memento. The commissioning and distribution of mourning jewellery amongst family and close friends to commemorate the memory of a loved one reached its height after the death of Prince Albert in 1861, but it had been fashionable among the well-to-do for more than 200 years. Betsy had arranged for mourning rings to be made following the deaths of her first husband and her father, and they were also commissioned and made for her mother.[15]

Mrs Reading's death meant that Betsy was once more alone and therefore free to do as she wished. Horace had not rescinded her banishment from St Clements, so she turned to arranging her removal to 15 Upper Close. The repairs and renovations were finally completed and on 15 April 1807 Betsy moved into her new home, although the contents of her wine cellar remained at St Clements until the end of the month, and she continued to make and bottle wine there until 1808. Despite the circumstances behind her departure from St Clements, Betsy remained on good terms with Horace's parents and other members of his family, and continued to visit, take tea and dine with them. A few weeks after her mother's death, James Beevor presented her with 'a Snuff Box with Mr. Pitt's head upon it', which could mean that Betsy, like her mother, was a snuff-taker.[16] Her relationship with Horace following his return to Norwich in early June 1807 seems to have been cordial enough, and Betsy continued to visit the young couple on a regular basis and to dine out with them.

After her removal to the Cathedral Close, Betsy had little to do for several months other than to settle in and resume her social life. During April and May a steady stream of friends and acquaintances visited the little house to present their compliments and to view her new premises. Prebendary Proctor enjoyed a friendly relationship with his new tenant during his periods of residence; the two neighbours found a common interest in whist and occasionally played cards at each other's houses. Betsy had probably expected to enjoy a great deal more of the company of Mrs Forster, wife of the headmaster of the Norwich School and thus a near neighbour, but tragically she was dead by the time Betsy moved house, having been fatally burned when her clothes caught fire at her home in School House. This was a dreadful warning of the dangers of getting too close to an open fire in the flimsy garments so popular at the time.[17]

Horace returned safely to England on 14 April 1807, and Mary set off the next day to meet him in London. On 8 June the couple returned to Norwich and quickly resumed their normal social and domestic life there. But only two weeks after their return Horace was summoned back to the East India Company offices in London. When he returned to Norwich six days later, he broke the news to Mary that he had been given orders to take the *Glory* back to Bombay in September. They stayed for only one more week in Norwich before leaving with Mary junior for Bury St Edmunds, where they left the little girl for a holiday with her great aunt and uncle before travelling on to London. Betsy left Norwich for London on 10 August, taking Horace junior with her. They stopped off at Bury St Edmunds on the way and joined Horace and Mary on 12 August.

Horace enjoyed only four short days with his wife and son after Betsy's arrival before he had to go to join the *Glory* at Gravesend, where it was to take on passengers for the journey to India before sailing to the Isle of Wight to pick up more passengers. Betsy, Mary and Horace junior left London the following day and arrived at Ryde on 19 August. There the two women took lodgings and subscribed to the library, clearly anticipating a stay of several weeks. The *Glory* docked at Ryde on 28 August with George Leathes aboard – he had travelled from Bury St Edmunds to join his brother-in-law at Gravesend for the short trip to the Isle of Wight.

The enlarged family party spent the next two weeks or so holidaying, sightseeing and socializing with the local gentry and the *Glory*'s passengers. But not everyone was happy; poor Mary, pregnant with her fourth child, endured agonies of toothache for several days before travelling with Horace to Portsmouth on 14 September to have the tooth extracted. They returned to Ryde the next day, when Horace reluctantly left his wife and son and began another long and hazardous voyage to India. George Leathes also left Ryde on 15 September and began his return journey to Bury St Edmunds. The two women stayed on until 5 October, when they too began a slow journey back to Norwich, stopping first in London for a few days and then at the Leathes home in Bury St. Edmunds for a week before finally arriving back in Norwich on 19 October.[18]

Mary slipped quickly back into her normal routine during Horace's absences at sea, but she must have regretted that they had enjoyed so little private time together during his five months' shore leave. However, she had her three children to care for and the arrival of a new baby to look forward to, so she probably had little time to dwell on what might have been.

17   Lost

When Betsy moved to her new house in the Close she was probably still feeling aggrieved and humiliated over her departure from St Clements House. It soon became clear, however, that the move was a blessing in disguise, because it restored her independence and freed her from the roles of chaperone, child-minder and housekeeper. It also enabled her to integrate herself fully into possibly the most exclusive social circle in Norwich. Lady Winterton was swift to recognize the advantages, and wrote to congratulate her on having exchanged a merely desirable situation for a much superior one.[1]

The precinct surrounding Norwich Cathedral, usually known as the Close, had largely been cleared of ruined priory buildings during the late 17th and 18th centuries. The ramshackle houses that had sprung up in and around the ruins were also demolished and their working-class occupants were encouraged to find lodgings elsewhere in the city. Fashionable new houses were erected, and were soon occupied by the cathedral clergy, the gentry and the professional classes. The upper and lower greens of the Close were landscaped, and in 1782 part of the lower green was enclosed by railings and converted into a garden to be used exclusively by occupants of the houses adjoining both greens. The upper green became known as Upper Close and the lower green as Lower Close, or Dean's Square. By 1790 the Cathedral Close had become a very desirable residential area.

Despite its apparent exclusivity, its population was still quite widely spread across the social spectrum in the 1780s. Most cathedral office holders lived there, as did a selection of gentlemen and gentlewomen of independent means, one baronet, several attorneys, two land agents, a brandy merchant, a shop keeper, three gardeners, a school master, two musicians, two builders, a stonemason, a baker, a tailor, a silk throwster and a dentist, as well as a number of young ladies and their teachers in the school at 20 Upper Close. Even modest households employed live-in servants, adding to the population mix. By 1783 only two inns survived: the Gate House Tavern, adjacent to the Ethelbert Gate, and the Three Cranes in Lower Close.[2] Both establishments were well patronised by male residents, including some of the minor canons.

The Cathedral Close survived as a discrete community, both legally and socially, well into the 19th century. It was completely walled and the gates were locked at night, so access was physically restricted. Additionally, the Close retained a separate jurisdiction and its occupants did not answer to the city authorities. It was to all intents and purposes a community set apart from the rest of the city.[3]

Betsy's social life did not change radically, but her social circle became significantly larger and developed more of a bias towards the Close and its inhabitants. She did not, however, neglect her acquaintances and friends elsewhere in the city; on the contrary, her existing acquaintances became friends and they in their turn

Cowgate, Norwich, looking towards the cathedral, a print by Henry Ninham

introduced her to more new acquaintances. For instance, Betsy had been socially acquainted for several years with Mrs and Miss Alderson, the wife and oldest unmarried daughter of Robert Alderson, steward of Norwich Corporation by 1807 and formerly minister at the Octagon Chapel on Colegate, but they did not feature regularly in the pages of her diary until 1808, a year during which the three women saw a good deal more of each other and became friends.

It must have been through the Alderson ladies that Betsy met Amelia Opie, the daughter of Robert's brother Dr James Alderson, a respected Norwich physician. Amelia had married the painter John Opie in 1798. The couple had then moved to London, where they quickly established themselves in the thriving literary and artistic circles of the capital. Amelia became a successful author of poems and novels, while John furthered his career as a portraitist. Following her husband's sudden and unexpected death in 1807 Amelia returned to her father's home in Norwich, where she continued her prolific literary career. As a vivacious, attractive and intellectually brilliant woman who was also an accomplished hostess, she quickly made an impact on Norwich society. Invitations to her parties were sought after, so Betsy must have been delighted to attend one of these gatherings in February 1809. The two women continued to meet at social events between 1809 and 1814, although they probably never became more than acquaintances.[4]

Manufacturers, merchants and bankers were amongst the wealthiest people in Norwich, and Betsy seems to have known most of the prominent families in this élite section of Norwich society. In 1809 she added James Hudson and his wife to her large acquaintance. Hudson and Robert Harvey had joined forces in 1792 to found Harvey and Hudson's Bank, known as the Norwich Crown Bank after 1808.[5]

Betsy first encountered Dr Warner Wright, a rising star in the Norwich medical firmament, in July 1809 when he was called to attend her at St Clement's House during a visit to Mary. Dr Wright was born in Norwich in 1775, and studied medicine at Edinburgh before returning there. He was elected physician to the Norfolk and Norwich Hospital in 1804, and was destined to become one of Norfolk's foremost physicians.[6] The Wrights featured increasingly regularly in Betsy's social life during 1809, and continued to be friends until her death.

Betsy's social life became less hectic than before she had moved to the Close, and its balance began to change. She went in more for dining out, tea parties, card parties and opportunist games of cards, where before she had favoured routs, assemblies, balls and theatre visits. She continued to play cards frequently, either at home with acquaintances, friends and close family members, or at the card parties, tea parties and supper parties thrown by her friends. Occasionally she held such parties herself. At one she entertained 12 people to tea, cards and supper, and on another occasion she invited 19 people to a card party, presumably making five tables for whist.[7] She played cards with her next-door neighbour Dr Proctor when he was in residence, and was occasionally invited to card parties at the Bishop's Palace. Bishop Bathurst was a sociable and popular man, and a skilled and enthusiastic whist player. Unfortunately he had less merit as a cleric and administrator, and Norwich was dubbed 'the Dead See' during his bishopric.[8]

Betsy's diaries for 1808 and 1809 regularly mention old friends and acquaintances. Unfortunately her diary for 1810 is missing. Sadly two of her old friends died during that year: her lawyer William Foster, and John Herring, the ex-mayor of Norwich. Her surviving correspondence seems to have been culled rather more stringently after 1805. Perhaps Betsy destroyed some letters because she did not wish them to be read by her descendants, or perhaps her children did so after her death. Many of Edward's letters to his mother remain, but there are far fewer from Elizabeth, Mary and George. The lone survivors from presumably many letters she received from friends after 1808 are a few from Lady Winterton, Lady Gordon, Mrs Man and Mrs Madan, and single letters from a few others. Fortunately we know something from her remaining correspondence, her surviving diaries and local newspapers of the local, national and international events that affected her wider family and her friends.

The seemingly endless war against France continued. A technological weapon was added to Britain's arsenal when a chain of telegraph stations was built to pass messages between the Admiralty office in London and sub-offices on the East coast. In December 1807 the chain of stations between London, Norwich and Yarmouth (including one on Strumpshaw Hill, near William Nelson's home) was completed by one on the hill at Thorpe St Andrew, just outside Norwich. Orders sent from the Admiralty office in London in January 1808 took just 17 minutes to arrive in Yarmouth.[9]

By 1805 the threat of invasion had receded once more, so volunteer regiments were gradually stood down or disbanded. Local defence forces were reorganized in July 1808 when the Local Militia was created, an infantry force consisting of men elected by ballot at county level to serve for four years, and attached to existing militia regiments. Volunteers were retained only if they could pay for themselves, effectively limiting them to the yeomanry, while the landed classes continued to provide officers for both militias and yeomanry.[10] Many former Norfolk Volunteers, presumably those from the poorer classes, transferred to the newly created Local Militia in July 1808.

The war had cast its shadow over much of Europe, and had extended as far as the West Indies, South America, South Africa and Egypt by 1808. News from the European front was mixed. A British expeditionary force of 40,000 men under the command of Lord Chatham sailed for the Scheldt estuary in July 1809 with orders to take Antwerp, but delays, ineptitude and disease meant the mission was a disaster. Some 3,000 men died and 11,000 sick and injured were evacuated during a protracted and ignominious retreat that was finally completed in December.

British forces in the Iberian peninsula were beginning to make headway against the French, although General Moore's death at Corunna in January 1809 and the subsequent retreat was a low point. Sir Arthur Wellesley pushed on into Spain after landing at Lisbon in April 1809, and was successful against the French at Talavera in July, for which he was created Viscount Wellington. The situation looked hopeful, but the French generals rallied and mounted a counter-attack that forced Wellington and his men to retreat to the comparative safety of southern Portugal in 1810.

Sir Orford Gordon, Lady Gordon's son, fought in Spain early in 1809, possibly at Corunna, then was invalided back to England. When Lady Gordon wrote to Betsy in July he had recovered and was on his way to Portsmouth to take ship for Spain, where he was to join General Picton, Wellington's second in command, as his aide-de-camp.[11]

The redoubtable Lady Winterton's letters to Betsy were full of family gossip. During 1809 the Turnour family was scandalized when the heir to the earldom, Edward, Lord Turnour, married against his father's wishes. He was 25, but by convention should still have obtained consent, and had already been warned of the dire consequences if he married a woman who was neither aristocratic nor affluent. Lucy Louisa was the 'penniless' daughter of John Heys of Upper Sunbury in Middlesex. Edward's family had already managed to extricate him from a previous youthful dalliance with a pretty woman with no money. Lord Winterton's besotted heir found himself cut out of his father's will and had his income reduced to a small yearly allowance. The estate was entailed so he could not be prevented from inheriting that or the title, but Lord Winterton made sure all the income was invested elsewhere. Lady Winterton gleefully told Betsy that when Edward succeeded, it would be to an empty house, 'as all the Furniture together with the Linen & Plate here is all ordered to be sold, therefore the young Lordling may be considered as an empty Title, all ways'. She felt Edward's new relatives richly deserved their impecunious son-in-law because they had actively encouraged the marriage.[12]

Betsy's own financial situation had become a good deal more secure by 1808. Her children were all grown and independent, and although Edward continued to ask periodically for loans, his mother now tended to ignore these requests. However, she did experience considerable inconvenience in 1808: her banker, Sir Roger Kerrison of Brooke Hall, died suddenly on 16 June, and his bank collapsed later that year.[13] It had been found to have tax and creditor debts of around £460,000 (approximately £15.5 million in today's terms). The creditors eventually received 16s.4d in the pound. Fortunately Betsy had rarely kept significant sums in the bank. She used it mainly to receive the half-yearly income from her investments and annuities, then withdrew sufficient cash to pay her bills and cover her living expenses, and reinvested the surplus. She had heard rumours just before the bank's failure and had wisely withdrawn her balance. However she had to change her banking arrangements, and opted for Harvey and Hudson's, where she went on 5 July to sign revised letters of attorney which were forwarded to the Bank of England.

Here the complications began. A zealous official at the Bank of England requested further proof of her widowed status. Betsy asked her friend Dr William Vyse, rector of Sundridge, for an attested copy of Edward Peach's burial entry in the Sundridge parish register. Dr Vyse duly obliged; Betsy received the required copy on Christmas Eve and immediately submitted it to the Bank of England.[14] But the Bank then asked for evidence of her first husband's death, her father's will, her second marriage and Peach's death. All this had to be attested by a justice of the peace. Betsy begged Dr Vyse to help once more, and fortunately he agreed. He and the parish clerk of Sundridge had to take the parish register to a magistrate who administered an oath before the copy of Peach's burial entry was signed and attested. Betsy received the completed document from Dr Vyse on 24 February 1809, and immediately sent it on to the Bank of England, where it was finally approved and the letters of attorney accepted.[15] So it took eight months before she could receive the interest on her investments and annuities via Harvey and Hudson's Bank. A widowed man would have had considerably less difficulty changing his financial arrangements.

Elizabeth and her children visited Betsy regularly, but she did not return the visits because she did not wish to meet James Thompson. George lived in lodgings at Bury St Edmunds and made his social life there. Edward had acted as his brother's curate at Limpenhoe, Southwood and Wickhampton, but this arrangement no longer suited him for tax reasons, so George had frequently to come from Bury St Edmunds to take services himself. He typically visited his mother on these weekends and used her house as a base.

In March 1809 the two brothers had a disagreement about George's failure to repay a loan from Edward. George pleaded temporary cash flow problems following the collapse of Kerrison's Bank, but Edward refused to accept this and worked himself up into a fury, firing off letters to both Betsy and George. Eventually George sent a messenger to Reedham with the cash. He must have felt these demands were uncalled for when Edward himself was notorious for failing to repay his debts.[16]

Edward had developed an obsession about the non-payment or late payment of tithes. Possibly his farmer parishioners found it hard to raise the money, but they might also have been using the general discontent with tithe payments to inconvenience and irritate their unpopular parish priest. In 1808 a Reedham farmer, Mr Baker, failed to set out his tithes according to the law, and Edward brought an action against him at the Norfolk Assizes. Lord Chief Justice Mansfield heard it at Norwich in August 1809. Mansfield ruled that Baker had acted contrary to tithe law and directed the jury to find in Edward's favour, although with a marked lack of impartiality he added that he was sorry to have to do so. The jury asked what was the lowest amount of damages and costs they could award. Damages were finally assessed at £8, which meant Edward must have been considerably out of pocket even though he had won.[17]

Undeterred, Edward brought a similar case against Mr Maddison, another Reedham farmer, at the Lent Assizes at Thetford on 19 March 1810. The (different) judge on this occasion was sympathetic to Maddison's explanation of the circumstances, and directed the jury to find in his favour.[18] Most reasonable people would have given up at this stage, but Edward was determined to bring his recalcitrant parishioners to heel, and in August 1810 he brought an identical action against Mr Long. Although the verdict went in his favour, damages were fixed at a derisory £12. To add insult to injury, Mr Baker sued him at the same Assizes for the losses he had sustained through the 1808 dispute, and was awarded £150 in damages.[19] Edward's tithe crusade ground to a halt for a while after this setback. Not only had his financial losses been heavy, his relationship with a significant number of his parishioners must have been damaged irreparably.

1808 saw the beginning of a sad and dramatic part of Mary's life. The year opened well enough with the safe delivery of her fourth child, Jessica, on 30 January, and continued without incident until Horace junior came down with the measles in mid-March. He made a safe recovery, and on 9 May Betsy, Mary, the three eldest children and their two nurses set off for Cromer to enjoy the sea air. It is doubtful whether they derived much benefit from the short holiday, as there were only two fine days of respite from wet, cold and windy weather. The visit was cut short by the news that Mary's father-in-law, James Beevor, had died on 21 May. They returned post-haste to Norwich the same evening, and joined in the family mourning. Sadly while James Beevor's burial service was taking place at St Saviour's in Norwich on 27 March, four-month-old Jessica died at Old Catton. Betsy's diary does not indicate the cause of death. Mary was devastated and sank into a deep depression.

Betsy could appreciate only too well how hard it was to bear the death of so young a child, since she had lost two children in infancy herself. The Leathes family and a few close friends gave Mary as much support as they could, but Horace was of course abroad, and she was inconsolable and completely incapable of dealing with the situation. Edward and George Leathes organized the funeral and Jessica was buried in the Leathes family vault at Reedham church on 2 June 1808. It took several months for Mary to recover, but by September she had begun to resume her social life.

At the end of August the *Glory* failed to return to England with the East India fleet.[20] It might simply have been that Horace's return had been delayed because his business in India had taken longer to transact than usual. Betsy did not record the progress of the *Glory*'s 1806–8 voyage to India in her diary, as she had done for Horace's previous voyages. Horace no longer wrote directly to her, and since she no longer lived in Mary's household, she did not necessarily know when a letter from him arrived at St Clements House.

Mary appeared to be fully returned to health by the beginning of 1809. In January she entertained a house guest for two weeks, and on 24 February she held a large dinner party. But her mother and brothers were only too well aware that she was still unstable, and they continued to monitor her state of mind through regular visits. Then her fragile composure was shattered on 26 April when she heard (presumably from the London offices of the East India Company) that since the *Glory* had failed to arrive home with the last two East India fleets, in the absence of any reports to the contrary she must be presumed missing.[21]

In late June Lady Gordon told Betsy that she had seen a newspaper report of the recent arrival of the latest East India fleet in which the *Glory* was listed as a missing ship. She sympathized wholeheartedly with Mary, recognizing the strain that the news must have imposed on her and on Horace's mother and siblings.[22]

Mary was once more completely unable to cope with the situation, and refused to leave St Clements House. Yet again Betsy, Edward and George did what they could to boost her spirits. Gradually she regained her composure and made occasional visits to relatives and close friends, lapsing spasmodically into illness and isolation before seeming to recover again. The final blow came on 10 December, when Mary received an official letter from the East India Company telling her that all hope for the *Glory* had been abandoned.[23]

Some of the circumstances were known. Between 1807 and 1809 British merchant shipping in the Indian Ocean was particularly vulnerable to predation by French privateers and by French naval vessels based on the islands of Ile de France and Bourbon (modern Mauritius and Réunion). So when the *Glory* sailed from Madras on 26 October 1808 with eight other Indiamen, they were accompanied by a naval escort, HMS *Albion*.[24] Hurricanes were also an ever-present danger to shipping in the Indian Ocean between November and March, so the voyage was likely to be more than averagely dangerous. The little fleet, one of two to sail from India between late 1808 and early 1809, was carrying saltpetre, which was vital to the British war effort in Spain and Portugal. They followed a route that ran east of Ceylon (Sri Lanka) then due south to avoid the Ile de France. On 20 November a storm blew up and by the following day it had become a hurricane; the fleet was scattered and each vessel was left to fend for itself for three days in appalling conditions. Between 12 and 16 January 1809 HMS *Albion* and six Indiamen, all of them badly damaged, limped into Table Bay, Cape Town. The three remaining Indiamen, the *Lord Nelson*, the *Experiment* and the *Glory*, vanished without trace.

Later in 1809 the East India Company held an enquiry into the loss of the three ships. The evidence it was given highlighted that the *Glory* was poorly built, handled badly and had difficulty keeping up with the other ships in the fleet. It also revealed inadequate manning levels on virtually all of the Indiamen, a perennial problem caused by royal navy captains who made up their own manning levels by impressing the best and fittest crewmen from the merchant ships that had the misfortune to be in port at the same time. The captains of the *Lord Nelson* and the *Glory* had advertised for more passengers a few days before their departure from Madras, so there were no surviving final passenger lists, and the East India Company could not even be sure of the identity of some of those on board. After examining the evidence and seeking further information from the Company's overseas agents, the enquiry was left with little alternative but to conclude that the ships had been irrevocably separated from the rest of the fleet by the hurricane and then overwhelmed by the sea.[25]

The process of getting her dead husband's will through probate and settling his estate was likely to take many months, so Mary was effectively left without sufficient means to support herself and her children in the short term. The lease of St Clement's House was in Horace's name and had to be surrendered, so Betsy offered to share her home with her daughter and grandchildren. George travelled to Norwich from Bury St Edmunds on 18 December to help Mary pack up her furniture and household belongings, and on 27 December she and her children moved into the Upper Close.

According to the will Horace had made in September 1807, just before he left Portsmouth for India for the last time, he had a seven-sixteenth share in the *Glory* and was additionally entitled to wages, profit and prize-money, all of which was to be paid to his widow in the event of his death. Mary's brother Edward was named as one of the executors, who were instructed to sell his share in the ship and to invest the capital in order to provide an income for his wife and family.[26] Horace's share of the *Glory* had been insured for £5,000, and together with his East India Company shares and other assets, this should have left Mary quite comfortably off. But the insurance claim proved complicated because the Company had insured the vessel and its cargo with many different underwriters. Mary had received an unspecified, but probably rather small, part of the £5,000 by March 1810, the rest being dependent on information from India. But the months passed by without news, and it became less and less likely that she would receive much more money.[27]

The pension she was granted by the East India Company seems to have been equally disappointing. Lord Winterton lobbied the Company's directors on Mary's behalf in an attempt to obtain a more generous settlement, but to no avail. The directors, it seems, were bound to abide by Company rules, and a spokesman wrote, 'I most sincerely wish the Pension had been more liberal, but make no doubt but what M[rs.] Beevor will receive such additional support from her Relatives & Connexions, as will enable her to live comfortably, and bring up her little family in a very respectable way.'[28] Unfortunately Mary seems to have received little practical or financial help from anyone other than her mother. So although her husband had made plans that should have left her comfortable, she found herself in very modest circumstances following his death, and there was little hope that her situation would improve.

18   Twilight

Betsy celebrated her 63rd birthday in May 1811. She was still physically and socially active, but suffered from increasingly poor health in the form of frequent coughs, colds, chest complaints and breathlessness. In December 1812 Lady Winterton, who was troubled in much the same way, warned her to take better care of her health during the coming winter months, and try harder to prevent a recurrence of the chest infection that she had suffered from during the previous winter. Asthma-like illnesses had troubled Betsy in the past and it seems that they continued to do so, because Lady Gordon referred to her tendency to be troubled by shortage of breath. She fell ill again in December 1813, but began to recover during January 1814, and by spring her friends were able to comment on the improvement in her health.[1]

It was just as well that Betsy was confined to her house during the winter: the atrocious weather of January and February 1814 saw freezing conditions and heavy falls of snow cripple road travel in and out of Norwich, bringing life almost everywhere to a standstill. The River Yare froze over and barges were unable to travel between Great Yarmouth and Norwich, preventing the movement of vital coal and food supplies, and causing great hardship in all the communities along the river. Towards the end of January Edward Leathes complained that Reedham was so effectively cut off from the rest of the world that he might as well have been living at the North Pole. The weather relaxed its grip early in February, but it took several more days for the river to thaw, so normal barge service did not resume until the middle of the month. It was fortunate that he had killed a pig in the middle of January, Edward told Betsy, so that at least he and his household did not starve.

How much worse must conditions have been for the poor everywhere. In Norwich alone some £2,600 was raised by subscription in January to relieve their sufferings by providing food and fuel. In addition the Friars' Society, Norwich's foremost philanthropic group, distributed 28,170 quarts of soup and the same number of penny loaves among the needy.[2]

Despite the physical restrictions imposed on her by the advancing years, Betsy still led a fairly active social life in the form of calls, visits, tea-drinking and parties. Balls, concerts, assemblies and theatre visits still figured in her life, but with diminishing frequency. Her favourite pastime continued to be card games, either with family or friends at one of the player's homes, or as part of a party, assembly or ball. This physically undemanding entertainment was particularly suited to ladies and gentlemen of more mature years. Whist was the game played most frequently, with quadrille and picquet the next favourites; tredrille or tresdrille (an adaptation of quadrille for three players) and commerce were also played occasionally. At the end of 1811 Betsy calculated that she had made a profit of 7s.6d from cards

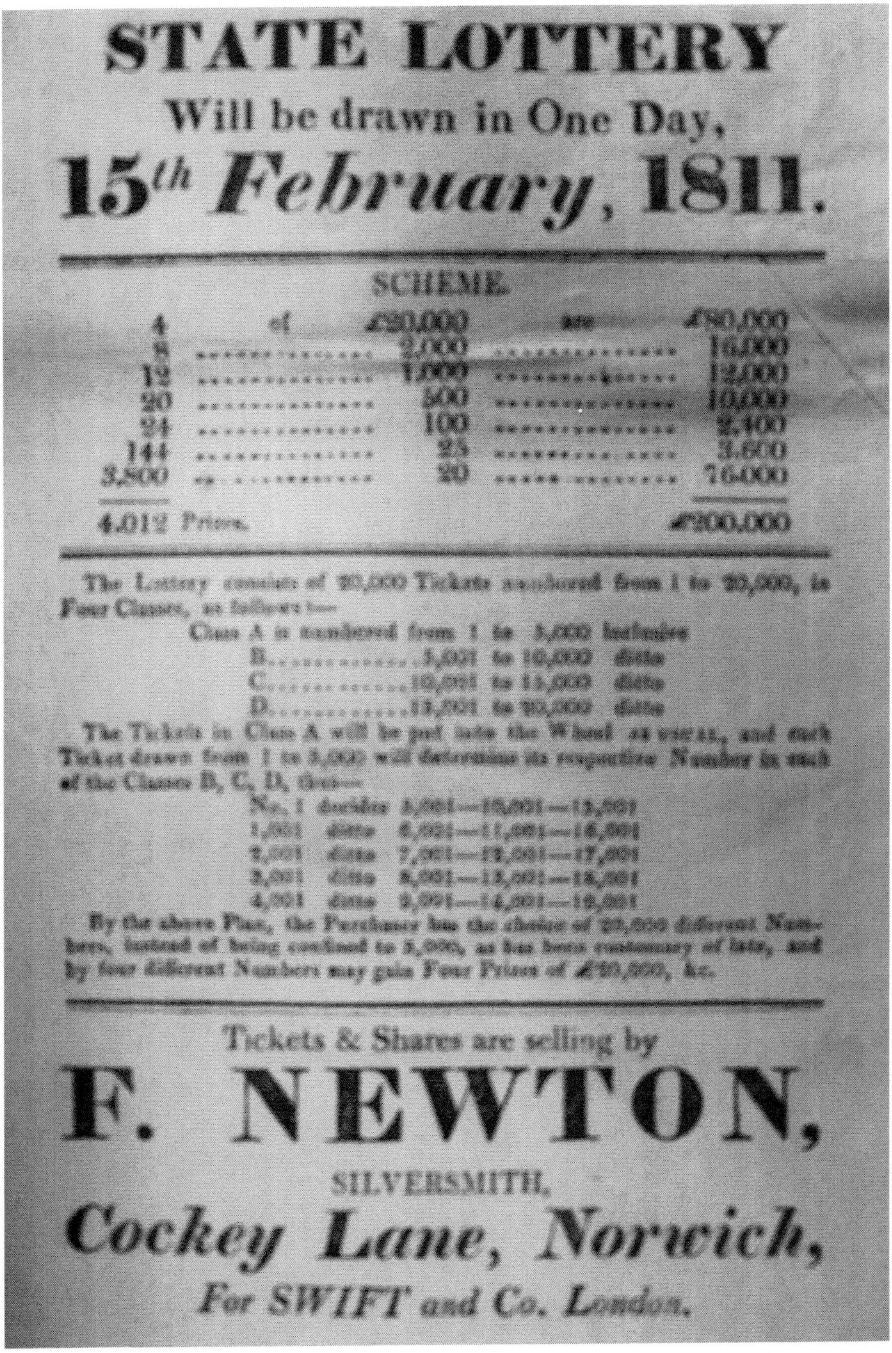

Lottery flyer dated 15 February 1811 (NRO BOL 2/122/4/1, 740 X3)

during the year. Cards were not her only vice, for she continued to enjoy a flutter on the state lottery, and purchased tickets, or shares in tickets, right up until the end of her life.[3]

Ladies belonging to the middle and upper ranks of society were expected to interest themselves in philanthropic activities. Betsy rarely took an active role in such endeavours, but was always ready to donate money when charitable subscriptions were raised in the city. She visited the 'Lancasterian School for Boys', as it was then known, three weeks after it was opened in Norwich on 2 April 1811, so she may well have contributed a modest sum to the public subscription that had funded it.[4] Lancaster was a Quaker who advocated the monitorial system of public elementary education, where teaching was carried out by the most able among the older students and supervised by a single teacher. His visit to Norwich on 23 March 1810 to give lectures on his system of education had inspired a number of interested individuals to open the public subscription, which soon reached its target.

Inspired by her late father's interest in astronomy, Betsy had a scientific turn of mind, and had in the past attended lectures, demonstrations and exhibitions on various subjects of popular scientific interest, a recreation that was considered entirely suitable for ladies of her rank. On another level, but still considered to be of scientific interest at the time, were the freak shows or raree shows that travelled around the country, stopping at inns and taverns to exhibit rare or deformed animals, animals who performed tricks and people with anatomical abnormalities. Such shows appealed to many visitors, ranging from those who had a genuine scientific interest to those who just came to gape or ridicule, with many shades of curiosity in between. On 9 April 1811 Betsy went to see just such an exhibition. 'The celebrated Miss Beffin, born deficient of arms, hands, and legs, aged 26, and only 37 inches high, exhibited herself in this city; using her needle, scissors, &c. drawing landscapes, and painting miniatures, and doing many other wonderful things, principally with her MOUTH.'[5] Although such displays would now be considered cruel and degrading, at least the income they generated gave people with extraordinary physical handicaps some sort of a living in an age when there was no welfare state.

Music was Betsy's favourite cultural pursuit, and she was swift to take advantage of the growing number of music festivals in Norwich, although she attended only those concerts that suited her musical tastes. A music festival under the direction of Charles John Beckwith, the Cathedral organist, ran for four days between 8 and 11 October 1811 and featured some of the most prominent vocalists of the era: Madame Catalani, Mrs Bianchi, Mr Braham and Mr Bellamy. It was patronised by the social élite of the city and county, and the total takings amounted to £1,800. Edward Leathes attended all four days of the festival, while Betsy attended the evening concert on 10 October and took her granddaughter Mary Beevor with her.[6] Another music festival was staged in Norwich between 5 and 8 October 1813 under the direction of Mr Pettet. Again, some of the country's best

To the Lovers of Natural Curiosities.

To be seen ALIVE,

IN A GENTEEL ROOM,

At Mr. PECK's, Church-Stile, Market-place, Norwich,

THE LARGEST

RATTLESNAKE

EVER SEEN IN ENGLAND,

Forty-two Years old, near nine feet long, in full Health and Vigour.

He is well secured, so that Ladies and Gentlemen may view him without the least Danger.

THE Proprietor of the Rattlesnake begs leave to return thanks to those Ladies and Gentlemen who have honoured him with a visit, and begs leave to inform them, that he has just arrived from America, TWO NON-DESCRIPT SNAKES ALIVE, allowed, by the best judges of Natural History, to be the most beautiful of all the reptile tribe. To be viewed the following week only as they leave Norwich at the expiration of that time.

N. B. A Quadruped to be put into the Rattlesnake's Cage at Twelve o'clock on Thursday next.

Admittance to Ladies and Gentlemen, 1s.

NORWICH: PRINTED BY STEVENSON AND MATCHETT.

Flyer giving details of a travelling snake show that visited Norwich in April 1801

vocalists performed and the festival was presumably as successful as its predecessors. A special three-day music festival was held in June 1814 to mark victory over the French. Betsy may well have attended some of the concerts in 1812, 1813 and 1814, but because the diaries for those years have not survived it is difficult to be certain.

The composition of Betsy's social circle in Norwich probably changed very little after 1810, but her diary for 1811 indicated that she had made a few new acquaintances. The Reverend Edward Valpy was appointed headmaster of Norwich Grammar School in 1811, following the resignation of Betsy's friend Dr Forster and his removal to Windsor. Betsy was swift to make Mrs Valpy's acquaintance and was soon on visiting terms. Another new figure on the cathedral scene was Dr Landon, appointed prebend in the place of Dr Philip Wodehouse, who had died

on 12 February 1811. Betsy again observed all the social niceties and the Landons'
names began to appear in the pages of her diary. Colonel Charles and Lady Anne
Chadd of Pinkney Hall near Fakenham also became well known to Betsy and her
family.

Lady Anne Chadd was the eldest daughter of Lord Winterton, and Charles
Chadd was the son and heir of Sir George Chadd of Thursford, although father
and son had been estranged for several years. The couple had married in 1810,
and by February 1811 Lady Anne was pregnant, much to the delight of Lady
Winterton. She gave birth to a boy in Norwich on 5 September 1811, and Betsy
was in attendance during the birth. As one of Lady Winterton's oldest friends,
she took the young couple under her wing. She took these responsibilities very
seriously, and scarcely a day of the Chadds' stay in the city went by without a
visit from Betsy and occasionally from Elizabeth Thompson. They returned to
Pinkney on 1 October. The baby was christened Edward Henry: Edward for his
maternal grandfather and Henry for his godfather, Henry Bathurst, bishop of
Norwich. Even the birth of his grandson failed to reconcile Sir George Chadd
with his son; he refused to act as godfather and forbade his daughter to act as
godmother.[7]

Details of the last three years or so of Betsy's life are hazy because her diaries
have not survived and her extant correspondence for those years is sparse. But it is
still possible to piece some of her story together, partly from the remaining letters
and partly from other contemporary sources. By 1811 most of her correspondents
were old friends connected with her childhood in Woodstock or her marriages.
Ann Man (formerly Ann Loggin of Woodstock) was perhaps Betsy's oldest friend;
their correspondence was infrequent, but they kept each other abreast of family
news. It seems unlikely that Betsy ceased to exchange letters with Elizabeth Merry,
her former sister-in-law, although none survive: perhaps they were removed or
destroyed at a later date. Betsy's contact with her uncle (by marriage) William
Nelson, rector of Strumpshaw and Braydeston since 1764, became increasingly
sparse after 1805, but they appear to have remained on good terms. Nelson died
in late November 1812, shortly after his second wife Susanna, and was buried
at Strumpshaw on 2 December. He left no direct heirs: his son Billy had died
suddenly in 1791 aged 22, leaving a daughter Sandra who died in 1803. Neither
Betsy nor her children were mentioned in his will.[8]

One old friend who had not figured in Betsy's correspondence or diaries for
many years was Edward Loveden of Buscot Park near Farringdon. Betsy wrote to
him at the beginning of April 1811, probably to send a message of comfort and
support while he was trying to divorce his adulterous fourth wife.[9] If he replied,
his letter has not survived. Two of her Sundridge friends, Mrs Madan and her
brother Dr Vyse, sympathized greatly with Mary Beevor's situation following
Horace's death, and corresponded with Betsy in 1811 during their attempt to get
Horace junior into a suitable school. Mrs Madan's last surviving letter to Betsy was

written in 1814 following the death of her husband, the bishop of Peterborough, and her removal to Lichfield, where she had purchased a house.[10]

Lady Gordon, who had outlived her husband and eldest son, wrote to Betsy in 1813 to say that her youngest son, Sir Orford Gordon, had at last returned home from Wellington's army in Spain after the victory at Vittoria in June 1813. He was all that a fond mother could wish for, she told Betsy, although she would have been much happier had he been a well man.[11]

The most regular of Betsy's correspondents was Lady Winterton, and the two women continued to exchange visits on rare occasions. They were on very friendly terms and exchanged interesting information about their families. Lord and Lady Winterton were very active on Mary Beevor's behalf in 1811, although they were somewhat preoccupied with Lady Anne Chadd's pregnancy and the death of Lady Winterton's sister that August. Like Dr Vyse and Mrs Madan, they tried to influence the governors of Christ's Hospital to secure Horace Beevor junior a place at the school.[12] The Wintertons made short visits to Norwich on at least two occasions in October and November 1811, while they were staying with their daughter, son-in-law and baby grandson at Pinkney Hall. On 13 October 1811 Lord and Lady Winterton met up with George Reading Leathes at his new living of Gissing, before leaving to tour the Winterton land holdings in Norfolk. They visited Norwich again in November before finally returning home.[13]

The eventful lives of her children sometimes overshadowed Betsy's own life, and certainly Edward Leathes and Mary Beevor kept her busy until the end of her life. Elizabeth Thompson gave birth to her seventh child, a daughter, on 9 March 1811. The demands of caring for seven children, ranging in age from infancy to 16, and coping with the undisguised hostility between her mother and her husband since 1802, meant that Elizabeth was under considerable strain. She visited Betsy from time to time, but her children were the most regular visitors to the house in Upper Close.

It is difficult to judge how stable the Thompson marriage was prior to 1812, but it seems likely that it broke down early that year. In April 1812 Lady Winterton wrote to Betsy referring to a traumatic event in Elizabeth's life, no doubt in response to what Betsy had told her. She judged Elizabeth's plight severe, and expressed the hope that she and her children would be happy once more when they were established in a new home in which she was independent of her husband. It would be a struggle for Elizabeth to bring the children up on her own, even if she received financial support from her estranged husband. Lady Winterton praised Elizabeth's forbearance and her attempts to make peace with her husband, an attitude that she hoped would eventually be returned with interest.[14]

George Reading Leathes had settled into a comfortable rut, moving between his house in Bury St Edmunds and his aunt's home at Herringfleet Hall. He occasionally visited his mother in Norwich and his brother Edward at Reedham, on the few occasions when he took services himself at Wickhampton, Limpenhoe and Southwood. In 1811, thanks to the patronage of Elizabeth Merry, George added the livings of Flordon and Gissing to the two he already held. He was duly instituted to Flordon on 7 March and to Gissing on 8 March.[15] He was then responsible for four parishes containing five churches: Gissing (near Diss), Flordon (near Wymondham), Wickhampton, and Limpenhoe with Southwood (two Broadland parishes close to Reedham). The last three churches formed a cohesive group, but the first two were several miles apart and widely separated from the Broadland group. George had already experienced considerable difficulty in commuting from Bury St Edmunds, where he was reader at St James's church, to serve his three Broadland churches, so it seemed unlikely he would be able to cope with five.

Betsy was clearly much impressed by her youngest son's good fortune. The livings yielded a reasonable income, and Gissing rectory was sufficiently large and well-appointed for him to entertain Lord and Lady Winterton and several of his own family members in November.[16] George was able to serve Flordon and Gissing churches on a regular basis, but relied on locum clergy for the three Broadland churches.

George did however face potential problems from Sir William Robert Kemp, the young baronet who lived at nearby Gissing Hall. His father, Sir John Kemp, had been patron of both livings when the previous incumbent was instituted in 1761, but the patronage had passed to the Leathes family of Herringfleet by the time of George's induction. Sir William had taken holy orders himself, and had expressed a desire to reacquire the patronage of the two livings. George perhaps did not realize this when he arrived at Gissing, and probably tried to ingratiate himself with Sir William, even though the latter made his intentions quite clear.[17] It was quite probable that George would eventually lose these livings as a result.

Mary's situation was far from ideal. Her pension from the East India Company was modest, and the fact that she and her children were still living with Betsy could well mean that the Company's insurers made no further payments to her after 1810. Lady Winterton described her case as particularly hard, since had lost not only her husband but all her property as well.[18] Attempts to intervene on her behalf came to nothing, so Mary had no choice but to make the best of what she had. Adjustments were made, and thanks to Betsy's willingness to give her daughter and grandchildren a permanent home, they all managed to settle down and enjoy life once more. Mary was popular and already well established in Norwich society, so her social life quickly became busy when she emerged from the formal mourning period. By early January 1811 she was being actively courted by one of her late husband's cousins, Charles Beevor, a barrister who later changed his name to Lombe when he inherited the Lombe estate at Great Melton, near Norwich.[19] He was assiduous in his attentions and a frequent visitor to the Upper Close, but seems to have spent as much of his time playing cards with Betsy as he did pleading his suit with Mary. Not surprisingly, he faded from the picture later that year.

A gentleman in evening dress and wearing slippers (left); a gentleman in morning or walking dress and wearing 'Hessian' boots (right); both c. 1810

One of Mary's many friends, Mrs Finch, then invited her to her home at Henny Street in Essex, just over the Suffolk county border near Sudbury. Betsy agreed to look after the three children, so Mary and her maid set off from Norwich for a visit that lasted for five months. During this stay Mary either met or renewed her acquaintance with 34-year-old Colonel John Cheetham Mortlock, the eldest son of John Mortlock III, mayor of Cambridge and banker to both the university and the town.[20] His brother Edmund was a friend of George Reading Leathes, so possibly he and Mary had met before her visit to Henny. Their relationship blossomed into romance between 17 June and Mary's return to Norwich on 15 October 1811. When John Mortlock travelled to Norwich on 7 November for a six-week stay, he did so as Mary's chosen suitor, and shortly afterwards they were engaged to marry. Lady Winterton met him when she and her husband visited Norwich in November; she heartily approved of Mary's choice and hoped that on this occasion she would have happier prospects in the 'Matrimonial Lottery'.[21]

The couple were married on 31 March 1812 by the Reverend John Walker at Gissing church, and the 27-year-old bride was given away by her brother George. The wedding was attended by a number of Mortlock relatives, including Sir Edmund and Lady Sarah Lacon of Ormesby Hall (the latter was related to both Beevor and Mortlock families) and the two Misses Lacon; Reverend Edmund, Thomas, William and Marianne Mortlock (the groom's brothers and sister); Margaret Crowe (née Beevor) and of course Betsy herself. Immediately after the wedding breakfast the bride and groom left for the Mortlock family seat at Abington, near Cambridge.[22]

Lady Winterton was swift to point out that for a young widow with little or no fortune and three children, Mary had been remarkably fortunate in her second marriage. As the eldest son, John Cheetham Mortlock was the heir to his father's considerable fortune and his position in Cambridge, so from his parents' perspective the marriage was less advantageous. But John Mortlock III and his wife Elizabeth pragmatically accepted their son's choice and welcomed Mary into their family. Lady Winterton was much impressed by their 'gratifying and respectful' behaviour towards the couple.[23]

By June Mary was pregnant. Betsy rushed to Cambridge to be present at the birth of Elizabeth in January 1813, and stayed for some weeks. Another daughter was born in 1814, and again Betsy went to stay with the couple for the birth and Mary's lying-in period. After a period of heartbreak and difficulties, Mary was now comfortably and happily settled.

Edward Leathes celebrated his 34th birthday in April 1811, but age had brought him neither wisdom nor contentment, and he continued to lead an unsettled and dissatisfied existence. He spent most of his time at Reedham, where he farmed his glebe and served his churches, leaving his mother to do much of his shopping, run his errands and change his library books. He visited Norwich only for musical events, occasional family gatherings and legal proceedings. His relationships with his leading parishioners were already poor, but they deteriorated even further in 1811. First Edward appealed against the Overseers' accounts in July, then in October he appealed against a conviction he had received under the Highways Act. Both appeals were dismissed, but his actions almost certainly exacerbated the situation.[24] 1812 began badly for Edward when his second appeal against his Highways Act conviction was dismissed without costs. Much worse was to come.[25]

In June 1812 he was involved in a court case so serious that it was transferred from the Lent Assizes at Thetford to the Court of King's Bench, for trial at the Norwich Summer Assizes by special jury. Edward asked his brother George to compile a list of local men he thought suitable to sit on a special jury, and send it to a firm of London solicitors. Soon afterwards he made a short visit to Norwich to prepare for the arrival of a Mr Trower, presumably his London lawyer. He asked Betsy to find this man lodgings in Norwich for Assize Week, of sufficient quality to keep him in a good mood.[26] Betsy and her children so thoroughly purged her correspondence of all mention of this affair that the only surviving reference is in a letter from Lady Winterton that eluded them. Our main source today is the report in the *Norwich Mercury* on Saturday 1 August 1812.

Edward faced two charges of intent to commit homosexual assault, one brought by David Wasey and the other by Adam Dent. These were serious charges that, if proved, could result in disgrace and imprisonment. Homosexuality was universally viewed as moral corruption in early 19th-century England; most people responded to known homosexuals with abhorrence, and the legal punishment was usually harsh. Had Edward been found guilty of sodomy, a capital offence until 1861, he might have been hanged.

The *Norwich Mercury* reporter described this as 'a crime at which nature shudders', to protect the delicate sensibilities of his readers. The case for the defence was eloquently and authoritatively presented by the Solicitor General, who took the line that the accusations were ridiculous and could not therefore be given credence. He concluded a powerful speech by saying he did not think it necessary to call any witnesses for the defence, to cross-examine the prosecution witnesses or question the defence attorney, because that would be tantamount to insulting the intelligence of the jury members and violating his own conscience. The special jury retired to consider the prosecution and defence, and quickly returned with a verdict of not guilty, which was 'most honourable to the Reverend defendant and to the satisfaction of a most respectable and crowded court'. So Edward was acquitted of both the charges.[27]

Although this case was not unique, it was extremely unusual. A year earlier the Right Reverend and Honourable Percy Jocelyn, bishop of Ferns and Leighlin, had been similarly accused. He was acquitted and successfully prosecuted his accuser for bringing false charges against him.[28] This case had been given massive publicity at the time, and might still have been fresh in the minds of many people, including the respectable crowd in the Norwich courtroom.

Although Edward was acquitted, he was left in a difficult position. He had already made himself locally unpopular through his court actions against delinquent tithe payers, and all these cases had been well aired in the regional press. Innocent or not, the lingering innuendo might well have made his life intolerable, not only in his own parishes but in wider local society. He was already somewhat reclusive, and the poisonous atmosphere that followed the trial must have made him even more so. Even so, his acquittal came as an enormous relief to his family and friends. It is clear from Betsy's correspondence that his family had tried to spread the opinion that the charges were false and malicious, and that Edward was completely free of blame. Lady Winterton hoped that after the acquittal Betsy and her family could put the unjust accusations and all the distress that they had caused behind them, but that does not mean they managed to do so.[29]

Edward did his best to return to some semblance of normality after the trial, and to pick up the threads of parish life. He continued to take divine service in his churches, and gave a dinner of turkey, roast beef and plum pudding to his workers on Christmas Day. However his autocratic manner, the impossibly high standards he imposed and the low wages he offered had always made it difficult for him to recruit and keep suitable servants, and after 1812 the situation became worse. He relied almost entirely on Betsy to recruit servants for him, but he continually found fault with their work and regularly sacked them. Not surprisingly, it became virtually impossible for her to find him cooks, washerwomen, maid-servants or farm workers. Edward was also permanently short of money, a situation doubtless made worse by his cumulative legal costs.

He seems to have managed to stay out of the Assize Court in 1813, but at the County Assizes in July 1814 he was sued by one of his Reedham parishioners for damages sustained when a number of sheep were worried by his dog Tiger. Damages of £60 were awarded, giving him yet another financial headache.[30] It seems his parishioners were more than willing to keep up the pressure on their unpopular parish priest.

The effects on Edward's family can only be guessed at, but they may well have contributed to the decline in Betsy's health and well-being between 1812 and 1815. She had always suffered from bouts of depressive illness during critical periods in her life, in all probability triggered by stress. There is no documentation, but it would be surprising if she had not suffered more from stress and depression during these years. This, in conjunction with her other known illnesses, would have drained her physical and mental resources.

Still, her spirits must have been raised when news arrived in Norwich on 6 April 1814 of the Allied Army's victorious entry into Paris on 31 March. This was marked in the city by bonfires and public displays of joy. More celebrations followed the news received on 9 April of Bonaparte's abdication and the restoration of the Bourbon monarchy. The war with France had lasted for 21 long years, and news that a peace treaty had been signed in Paris on 30 May was greeted with great relief and joy. There were enthusiastic celebrations all over the country, with illuminations, fireworks, congratulatory addresses to the great and good by local worthies, the conferring of knighthoods and peerages by the king, church and cathedral services, celebratory dinners, public dinners for the poor, and in Norwich a special three-day music festival. No one suspected that the peace they had craved for so long would be brief, and that by June 1815 the Allies would again be fighting for national survival following Napoleon's escape from Elba on 1 March.

Betsy's diary for 1815 opened with the usual round of visits made and received, tea parties and card parties. Cold, snowy weather set in on 8 January and continued throughout the month, occasionally confining her to the house. She was visited fairly regularly by Elizabeth Thompson and the younger Thompson grandchildren, and Elizabeth accompanied her mother to some of her card parties.

Betsy always prepared her diary in advance for the year ahead, marking the dates of Sundays and the times of full and new moons. On Monday 23 January she recorded that a Ben Chapman had called, then she left a piece of well-used blotting paper in the page, ready to record the next day's events. The entry was never made. Betsy died at her house in Upper Close on Tuesday 24 January, aged 66.

She was buried at Reedham church in the family vault, where her coffin joined those of her first husband, Edward Leathes; their two sons, John and Reading, who had died in infancy; her father, James Reading; her mother, Elizabeth Reading; and her granddaughter, Jessica Beevor. On Saturday 28 January notice of her death was recorded in the pages of the *Norwich Mercury*, just as the conventions of polite society demanded and she would have wished.

Postscript

Betsy made at least three wills during her lifetime, the last of them on 18 February 1814. Her youngest son, George Reading Leathes, and her son-in-law, John Cheetham Mortlock, were named as executors, and the will was proved by them at London on 10 February 1815.[1] The will suggests that she wanted to redress the balance between her sons, who had benefited financially during her lifetime, and her daughters, who had had much less financial support.

Elizabeth Thompson received all of her mother's remaining investments, £400 of which was to be paid within 12 months; all of her household furniture (excluding plate, linen and china); and half of her clothes – all in all, a considerable bounty for a woman in difficult circumstances. The Thompsons were reunited after Betsy's death, and a sixth daughter, Amelia Mary, was born to them in August 1819. James died on 3 August 1849, aged 73, and Elizabeth on 6 July 1853, aged 77. They were buried side by side in Reedham churchyard.

In 1821 their eldest daughter Elizabeth married her cousin Frederick Leathes, who succeeded her uncle Edward as the incumbent of Reedham and Freethorpe in 1844. Their youngest daughter, Amelia Mary, became the fourth wife of Major-General Henry Prior in 1852; her cousin Elizabeth Mortlock had been his second wife.[2] Amelia gave Henry Prior three (of his total of 12) children before dying in 1857. It is from their eldest son, Leathes Prior, that the Prior family of Norwich traces its descent to the present day.[3]

Edward Leathes had owed his mother approximately £2,000 in 1810, over and above the 'loans' she had written off over the years, and perhaps this debt grew (to an unknown size) before her death.[4] Probably for this reason, in her will she remitted all his debts to her, with the exception of one that had been secured by bond, but left him nothing else, except for her harpsichord and music manuscripts. The amount covered by the bond is not mentioned in her will, but Edward had to pay the interest on it to the estate, presumably until the loan was repaid. He had other debts too, and had doubtless been relying on a substantial bequest.

Subsequent events had an air of inevitability. In June 1816 all of Edward's household furniture, most of it paid for with Betsy's money, was removed by order of the sheriff and put up for sale by auction.[5] Edward could not face the prospect of this public humiliation, and fled from Reedham before the sheriff's men descended, abandoning his ministerial duties. He may have gone abroad, financed by a family member or a friend. He stayed away for eight months, then returned to Reedham in early March 1817.

In absconding Edward had failed to provide a deputy to serve his churches, and the church authorities took this dereliction of duty very seriously. Just over a month after his return he was summoned by the Consistory Court at Norwich to answer a charge of neglect of duty. Following the legal preliminaries, the court proceedings began on 2 October 1817 and concluded on 19 May 1818. Edward was found guilty, suspended from his living for two years, and ordered to pay costs.[6] The sentence was sufficiently rare to merit mention in *The Times*.[7]

Edward received no income from his livings for the duration of the suspension. What he lived on for these two years, and where, is a mystery. Perhaps the person or persons who had financed his disappearance in 1816 (conceivably Elizabeth Merry, or John and Mary Mortlock) helped him again. He must have been a complete embarrassment to his family by this time, and they probably wished he would go as far away from them as possible. He resumed his ministerial duties at Reedham and Freethorpe in 1820, and retained the livings for another 14 years, but after 1834 the two churches were served by a succession of licensed curates, including his brother-in-law, James Thompson. It seems likely that Edward went abroad, where he could live more cheaply on the residual income from his parishes. He died at Milan in January 1844, aged 66.[8]

George had not been quite as profligate as his brother, so he benefited more in material terms from the will. All of his debts were remitted; an annuity that Betsy had purchased from him was returned (less any arrears owing); and he inherited all the rights and interests in the insurance policy she had taken out on his life. He also inherited all her paintings and her 'India Clock'. George's career suffered a setback in or around March 1816 when his aunt, Elizabeth Merry, sold the patronage of the livings of Flordon and Gissing to Sir William Robert Kemp. George had no alternative but to resign, and Sir William was instituted to the livings soon afterwards. This meant a considerable loss of income for George, who also lost the large rectory at Gissing. He had to fall back on his modest income from the livings of Wickhampton and Limpenhoe with Southwood, and to find alternative accommodation. Of course, he might well have been compensated in some way by his aunt or Sir William.

In 1821 George married Sarah, the daughter of Lieutenant-General James Hethersett of Shropham Hall, and they lived happily together until George died at the age of 55 on 1 January 1836 after suffering a stroke on Christmas Day 1835.[9]

Mary was comfortably situated after her marriage to John Cheetham Mortlock in 1812, and probably had the least need to benefit financially from her mother's will. To her three Beevor grandchildren Betsy bequeathed all the gifts she had had from their father (Mary's first husband Horace). Mary inherited her mother's rings, half her clothes, and the residue of her personal estate after payment of her debts, funeral costs and testamentary expenses. This probably did not amount to a great deal, although that rather depends on the size of Edward's outstanding debt and whether it was ever repaid.

On 1 July 1816 Mary became Lady Mortlock when her husband was knighted after presenting a congratulatory address to the Prince Regent on the occasion of his marriage to the Princess Charlotte. How Betsy would have relished that!

Sir John went on to serve as Commissioner of Excise from 1819 until 1845, and for many years held the post of Auditor as well. Seven children were born to the couple between 1814 and 1823, six daughters and one son. The little boy, Mary's tenth and penultimate child, lived for only a few months. Mary died on 10 June 1833, aged 50; John lived on for another 12 years before he died in November 1845. They are buried at Little Marlow in Buckinghamshire.[10]

Notes

Chapter 1

1 William Pocock was the brother of Admiral Sir George Pocock, commander of the East India squadron from 1757 to 1761.
2 NRO, BOL 2/3/3, 5 July 1771.
3 NRO, BOL 2/3/4, 10 July 1771.
4 Hill Mussenden died in November 1772 and the Herringfleet estate duly passed to his brother, Carteret Leathes. Edward Mussenden was left an annuity of £800 a year in his father's will.
5 NRO, BOL 2/3/7, 15 August 1771.
6 NRO, BOL 2/48/12, 20 January 1779.
7 NRO, BOL 2/4/13, 26 September 1772.
8 Stone (1993), p. 248.
9 NRO, BOL 2/42(iii) a, 9 September 1774.
10 The practice of throwing the stocking continued a tradition of some antiquity whereby guests entered the bridal couple's bedroom following the wedding and the male guests took the bride's stockings and the female guests took the bridegroom's stockings. Individuals from the two groups then took in turn to throw a stocking backwards over their heads in an attempt to hit the bride or groom on the nose; the first guest to do so would be the next to wed. The current custom of throwing a bouquet or garter is probably descended from this tradition.
11 NRO, BOL 2/138/5, 14 September 1774.
12 Diary, 15 September 1774.
13 NRO, BOL 2/6/15, 15 September 1774.

Chapter 2

1 NRO, BOL 2/148/26, 19 September 1774 (*Bills paid in the Year 1774*).
2 NRO, BOL 2/6/23, 15 October 1774. Vansommer was a popular London merchant and designer, as well as a partner in a weaving firm; see Ashford (1996), p. 154.
3 NRO, BOL 2/148/8, 22 December, 1774 and BOL 2/148/12, February and March 1774.
4 The ferry and the inn are still owned and run by the landlord today; a park for touring caravans has been added and the ferry is now powered by an engine.
5 The Old Rectory is now a residential care home; the River Yare is no longer an essential transport artery, but it is busy with pleasure craft.
6 NRO, BOL 2/24/26, 28 August 1775.
7 NRO, BOL 2/25/4, 4 February 1776.
8 NRO, BOL 2/148/26, bills paid, unpaid or not accounted for between August and September 1777.
9 NRO, BOL 2/25/15, 29 August/1 September 1776.
10 NRO, BOL 2/2/148/26 (*Bills unpaid at 25 August 1777*) and BOL 2/148/9 (undated bill from William Nelson).
11 See NRO, BOL 2/148/9, BOL 2/2/148/12, and BOL 2/148/26 for details of loans and bills in 1776.
12 NRO BOL 2/25/18, 8 December 1776; BOL 2/27/1, 6 January 1777; BOL 2/27/3, 26 January 1777.
13 NRO, BOL 2/92/9, 14 April 1777.
14 NRO, BOL 2/92/11, 26 April 1777.
15 NRO, BOL 2/48/4, 15 July 1777.

Chapter 3

1 According to William Chase's *Norwich Directory* for 1783, Richard Bacon was an 'Auctioneer, Appraiser and Brandy Merchant', whose premises were at 12 Lower Goat Lane.
2 NRO, BOL 2/148/12, 20 February 1777.
3 NRO, BOL 2/148/26 and BOL 2/148/27. Edward's total debts amounted to more than £200,000 at 2007 equivalent rates (see National Archives Currency Converter at www.ex.ac.uk/~RDavies/arian/current/howmuch.html).
4 This state of affairs continued until December 1784, when the remaining glebe lands were let and the working horses were sold.
5 NRO, BOL 2/28/13, 14 June 1778.
6 NRO, BOL 2/28/14, 15/17 June 1778.
7 NRO, BOL 2/28/19, 10 November 1778.
8 *Victoria County History of the County of Oxford*, Vol. XII (1990), p. 416.
9 NRO, BOL 2/42(i)m, 23 April 1779 and BOL 2/29/4, 28 April 1779.
10 Hotchkin (1890), pp. 241-2.
11 NRO, BOL 2/19/3, 7 April 1788.
12 NRO, BOL 2/19/4, 26 May 1789.
13 NRO, BOL 2/53/5, 30 November 1777.
14 NRO, BOL 2/28/21, 8 December 1778
15 NRO, BOL 2/29/7, 21 June 1779.
16 NRO, BOL 2/29/9, 6 August 1779.
17 NRO, BOL 2/30/1, 9-12 January 1780.
18 NRO, STA 705, probate copy of the will of Carteret Leathes.
19 NRO, BOL 2/95/8, 10 May 1780.
20 NRO, BOL 2/30/11, 18 June 1780.

Chapter 4

1 NRO, BOL 2/31/2(ii), 21 January 1781.
2 NRO, BOL 2/96/5, 19 February 1781.
3 Peruvian bark was another name for the bark of the South American cinchona tree from which quinine was first extracted to treat malaria. Laudanum consisted of opium dissolved in alcohol, a highly addictive narcotic favoured by the upper classes in the 18th and 19th centuries.
4 NRO, BOL 2/167.
5 Buscot Park is now a National Trust property.
6 NRO, BOL 2/32/2, 7/10 May 1782.
7 William Reading's sermons were collected and published posthumously in 1775 as *One Hundred and Sixteen Sermons*.
8 NRO, BOL 2/135/1, 15 March, 1782.
9 NRO, BOL 2/32/3, 13 May 1782.
10 NRO, BOL 2/33/11, 20 June 1782.
11 NRO, BOL 2/58/2/7, 26 June 1782.
12 NRO, BOL 2/33/20, 30 August 1782.
13 NRO, BOL 2/43/14, 20 June 1783.

Chapter 5

1 NRO, BOL 2/36/5, 9 March 1784.
2 NRO, BOL 2/35/12, 17 October 1784.

3 Ibid.
4 Ibid.
5 NRO, BOL 2/148/28.
6 NRO, BOL 2/148/30, 1784-86.
7 NRO, BOL 2/100/6, February 1785.

Chapter 6

1 NRO, BOL 2/153/1, bundle 1.
2 NRO, BOL 2/148/2, accounts for 1786-87. Carcavella was a Portuguese wine made at a small vineyard near Lisbon. It was made from a rare and distinctive grape and was generally falling out of favour by the 1780s.
3 NRO, BOL 2/150/4, a small bundle of bills relating to work done by Daniel Coppin between 1782 and 1785.
4 Probate copy of the will of John Leathes, NRO, STA 705.
5 NRO, BOL 2/39/10, 4 November 1787.
6 NRO, BOL 2/36/9, 26 November 1784; BOL 2/36/16, 26 December 1784; BOL 2/100/18, 14 September 1785; BOL 2/104/4, 14 February 1788; BOL 2/42 (vi)3d, 30 June 1788.
7 NRO, BOL 2/153/bundle 4, a bill from John Brunning for building the vault between March and August 1788 at a total cost of £4.7s.6d. For the positioning of the vault see HC, Reedham Burial Register, Microfiche 1/2. The coffins of John and Reading Leathes were moved to join their father's coffin in the vault. James and Elizabeth Reading were also laid to rest there in due course, as was Betsy herself. Unfortunately the fabric of the church was severely damaged by fire in 1981 and the vault was destroyed. The church was restored with the help of a substantial grant from English Heritage.

Chapter 7

1 Will of Edward Leathes, see Norfolk Records Society, *Index of Wills proved at Norwich*, Vol. XXXIII (1969), NRO, MF451.
2 For bills paid during this period see NRO, BOL 2/153. bundles 2–4; BOL 2/148/2; BOL 2/148/9; BOL 2/148/27; BOL 2/150/3; BOL 2/155; BOL 2/129.
3 NRO, BOL 2/159. The total of the bill for 13 August 1788 to 13 February 1789 has been adjusted to take account of Miss Olier's accounting errors.
4 NRO, BOL 2/140/1/2, 10 March 1789.
5 NRO, BOL 2/140/1/4, 1 April 1789.
6 NRO, BOL 2/63/10, 23 May 1789.
7 NRO, BOL 2/105/7, 6 October 1789.
8 NRO, BOL 2/140/2/29, 15 September 1790.
9 NRO, BOL 2/140/2/33, 5 October 1790.
10 NRO, BOL 2/140/1/29, 6 October 1790.
11 NRO, BOL 2/109/19, 13 November 1790.

Chapter 8

1 NRO, BOL 2/10/1, 27 May 1791; BOL 2/10/3, June/July undated.
2 For details of the estate see *Maidstone Journal and Kentish Advertiser*, 10 April 1798, 7 May 1805; Diary, 5 August 1807.
3 NRO, BOL 2/111/10, 17 September 1792.
4 NRO, BOL 2/59/6, 23 November 1791.

5 NRO, BOL 2/148/7.
6 Lady Hester Lucy Stanhope (1776-1839) travelled extensively in the Middle East between 1810 and 1820, usually dressed in Turkish male clothes. She settled at Joun, near Sidon, in 1820 and died there in 1839. See Gibb (2005) for the story of her life.
7 Beilby Porteus, Bishop of London 1787–1809 and chaplain to George III, was one of the most underrated churchmen of the 18th century. He was a leading advocate of the abolition of slavery, favoured reform of the Church of England and numbered several leading nonconformists among his friends. He was buried at Sundridge church.
8 NRO, BOL 2/10/4, 6 July 1791. To 'figure off' is to make a good impression.
9 NRO, BOL 2/10/5, 22 July 1791.
10 NRO, BOL 2/140/4/8, 22 July 1791.
11 NRO, BOL 2/10/10, 23/24 September 1791.
12 NRO, BOL 2/10/14, 13 November 1791.

Chapter 9

1 NRO, BOL 2/111/16, 19 December 1792.
2 NRO, BOL 2/112/1, 9 January 1793.
3 NRO, BOL 2/111/16, 19 December 1792.
4 NRO, BOL 2/12/1, 10 January 1793 and BOL 2/12/2, 10 January 1793.
5 NRO, BOL 2/11/7, 5 May 1792.
6 NRO, BOL 2/12/5, 19 February 1793.
7 NRO, BOL 2/12/10, 8 April 1793.
8 For Edward's opinions of Dr Forster see NRO, BOL 2/142/5, 14 April 1793; BOL 2/142/6, 1 May 1793; BOL 2/142/10, 15 September 1793. For his antipathy to Mr Wilkinson see NRO, BOL 2/142/12, 16 October 1793.
9 NRO, BOL 2/165; BOL 2/166.
10 NRO, BOL 2/112/9, 19 December 1793.
11 NRO, BOL 2/143/1, 19 January 1794
12 NRO, BOL 2/72/12(i) is a copy in Betsy's handwriting of amendments made to the deed of separation in 1802; the original deed has not survived.
13 See Stone (1993), pp. 19–21.
14 Diary, 4 and 7 March 1794.

Chapter 10

1 Norwich Heritage Projects (2010), p. 4.
2 Larwood (1800), pp. 112–13.
3 NRO, BOL 2/60/2, 7 September 1794.
4 NRO, BOL 2/113/17, 29 October 1794.
5 NRO, BOL 2/69/6, 12 November 1794.
6 NRO, BOL 2/69/9, 2 August 1795.
7 NRO, BOL 2/114/4, 29 June 1795.
8 NRO, BOL 2/13/6, 13 October 1795.
9 Beresford (1981), Vol. IV, pp. 17–18.
10 Diary, £5.5s.0d on 3 November, £2.2s.0d on 16 December 1795 and £2 on 6 January 1796.

Chapter 11

1 Carter (1993), p. 58.

2 NRO, BOL 2/74/7, 29 February 1796.

3 NRO, BOL 2/68/9, 5 April 1796.

4 Leathes Johnstone was the son of Jane Johnstone (née Mussenden), sister to Carteret and Hill Mussenden (later Leathes) and therefore the cousin of Betsy's first husband, Edward Leathes. William Leathes, British Minister at The Hague, was Jane Johnstone's brother; he died without issue in 1700 leaving his estates divided between his two nephews, Carteret and Hill, both of whom added Leathes to their surnames as a condition of their inheritance. Hill died without issue in 1772 and left the Herringfleet estate to his brother Carteret, who died in 1778, leaving the whole estate to his eldest son John, who died without issue in 1787. John left the estate to his wife Elizabeth for her lifetime; after her death it devolved to his brother George. John also left substantial legacies to both of his brothers and their children.

5 NRO, BOL 2/115/7, 11 May 1796.

6 Diary, 5 May 1796.

7 NRO, BOL 2/63/3, 12 April 1796; BOL 2/63/4, 8 June 1796; BOL 2/63/7, 7 August 1796; BOL 2/63/12, 28 August 1796.

8 Beresford (1981), Vol. IV, pp. 280-1.

9 Hague (2004), p. 381.

10 Diary, 17 October 1797. Some ships of the North Sea fleet ships were also moored there, including the *Ardent*, which had been heavily damaged during the action and was therefore of most interest to the curious public who came to stare. The captured Dutch ships were the *Hercules*, the *Wassenaar*, the *Alkmaar*, the *Jupiter* and the *Vryheid*, plus others unnamed in the newspaper report – see *Norwich Mercury*, 21 October 1797.

11 NRO, BOL 2/116/1, 7 January 1797.

12 NRO, BOL 2/76/6, 28 November 1797.

13 Diary, 27 February and 2 March 1797 and NRO, BOL 2/77/1, 1 March 1797.

14 Diary, 25 September and 24 October 1797.

15 Diary, 5, 6, 23, 24 April 1797; NRO, BOL 2/14/1, 26 April 1797.

16 NRO, BOL 2/14/3, 25 June 1797.

17 Diary, 14 November 1797.

Chapter 12

1 NRO, BOL 2/71/11, 17 January 1798.

2 NRO, BOL 2/42(v)n, 6 May 1798.

3 NRO, BOL 2/76/8, 23 December 1798.

4 NRO, BOL 2/69/11, 7 October 1798.

5 NRO, BOL 2/117/12, 21 October 1798.

6 NRO, BOL 2/69/10, 30 August 1798.

7 NRO, BOL 2/48/37, 5 July 1800.

8 NRO, BOL 2/48/34, 7 August 1798.

9 Carter (1993), pp. 95–8.

10 Sutton (1981), pp. 42–6. In 1793 the Company decreed that there should be 36 ships of over 1,000 tons for the China trade, 40 ships of 800 tons for the India trade, plus a variable number of ships of between 500 and 600 tons to be used as circumstances dictated: see Sutton p. 46.

11 William Grimaldi's other claim to fame was that he and his son Stacey, a London solicitor, published the first pop-up book for children in 1821.

12 NRO, BOL 2/42(iii)d, 12 February 1798.

13 NRO, BOL 2/42(iii)c, 5 August 1797. Betsy had written on the bottom of this letter: *Sorry, very sorry that I have burned all Mrs. Cuthbertson's Letters except two.*

14 Diary, 16 February 1798.

15 Blackwell and Blackwell (2007).
16 Philip Meadows Martineau (1752–1829) was of Huguenot descent and the last of several surgeons of that name. He practised as a surgeon at the Norfolk and Norwich Hospital and achieved international fame for his technique of removing bladder stones. He did not confine himself to surgery, as he also practised as a man-midwife or gynaecologist, a mixture of surgical and medical skills that was not unusual at the time.
17 Diary, 23 and 24 March 1799.
18 NRO, BOL 2/79/1, 1 January 1800.
19 Edward South Thurlow (1764–1847) was a prebendary of Norwich Cathedral from 1788 until 1847. One of his uncles became Lord Chancellor, while the other was successively bishop of Lincoln and of Durham, so he was a very well-connected man whose acquaintance was worth cultivating.
20 NRO, BOL 2/76/9, 3 July 1799.
21 Diary, 1 January and 16 July 1799.
22 For the complex Beevor family tree see Carter (1993), pp. 274–89.
23 According to Chase's *Norwich Directory* of 1783 John Herring's work rooms were situated at number 66 Gilden Gate and his house at number 67; the Maltbys lived at number 6 Tombland.

Chapter 13

1 NRO, BOL 2/79/3, 6 December 1800.
2 Hague (2004), p. 455.
3 NRO, BOL 2/42(iv) h, 6 March 1800; NRO, BOL 2/119/7, 10 May 1800.
4 Beresford (1981), Vol. V, p. 241, 25 February 1800.
5 Jewson (1975), pp. 99–102.
6 Diary, 7 January and 26 June 1799.
7 Diary, 7 May 1799. *The Gallery of Fashion*, a series of volumes of fashion plates, was first published by Heideloff in 1794; it appeared in monthly parts that built into volumes and cost 3 guineas a year. An average of 30 hand-coloured aquatint plates was published in each year and by the time publication ceased in 1802 nine volumes were complete, containing 251 plates.
8 Diary, 30 September 1799; 15 September 1800.
9 Clabburn (1995).
10 Ibid. and Diary, 26 October 1800.
11 Diary, 25 June 1800.
12 NRO, BOL 2/122/4/10, 27 June; BOL 2/122/4/9, 29 June 1800.
13 Dilapidations: the sum needed to effect necessary repairs to a property at the end of a tenancy. They were the subject of frequent disputes between the outgoing clergyman (or more usually his widow) and the incoming clergyman; the sum to be handed over was usually achieved only agreed after lengthy negotiation. Parson Woodforde had a tussle with the widow of his predecessor at Weston Longville; see Beresford (1981), Vol. 1, pp. 154–5, and 194.
14 NRO, BOL 2/119/9, 26 June 1800.
15 Sutton (1981), pp. 26, 33–46.
16 NRO, BOL 2/79/3, 6 December 1800.
17 Diary, 20 March 1801.
18 Hague (2004), pp. 471–84.
19 NM, Saturday 24 October 1801.

Chapter 14

1 Hilton (2006), pp. 98–103.

2 Barney (2000), pp. 24 and 51–7. Sea fencibles were auxiliary corps recruited from inshore fishermen and longshoremen who were protected from being pressed into the navy. They were engaged to defend the coast on land or at sea and were commanded by officers of the regular navy.

3 NRO, BOL 2/122/2/20, 18 June 1802.

4 R. Wilson, 'The textile industry', in Rawcliffe and Wilson (2004), p. 235.

5 R. Ryan, 'Banking and Insurance', in Rawcliffe and Wilson (2004), pp. 363–5.

6 Betsy made her own copy of the amendments to the deed: see NRO, BOL 2/72/12(i).

7 The separation trust money included £800 that was held in reserve by the trustees as an indemnity for Edward Peach against 'certain contingencies', according to NRO, BOL 2/118/9, 29 October 1799.

8 Vickery (2009), p. 216.

9 Stabler (2006), pp. 141–2 and 168.

10 NRO, BOL2/162, bills and purchases 1801.

11 NRO, BOL 2/163, housekeeping expenses 1801–2.

12 Austen (2003), p. 39.

13 *Oxford Dictionary of National Biography*.

14 NRO, BOL 2/79/4, 24 March 1802.

15 NRO, BOL 2/79/6, 30 January 1803.

16 For an account of Merry's career in Washington see Lester (1978).

17 Ibid., pp. 22, 42.

18 NRO, BOL 2/123/22 and BOL 2/123/23, 8 October 1803.

19 Diary, 5 July 1802. The ascent was one of several made by Garnerin in London and the provinces during his visit to England in 1802, see Rolt (2006), p. 107.

20 NRO, BOL 2/48/42, 24 September 1802.

21 Diary, 20 November 1802.

22 NRO, BOL 2/48/43, 23 November 1802.

23 Diary, 30 November and 2 December 1802.

24 NRO, BOL 2/48/45, 28 December 1802.

25 NRO, BOL 2/42(v)y, 4 March 1803.

26 NRO, BOL 2/79/7, 29 April 1804.

27 Diary, 5 January 1804.

Chapter 15

1 NM, 21 December 1805.

2 NC, 21 December 1805.

3 NRO, BOL 2/61/3, 6 December 1805.

4 Crosse (1968), p. 87. Dalrymple was born in Norwich to Scottish parents and attended Norwich Grammar School under the famous Dr Parr. Having chosen medicine as a career, he was apprenticed in London and studied at Guy's and St Thomas's hospitals. He returned to Norwich in 1793, where he set up a surgical practice. He was elected assistant surgeon at the Norfolk and Norwich Hospital in 1812 and full surgeon in 1814.

5 Glover held two other curacies: Barmer in Burnham Deanery from 1791–1810 and St Lawrence, Norwich from 1811: see Turner (1847). His daughter Sarah was a Sunday School teacher and developed the Norwich Sol-fa system in order to help her pupils learn hymn tunes.

6 Cozens-Hardy and Kent (1938), pp. 137–8.

7 Henry Bathurst (1744–1837) was the son of Benjamin Bathurst of Lydney Park in Gloucestershire, and cousin to Earl Bathurst of Cirencester. He was 61 when he became bishop of Norwich and 92 when he died, Norwich's only nonagenarian bishop. A lifelong Whig, he was a supporter

of Roman Catholic emancipation and the only bishop to vote for the Great Reform Act of 1832. For a summary of his life see Linnell (1961), pp. 130–56.

8 NRO, BOL 2/125/43, 18 October 1805.

9 Diary, 2 February and 24 April 1804.

10 Diary, 6 April 1804.

11 Diary, 7 February 1804.

12 Diary, 3 and 24 June, 1 and 15 July 1804.

13 NM, Saturday 9 August 1806.

14 Diary, 23, 25, 30 October and 1, 13, 15 November 1805.

15 NRO, BOL 2/125/17, 22 May 1805.

16 Diary, 23 August, 2 November, 10 December 1805.

17 NRO, BOL 2/140/5/18, 19 November 1804.

18 For Edward's difficulties with tithe payments and income tax in 1804 see NRO, BOL 2/124/16, 10 April 1804; BOL 2/124/18, 16 April 1804; BOL 2/124/35, 21 December 1804.

19 Maintenance and repair of Southwood church was charged to the parish in 1794, according to the Glebe Terrier: see NRO, DN/TER 135/6/6. However, a letter from Edward Leathes to his mother indicated that the vicar was responsible for repairs to the chancel thatch: see NRO, BOL 2/168/22, 25 April 1806.

20 Diary, 26 and 28 August, 1805.

21 Sutton (1981), p. 46.

22 Taylor (2007), p. 53.

23 NRO, BOL 2/140/5/23, 12 January 1805.

24 NRO, BOL 2/83/1, 25 January 1805.

25 NRO, BOL 2/83/2, 28 April 1805.

26 NRO, BOL 2/65/3, 29 October 1805.

27 Betsy made a handwritten copy of the deed of separation as amended in 1802: see NRO, BOL 2/72/12 (i) and (ii). There is no extant copy of the original deed of separation signed in 1794, so it is impossible to say how complete or accurate Betsy's 1802 copy is. That Betsy signed a deed empowering Edward Peach's executors to sell three cottages worth £250 at Tunbridge later in 1805 probably indicates that the 1794 deed also involved some property; see Diary, 28 August 1805.

28 NRO, BOL 2/72/11, 26 March 1805.

Chapter 16

1 For Lady Gordon's letter see NRO, BOL 2/62/4, 21 July 1806; for Lady Winterton's letter see NRO, BOL 2/83/4, 17 July 1806.

2 Voting by secret ballot and an increase in the number of polling places were not introduced until the Ballot Act became law in 1872. The franchise was widened successively by the Representation of the People Acts of 1867 and 1884; the right to vote was finally given to all men over 21 and to women over 30 (providing they were ratepayers or the wives of ratepayers) by the Representation of the People Act 1918. It was 1928 before the franchise was extended to all women over the age of 21.

3 For an account of the 1806 Norfolk county election, see Ketton-Cremer (1948), pp. 215–37; Wade-Martins (2009), pp. 135–7. Thomas William Coke was created earl of Leicester in 1837.

4 NRO, BOL 2/168, Mrs Peach's Wine Book 1803–13.

5 NRO, BOL 2/126/18, 28 March 1806.

6 Diary, 17 November 1805; 10 January 1806; 26 February 1806; 19 April 1806; 21 April 1806; 10 May 1806; 14 June 1806; 23 November 1806.

7 NRO, BOL 2/62/4, 21 July 1806.

8   According to Betsy's diary for 1806, Mary received a letter from Horace on 19 April, in which he may well have confirmed an earlier verbal request for Betsy to leave the house.

9   Diary, 12 September 1806.

10 This is the only house that fits: see A. B. Whittingham, 'The development of the Close since the Reformation', in Metters (1985), pp. 105, 116–17. According to the plan at pp. 116–17, this was the only one of the prebendary houses that had an unobstructed view of the Cathedral, matching the reference to Prebendary Proctor's house made in Winkles (1842), p. 86.

11 NRO, BOL 2/126/42, 26 September 1806.

12 NRO, BOL 2/41/10, 2 February 1807.

13 Diary, 4 February 1807.

14 For Elizabeth Reading's will see Norfolk Records Society, *Index of Wills proved at Norwich*, Vol. XXXIII (1969); NRO, MF 458.

15 Diary, 13 and 24 February 1807.

16 Diary, 26 February 1807.

17 Diary, 19 March 1807. Mrs Forster was buried on 25 March.

18 For the events of April-October, see Diary, 1807.

Chapter 17

1   NRO, BOL 2/83/6, 17 January 1808.

2   See Chase, *Norwich Directory* 1783.

3   For a full account of the development of the Cathedral Close see I. Atherton, 'The Close', in Atherton et al. (1996), pp.634–64.

4   Diary, 24 February 1809 et seq. In 1814 Amelia Opie began to attend Quaker services and she became a Quaker in 1825, after which she turned her back on fiction and poetry and spent the rest of her life engaged on good works.

5   Preston (1994).

6   Crosse (1968), p. 87.

7   Diary, 1 and 27 January 1808.

8   In his defence he was very elderly (92 when he died in 1837) and after Mrs Bathurst's death in 1823, very infirm. For more details see R. G. Wilson, 'The Cathedral in the Georgian period', in Atherton et al. (1996), pp. 581–3.

9   Matchett (1822), p.102. For the years from 1760, the *Norfolk and Norwich Remembrancer* was compiled largely from the pages of the *Norfolk Chronicle*, which was certainly one of the newspapers taken by Betsy.

10 For a detailed discussion, see: Barney (2000), pp. 59–72.

11 NRO, BOL 2/73/5, undated except for July, but references in the letter to the *Glory* and the Peninsular War indicate that it was written in 1809.

12 NRO, BOL 2/87/1, 30 June, 1809. The young couple had a son (another Edward) in May 1810 and Edward senior eventually succeeded to the title when his father died in 1831.

13 Matchett (1822), p. 105.

14 Diary, 24 December 1808; Dr Vyse's letter is at NRO, BOL 2/84/4, 21 December 1808.

15 NRO, BOL 2/84/5(iii), 17 January 1809; BOL 2/84/5(i), 20 January 1809; BOL 2/84/6(ii), 24 February 1809. Betsy also made a copy of the Bank of England's required form of words, see BOL 2/84/5(ii), 20 January 1809.

16 NRO, BOL 2/128/1/3, 27 March 1809; NRO, BOL 2/128/2/7, 14 April 1809; Diary, 15 April 1809. For Edward's continuing failure to repay his debts to Betsy, see NRO, BOL 2/129/1/2, 2 February 1810 and BOL 2/129/1/12, 16 November 1810.

17 Mackie (1901), 31 July 1809. Why Mackie assigned this account of the case to 31 July 1809,

when it was heard first on 3 August and again on 21 August (see Diary, 3 and 21 August 1809), is a mystery.

18 NM, 24 March 1810.

19 Ibid., 25 August 1810.

20 NRO, BOL 2/42(v)H, 3 September 1808. All the other events referred to in this paragraph are mentioned in the Diary, January–September 1808.

21 Diary, 26 April 1809.

22 NRO, BOL 2/87/1, 30 June 1809.

23 Diary, 10 December 1809.

24 East India Company ships on the India run were usually known as Indiamen.

25 Taylor (2007), pp. 47–78.

26 Carter (1993), p. 102.

27 Letters received by Betsy from Ann Man, NRO, BOL 2/73/11, 4 January 1810 and BOL 2/73/12, 2 March 1810.

28 NRO, BOL 2/87/3, 10 April 1810.

Chapter 18

1 Lady Winterton: NRO, BOL 2/87/15, 2 December 1812; Lady Gordon: NRO, BOL 2/73/6, 14 October 1813; Edward Leathes: NRO, BOL 2/129/5/36(i), 17 December 1813; Mrs Smythe: NRO, BOL 2/73/19, 6 May 1814.

2 NRO, BOL 2/130/3, 10 January 1814; NRO, BOL 2/130/5, 28 January 1814; NRO, BOL 2/130/6, 2 February 1814; NRO, BOL 2/130/8, 8 February 1814. See also Matchett (1822), 9, 19, and 25 January 1814.

3 Betsy sorted her correspondence into separate bundles and used an assortment of old letters and various printed ephemera to wrap them in. The wrapper of one bundle (NRO, BOL 2/122/4/11) is a flyer advertising tickets for the state lottery draw on 15 February 1811.

4 Diary, 21 May 1811; see also Matchett (1822), 23 March 1810, 17 April 1810, 2 April 1811. A rival monitorial system was successfully promoted by an Anglican clergyman, Andrew Bell.

5 *Norfolk and Norwich Remembrancer*, 6 April 1811; Diary, 9 April 1811. For more on the exploitation of humans and animals see A. Dain, 'An enlightened and polite society', in Rawcliffe and Wilson (2004), Vol. 2, pp. 200–2.

6 Matchett (1822), 8 October 1811; NM, 12 October 1811; Diary, 8–11 October 1811.

7 NRO, BOL 2/87/8, 5 November 1811.

8 NRO, MF 354; bequests were made to his executor, his executor's children and his late wife's sisters; the

9 For the full story see Stone (1993), pp. 248–69.

10 NRO, BOL 2/86b, 3 April 1811; NRO, BOL 2/86a, 7 April 1811; NRO, BOL 2/88, 24 March 1814.

11 NRO, BOL 2/73/6, 14 October 1813.

12 NRO, BOL 2/87/5, 19 April 1811.

13 NRO, BOL 2/87/7, 29 September 1811; NRO, BOL 2/87/8, 5 November (*recte* October) 1811; NRO, BOL 2/87/11, 7 October 1811; NRO, BOL 2/87/9, 9 November 1811; Diary, 14, 15 October and 13 November 1811. The Winterton family's Norfolk estates were at Attleborough and Somerton.

14 NRO, BOL 2/87/12, 22 April 1812. Whatever happened between them during and after 1812, James and Elizabeth Thompson were buried side by side in Reedham churchyard.

15 Turner (1847), pp. 53 and 55; Diary, 8 March 1811.

16 Diary, 13–15 November 1811.

17 NRO BOL 2/87/10, 1 December 1811.

18 NRO, BOL 2/87/5, 19 April 1811.

19 Carter (1993), p. 102.

20 John Cheetham Mortlock commanded the Cambridge Local Militia, a volunteer force that he had been instrumental in raising in or around 1808.

21 NRO, BOL 2/87/10, 1 December 1811.

22 Carter (1993),p. 102, quoting from the now missing Peach diary for 1812.

23 NRO, BOL 2/87/12, 22 April 1812.

24 Diary, 16 July and 26 October 1811; NM, 20 July 1811 and 18 January 1812.

25 *NM*, 18 January 1812.

26 NRO, BOL 2/129/3/14, 18 June 1812; NRO, BOL 2/129/3/15, 9 July 1812.

27 NM, 1 August 1812.

28 In 1822 he was caught *in flagrante* with a soldier and fled the country before charges could be brought against him; see Harvey (2002), pp. 137–8.

29 NRO, BOL 2/87/15, 2 December 1812.

30 NC, 1 August 1814.

Postscript

1 National Archives, PCC PROB 11/1565.

2 Henry Prior held the rank of major in the Indian Army when he married Elizabeth Mortlock, the first daughter of John and Mary Mortlock, at Madras in 1836. The couple were childless when she died of cholera in 1839. He was later promoted to major-general.

3 The descent of the Priors of Norwich is outlined in *Norfolk Genealogies*, vol. 22, pp. 130-33.

4 See NRO, BOL 2/164 for Edward's recorded debts to Betsy up to 1810.

5 NC, 29 June 1816.

6 Consistory Court Act Book 1798-1821, NRO, DN/Act 104 (MF/X 56/5); Consistory Court Case Papers, NRO DN/CON/124.

7 *The Times*, 26 May 1818.

8 *Alumni Cantab.*

9 Ibid.

10 Ibid.; see also R. J. H. Griffiths, 'The banking Mortlocks', www.Mortlock-info/mortlock-encyclopaedia, pp. 11–14.

Select bibliography

Primary sources

Documents

Norfolk Record Office

Bolingbroke Collection, MS 33314; BOL 2, Leathes/Peach correspondence.
Standley Deposit, papers relating to the Herringfleet estate; STA/684, STA/703, STA/729.
Consistory Court Act Book 1797–1821, DN/Act/104 on MF/X 56/5.
Consistory Court Papers 1817–18, DN/CON/124.

Norfolk Heritage Centre, Norwich

Parish Registers and Burial Registers for Reedham, Freethorpe and Strumpshaw (on microfiche).

Printed sources

Norfolk Record Office

Chase, W., *The Norwich Directory, 1783* (facsimile edn, 1991).
Norfolk Record Society, *Index of Wills proved at Norwich*, vol. XXXIII (1969).

Norfolk Heritage Centre, Norwich

Norfolk Chronicle.
Norwich Mercury.

Kent Record Office

Maidstone Journal and Kentish Advertiser.

Secondary sources

Ashford, J., *The Art of Dress: Clothes through history 1500–1914* (London, 1996).
Atherton, I. et al. (eds), *Norwich Cathedral: Church, City and Diocese, 1096–1996* (London, 1996).
Austen, J., *Northanger Abbey* (1818/Penguin, 2003).
Barney, J., *The Defence of Norfolk 1793–1815* (Norwich, 2000).
Beresford, J., *The Diary of a Country Parson*, 5 vols (Oxford, repr. 1981).
Berg, M., *Luxury and Pleasure in Eighteenth-Century Britain* (Oxford, 2005).
Black, J., *A Subject for Taste: Culture in eighteenth-century England* (London, 2005).
Blackwell, M. and Blackwell, C., *Norwich Theatre Royal* (Norwich, 2007).
Carter, A., *The Beevor Story* (Norwich, 1993).
Clabburn, P., *The Norwich Shawl* (Norwich, 1995).
Cozens-Hardy, B. and Kent, E., *The Mayors of Norwich 1403–1835* (Norwich, 1938).
Crosse, V. M., *A Surgeon in the Early Nineteenth Century: The life and times of John Green Crosse M.D., F.R.C.S., F.R.S.* (London and Edinburgh, 1968).
Donnison, J., *Midwives and Medical Men: A history of the struggle for the control of childbirth* (London, 1988).
Foster, J., *Alumni Oxonienses, Vol. II, 1715–1886* (1891).
Gallery of Fashion 1790–1822, from plates by Heideloff and Ackerman (Batsford, 1949).

Gibb, L., *Lady Hester, Queen of the East* (London, 2005).

Glynn, I. and J., *The Life and Death of Smallpox* (London, 2004).

Hague, W., *William Pitt the Younger* (London, 2004).

Harvey, A. D., *Sex in Georgian England* (London, 2002).

Harvey, R., *The War of Wars: The epic struggle between Britain and France 1793–1815* (London, 2006).

Hilton, B., *A Mad, Bad and Dangerous People? England 1783–1846* (Oxford, 2006).

Hotchkin, S. F., *Early Clergy of Pennsylvania and Delaware* (Philadelphia, 1890).

Jacob, W. M., *The Clerical Profession in the Long Eighteenth Century* (Oxford, 2007).

Jewson, C .B., *Jacobin City* (Glasgow, 1975).

Ketton-Cremer, R. W., *A Norfolk Gallery* (London, 1948).

Larwood, Joshua, E*rratics: By a sailor; containing rambles in Norfolk, and elsewhere* (London, 1800; Ecco facsimile repr.edn).

Lester, M., *Anthony Merry* Redivivus: *A reappraisal of the British Minister to the United States, 1803–6* (Charlottesville, Va., 1978).

Linnell, C., *Some East Anglian Clergy* (London 1961).

Mackie, C., *Norfolk Annals, Vol. 1* (Norwich, 1901).

Matchett, J., *The Norfolk and Norwich Remembrancer and Vade Mecum* (facsimile repr. of Norwich, 1822 edn).

Metters, G. A. (ed.), *The Parliamentary Survey of Dean and Chapter Properties in and around Norwich in 1649* (Norwich Records Society, vol. 51, 1985).

Mingay, G. E., *English Landed Society in the Eighteenth Century* (London, 1963).

Norwich Heritage Projects, *A Market For Our Times: A History of Norwich provision market* (Norwich, 2010).

Porter, R., *English Society in the Eighteenth Century* (London, 1991).

Porter, R. and Porter, D., *Patient's Progress: Doctors and doctoring in eighteenth-century England* (Oxford, 1989).

Porter, R. and Rousseau, G. S., *Gout: The Patrician Malady* (London, 2000).

Preston, H., *Early East Anglian Banks and Bankers* (Thetford, 1994).

Priestley, U., *The Fabric of Stuffs: The Norwich shawl industry from 1565* (Norwich, 1990).

Rawcliffe, C. and Wilson, R. (eds), *Norwich Since 1550* (London, 2004).

Rolt, L. T. C., *The Balloonists: The history of the first aeronauts* (Stroud, 2006).

Sandon, E., *Suffolk Houses: A Study of Domestic Architecture* (Woodbridge, 1977).

Stabler, J., *Norfolk Furniture Makers 1700–1840* (2006).

Stone, L., *Broken Lives: Separation and divorce in England 1660–1857* (OUP, 1993).

Sutton, J., *Lords of the East: The East India Company and its ships* (London, 1981).

Swafford, J., *The New Guide to Classical Music* (London, 1992).

Taylor, S., *Storm and Conquest: The battle for the Indian Ocean 1809* (London, 2007).

Turner, D. (ed.), *List of Norfolk Benefices* (Norwich, 1847).

Uglow, J., *In These Times: Living in Britain through Napoleon's wars, 1793–1815* (London, 2014).

Venn, J. A., *Alumni Cantabrigienses, Part 2, 1752–1900* (1951).

Vickery, A., *Behind Closed Doors: At home in Georgian England* (New Haven and London, 2009).

Vickery, A., *The Gentleman's Daughter: Women's lives in Georgian England* (London, 1998).

Victoria County History of the County of Oxford, Vol. XII (Oxford, 1990).

Wade-Martins, S., *Coke of Norfolk 1754–1842* (Woodbridge, 2009).

Winkles, R. B., *History of the Cathedral Church in Norwich* (Norwich, 1842).

Index

References to illustrations are given in **bold.**
Individuals are generally indexed under their
final name, when their names have changed
during their lifetime. Notes are referenced in
the form 152n1-3 for note 3 to chapter 1, on
page 152.

A

Abingdon Races, 11–12
Addington, Henry, 137, 139, 150
ague, the, 39
alcohol
    consumption of, 27, 43, 59–60
    winemaking, 162
Alderson family, 169
Algeciras Bay, battle of, 143
America, 30–1, 143
Amherst, Lord and Lady, 81
Arnam, John, 15, 28
arts, visual, 153–4, 169
Ashbrook, Lady Elizabeth, 65
astronomy, 56
Austen, Jane, 1, 142

B

Bacon, Sir Edmund and Lady, 62
Bacon, Richard, 27, 192n3-1
balloon ascent, 145
bankruptcies, 27
banks and banking, 70, 79–80, 112, 140, 171,
    169
    bank collapse, 171
    banking crisis, 111
baptism, 48
Bath, 100
Bathurst, Henry, 152, 169–70, 180,
    197–8n15-7, 199n17-8
Bathurst, Mrs, 152
Beauchamp Proctor, Sir Thomas and Lady, 62
Beevor family, 106–7, 121–2, 165
Beevor, Ann, 141
Beevor, Augustus, 106, 121, 145
Beevor, Charles, 182
Beevor, Horace/Horatio, 120–2, 126, 135–6,
    145, 147–9, 157–8, 162, 165–6, 173–5
Beevor, James, 106–7, 120, 126, 165, 173

Beevor, John, 107
Beevor, Robert, 145
Beevor, Sir Thomas (18th century), 107
Beevor, Sir Thomas (contemporary), ix–x
Bignold, Samuel, 140
birth
    arrangements for, 17–18
    of boys, importance of, 23–4
    dangers of and problems following, 31, 36,
        49
    see also entries for individuals
Bodicote, Harriet *see* Winterton, Lady
Bodicote, John, 81
Bolingbroke, Leonard, ix
books, 47, 114, 142
Bowness, Rev. Francis, 67–92 *passim*, 98– 103
    passim, 116, 125, 133, 134–7
    death, 137
    letters from, 102, 108–9, 111, 119, 128
Branthwayt, Jane, 107
breach of promise, 10
Brett, Robert, 97
Brittan, Henry, 59
Browne, Philip, 154
Browne, Samuel, 28
Burney, Fanny, 47
Bury St Edmunds
    Assembly Rooms, 53–4
    Fair, 52–3
    Northgate Street, 19, **20**, 51
    St James's Church/Cathedral, 157, 182

C

Cambridge
    Caius College, 97, 100
    lodgings in, 100–1, 103
    St Catherine's Hall, 163
    Trinity College, 103, 112
Campbell, Lord and Lady Frederick, 81, 82,
    145
Camperdown, battle of, 111
Cantley, living of, 57, 64, 66
Capps, Jane, 43
Carlos, James, 15, 28
Carter, Anne, x
Chadd, Charles and Lady Anne, 180

For details of hard copy and electronic editions of titles published by the Lasse Press, visit:

www.lassepress.com